Strategies and Theories of Vocational Education

Strategies and Theories of Vocational Education

Darpan Verma

RANDOM PUBLICATIONS
NEW DELHI - 110 002 (INDIA)

Strategies and Theories of Vocational Education

ISBN 978-93-51112-96-9

Published in 2014 in India by

RANDOM PUBLICATIONS

4376-A/4B, Gali Murari Lal, Ansari Road
New Delhi-110 002
Phone: +9111-43580356, 23289044
E-mail: randomexports@gmail.com; sales@randompublications.com; info@randompublications.com

Reprinted 2021

Type Setting by: Friends Media, Delhi-110089
Digitally Printed at: Replika Press Pvt. Ltd.

Preface

Vocational education consists basically of practical courses through which one gains skills and experience directly linked to a career in future. It helps students to be skilled and in turn, offers better employment opportunities. These trainings are parallel to the other conventional courses of study (like B. Sc., M. Sc. etc.). Time management and meeting deadlines play an important role in success in a vocational course and during their studies students normally produce a portfolio of evidence (plans, reports, drawings, videos, placements), which is taken as a demonstration of students' capabilities for a job. After finishing the courses, students are often offered placements in jobs. Vocational trainings in a way give students some work related experiences that many employers look for.

Vocational education or Vocational Education and Training (VET), also called Career and Technical Education (CTE), prepares learners for jobs that are based in manual or practical activities, traditionally non-academic and totally related to a specific trade, occupation or vocation, hence the term, in which the learner participates. It is sometimes referred to as technical education, as the learner directly develops expertise in a particular group of techniques or technology. Generally, vocation and career are used interchangeably. Vocational education might be classified as teaching procedural knowledge. This may be contrasted with declarative knowledge, as used in education in a usually broader scientific field, which might concentrate on theory and abstract conceptual knowledge, characteristic of tertiary education. Vocational education can be at the secondary or post-secondary level and can interact with the apprenticeship system. Increasingly, vocational education can be recognised in terms of recognition of prior learning and partial academic credit towards tertiary education (e.g., at a university) as credit; however, it is rarely considered in its own form to fall under the traditional definition of a higher education. Up until the end of the twentieth century, vocational education focused on specific trades such as for example, an automobile mechanic or welder, and was therefore associated with the activities of lower social classes. As a consequence, it attracted a level of stigma. Vocational education is related to the age-old apprenticeship system of learning. However, as the labour market becomes more specialized and economies demand higher levels of skill, governments and businesses are increasingly investing in the future of vocational education through publicly funded training organizations and subsidized apprenticeship or traineeship initiatives for businesses. At the post-secondary level vocational education is typically provided by an institute of technology, or by a local community college.

This book offers a comprehensive description of the applications of various fields in this subject. The book will be appropriate as a guide for students.

I thank all members of my team who have helped in the preparation of the book. My special thanks go to "Random Publications" who have published the book.

—Darpan Verma

Contents

1

Introduction

Vocational education has an overall goal of the development of working competence and six specifically desired outcomes:

1 Routine expertise: mastery of everyday working procedures in the domain.

2 Resourcefulness: having the knowledge and aptitude to stop and think effectively when required.

3 Functional literacies: adequate mastery of literacy, numeracy and digital literacy.

4 Craftsmanship: an attitude of pride and thoughtfulness towards the job.

5 Business-like attitudes: understanding the economic and social sides of work.

6 Wider skills for growth: having an inquisitive and resilient attitude towards constant improvement – the 'independent learner'.

A Vocational Pedagogy

All over the world education plays an increasingly important role for economic success.

Pedagogy is the science and art of education, specifically instructional theory. An instructor develops conceptual knowledge and manages the content of learning activities in pedagogical settings. Modern pedagogy has been strongly influenced by the cognitivism of Piaget, 1926, 1936/1975; the social-interactionist theories of Bruner, 1960, 1966, 1971, 1986; and the social and cultural theories of Vygotsky, 1962. These theorists have laid a foundation for pedagogy where sequential development of individual mental processes, such as recognize, recall, analyze, reflect, apply, create, understand, and evaluate, are scaffolded. Students learn as they internalize the procedures, organization, and structures encountered in social contexts as their own schema. The learner requires assistance to integrate prior knowledge with new knowledge. Children must also develop metacognition, or the ability to learn how to learn.

The Need for a Vocational Pedagogy

The effectiveness of all education systems depends critically on the quality of teaching and learning in the classrooms, workshops, laboratories and other spaces in which the education takes place. While outstanding teachers (including lecturers, trainers, tutors, and coaches), engaged students, well-designed courses, facilities which are fit for purpose, and a good level of resources are necessary if any kind of educational provision is to be excellent, they alone are not sufficient. The real answers to improving outcomes from vocational education lie in the 'classroom', in understanding the many decisions 'teachers' take as they interact with students.

Pedagogy has been neglected partly because it is undeniably complex, leading some agencies to prefer to focus on more controllable factors such as qualifications, funding or a nebulous notion of 'teacher quality'. Teaching methods can also become political footballs, one method being labelled 'traditional' while another, equally unhelpfully, seen as 'trendy'. When vocational education and training systems were initially created, discussions about vocational pedagogy were likely to be derived from the principles of general education. Even today, there is a sense in which vocational pedagogy sits in a no man's land between what is taught, in colleges and by training providers, and what is needed in the workplace.

And too often employers complain that the content taught does not connect closely enough with the requirements of a particular occupation. Vocational education faces two major challenges. Firstly, the dual worlds of educational institution and workplace require two sets of expertise – teachers with current experience of the workplace and workers who can teach. And many vocational learners have diverse needs which may be challenging. Of whatever age, vocational learners may not have had fulfilling experiences in their general education to date leaving their motivation impaired.

Alternatively they may be so hungry for paid employment in the real world that they are impatient to leave formal education.

Poor Analogies for Vocational Education

Historically descriptions of vocational education have tended to be rather imprecise. The mental models or metaphors which have been deployed are often drawn from other areas of learning without clear examination of their appropriateness. So, for example, vocational education has been seen as being:

Like 'school' but with work experience, or Like 'learning to drive' but often without a car (ie the actual equipment ultimately to be used), or Like 'sitting by Nellie' but with no real understanding about who Nellie is, whether the ways she is working are good ways and what she might be doing to ensure that vocational education is really happening, or Like 'working' but without any remuneration.

While general education and informal learning have, over the years, developed much useful theory which could inform vocational pedagogy, when such thinking is transferred to vocational education it tends to be bolted on rather than fully integrated. So approaches such as problem-based learning may sit side by side with didactic instruction with no apparent justification or thought as to the situations in which one might be chosen in preference to the other. Vocational subjects are distinct from academic subjects in a number of ways, each of which raises its own concerns for the organisation, teaching, and assessment of such subjects.

The Teacher and the Teaching Factors

A teacher or schoolteacher is a person who provides education for pupils (children) and students (adults). The role of teacher is often formal and ongoing, carried out at a school or other place of formal education. In many countries, a person who wishes to become a teacher must first obtain specified professional qualifications or credentials from a university or college. These professional qualifications may include the study of pedagogy, the science of teaching. Teachers, like other professionals, may have to continue their education after they qualify, a process known as continuing professional development. Teachers may use a lesson plan to facilitate student learning, providing a course of study which is called the curriculum.

A teacher's role may vary among cultures. Teachers may provide instruction in literacy and numeracy, craftsmanship or vocational training, the arts, religion, civics, community roles, or life skills. A teacher who facilitates education for an individual may also be described as a personal tutor, or, largely historically, a governess. In some countries, formal education can take place through home schooling. Informal learning may be assisted by a teacher occupying a transient or ongoing role, such as a family member, or by anyone with knowledge or skills in the wider community setting.

Teaching may be carried out informally, within the family, which is called home schooling, or in the wider community. Formal teaching may be carried out by paid professionals. Such professionals enjoy a status in some societies on a par with physicians, lawyers, engineers, and accountants (Chartered or CPA).

A teacher's professional duties may extend beyond formal teaching. Outside of the classroom teachers may accompany students on field trips, supervise study halls, help with the organization of school functions, and serve as supervisors for extracurricular activities. In some education systems, teachers may have responsibility for student discipline. Around the world teachers are often required to obtain specialized education, knowledge, codes of ethics and internal monitoring. There are a variety of bodies designed to instill, preserve and update the knowledge and professional standing of teachers. Around the world many governments operate teacher's colleges, which are generally established to serve and protect the public interest through certifying, governing and enforcing the standards of practice for the teaching profession.

The functions of the teacher's colleges may include setting out clear standards of practice, providing for the ongoing education of teachers, investigating complaints involving members, conducting hearings into allegations of professional misconduct and taking appropriate disciplinary action and accrediting teacher education programs. In many situations teachers in publicly funded schools must be members in good standing with the college, and private schools may also require their teachers to be college peoples. In other areas these roles may belong to the State Board of Education, the Superintendent of Public Instruction, the State Education Agency or other governmental bodies. In still other areas Teaching Unions may be responsible for some or all of these duties.

Pedagogy and Teaching

In education, teachers facilitate student learning, often in a school or academy or perhaps in another environment such as outdoors. A teacher who teaches on an individual basis may be described as a tutor.

Figure: *A primary school teacher in northern Laos*

The objective is typically accomplished through either an informal or formal approach to learning, including a course of study and lesson plan that teaches skills, knowledge and/or thinking skills. Different ways to teach are often referred to as pedagogy. When deciding what teaching method to use teachers consider students' background knowledge, environment, and their learning goals as well as standardized curricula as determined by the relevant authority. Many times, teachers assist in learning outside of the classroom by accompanying students on field trips. The increasing use of technology, specifically the rise of the internet over the past decade, has begun to shape the way teachers approach their roles in the classroom.

The objective is typically a course of study, lesson plan, or a practical skill. A teacher may follow standardized curricula as determined by the relevant authority. The teacher may interact with students of different ages, from infants to adults, students with different abilities and students with learning disabilities.

Teaching using pedagogy also involve assessing the educational levels of the students on particular skills. Understanding the pedagogy of the students in a classroom involves using differentiated instruction as well as supervision to meet the needs of all students in the classroom. Pedagogy can be thought of in two manners. First, teaching itself can be taught in many different ways, hence, using a pedagogy of teaching styles. Second, the pedagogy of the learners comes into play when a teacher assesses the pedagogic diversity of his/her students and differentiates for the individual students accordingly.

Perhaps the most significant difference between primary school and secondary school teaching is the relationship between teachers and children. In primary schools each class has a teacher who stays with them for most of the week and will teach them the whole curriculum. In secondary schools they will be taught by different subject specialists each session during the week and may have 10 or more different teachers.

The relationship between children and their teachers tends to be closer in the primary school where they act as form tutor, specialist teacher and surrogate parent during the course of the day.

***Figure:** GDR "village teacher", a teacher teaching students of all age groups in one class in 1951*

This is true throughout most of the United States as well. However, alternative approaches for primary education do exist. One of these, sometimes referred to as a "platoon" system, involves placing a group of students together in one class that moves from one specialist to another for every subject.

The advantage here is that students learn from teachers who specialize in one subject and who tend to be more knowledgeable in that one area than a teacher who teaches many subjects. Students still derive a strong sense of security by staying with the same group of peers for all classes.

Co-teaching has also become a new trend amongst educational institutions. Co-teaching is defined as two or more teachers working harmoniously to fulfill the needs of every student in the classroom. Co-teaching focuses the student on learning by providing a social networking support that allows them to reach their full cognitive potential. Co-teachers work in sync with one another to create a climate of learning.

Teacher Enthusiasm

Since teachers can affect how students perceive the course materials, it has been found that teachers who showed enthusiasm towards the course materials and students can affect a positive learning experience towards the course materials. On teacher/course evaluations, it was found that teachers who have a positive disposition towards the course content tend to transfer their passion to receptive students. These teachers do not teach by rote but attempt to find new invigoration for the course materials on a daily basis. One of the difficulties in this approach is that teachers may have repeatedly covered a curriculum until they begin to feel bored with the subject which in turn bores the students as well. Students who had enthusiastic teachers tend to rate them higher than teachers who didn't show much enthusiasm for the course materials.

Teachers that exhibit enthusiasm can lead to students who are more likely to be engaged, interested, energetic, and curious about learning the subject matter. Recent research has found a correlation between teacher enthusiasm and students' intrinsic motivation to learn and vitality in the classroom. Controlled, experimental studies exploring intrinsic motivation of college students has shown that nonverbal expressions of enthusiasm, such as demonstrative gesturing, dramatic movements which are varied, and emotional facial expressions, result in college students reporting higher levels of intrinsic motivation to learn. Students who experienced a very enthusiastic teacher were more likely to read lecture material outside of the classroom.

There are various mechanisms by which teacher enthusiasm may facilitate higher levels of intrinsic motivation. Teacher enthusiasm may contribute to a classroom atmosphere full of energy and enthusiasm which feed student interest and excitement in learning the subject matter. Enthusiastic teachers may also lead to students becoming more self-determined in their own learning process. The concept of mere exposure indicates that the teacher's enthusiasm may contribute to the student's expectations about intrinsic motivation in the context of learning. Also, enthusiasm may act as a "motivational embellishment"; increasing a student's interest by the variety, novelty, and surprise of the enthusiastic teacher's presentation of the material. Finally, the concept of emotional contagion, may also apply. Students may become more intrinsically motivated by catching onto the enthusiasm and energy of the teacher.

Research shows that student motivation and attitudes towards school are closely linked to student-teacher relationships. Enthusiastic teachers are particularly good at creating beneficial relations with their students. Their ability to create effective learning environments that foster student achievement depends on the kind of relationship they build with their students. Useful teacher-to-student interactions are crucial in linking academic success with personal achievement. Here, personal success is a student's internal goal of improving himself, whereas academic success includes the goals he receives from his superior. A teacher must guide his student in aligning his personal goals with his academic goals. Students who receive this positive influence show stronger self-confidence and greater personal and academic success than those without these teacher interactions.

Students are likely to build stronger relations with teachers who are friendly and supportive and will show more interest in courses taught by these teachers. Teachers that spend more time interacting and working directly with students are perceived as supportive and effective teachers. Effective teachers have been shown to invite student participation and decision making, allow humor into their classroom, and demonstrate a willingness to play.

The way a teacher promotes the course they are teaching, the more the student will get out of the subject matter. The three most important aspects of teacher enthusiasm are enthusiasm about teaching, enthusiasm about the students, and enthusiasm about the subject matter. A teacher must enjoy teaching. If they do not enjoy what they are doing, the students will be able to tell. They also must enjoy being around their students. A teacher who cares for their students is going to help that individual succeed in their life in the future. The teacher also needs to be enthusiastic about the subject matter they are teaching. For example, a teacher talking about chemsitry needs to enjoy the art of chemistry and show that to their students. A spark in the teacher may create a spark of excitement in the student as well. An enthusiastic teacher has the ability to be very influential in the young students life.

Many people emphasize the importance of good teachers, and many local, state, and federal policies are designed to promote teacher quality. Research using student scores on standardized tests confirms the common perception that some teachers are more effective than others and also reveals that being taught by an effective teacher has important consequences for student achievement.

- Teachers matter more to student achievement than any other aspect of schooling.

Many factors contribute to a student's academic performance, including individual characteristics and family and neighborhood experiences. But research suggests that, among school-related factors, teachers matter most. When it comes to student performance on reading and math tests, a teacher is estimated to have two to three times the impact of any other school factor, including services, facilities, and even leadership.

- Nonschool factors do influence student achievement, but they are largely outside a school's control.

Some research suggests that, compared with teachers, individual and family characteristics may have four to eight times the impact on student achievement. But policy discussions focus on teachers because it is arguably easier for public policy to improve teaching than to change students' personal characteristics or family circumstances. Effective teaching has the potential to help level the playing field.

- Effective teachers are best identified by their performance, not by their background or experience.

Despite common perceptions, effective teachers cannot reliably be identified based on where they went to school, whether they're licensed, or (after the first few years) how long they've taught. The best way to assess teachers' effectiveness is to look at their on-the-job performance, including what they do in the classroom and how much progress their students make on achievement tests. This has led to more policies that require evaluating teachers' on-the-job performance, based in part on evidence about their students' learning.

- Effective teachers tend to stay effective even when they change schools.

Recent evidence suggests that a teacher's impact on student achievement remains reasonably consistent even if the teacher changes schools and regardless of whether the new school is more or less advantaged than the old one.

Learning Theories in the Early Childhood Classroom Environment

During the early stages of development, children learn by playing. Play, in a developmentally appropriate environment, inspires the child to relate oneself to the environment while making sense of the infinite elements uniting internal processes with external influences. As children play, they learn. They learn about the size, shape, smell, taste, and tactile quality of their world.

As they internalize the sensations of the environment, they integrate personal experiences to hypothesize the impossible. Imaginary play is constant as children relate their hopes and experiences to new sensations. As their minds translate external experiences with personal meaning, children become masters of their environment. The child's environment may be defined as a continuum between the imaginary and the sensory.

Complex yet accessible relationships occurring in the classroom enrich the mental processes of young students. "The rationale for emphasizing the construction of relationships in education is that it is basically by constructing relationships that children elaborate their knowledge and develop their intelligence".

When children reflect on their environment, they instinctively classify experiences according to both individual personality and the surrounding culture. As children become familiar with the syntax of social knowledge, their worlds are shared with one another to form a social imagination.

As the child struggles to comprehend new experiences, he or she will naturally utilize scientific notions of problem solving and critical thinking.

The Lesson Plan

In an early childhood classroom operating within a public elementary school, the teacher prepares a lesson on food production. According to the classroom curriculum standards, the teacher should provide the children with an awareness of the process of taking food from the farm producer and preparing it for the grocery store consumer. The generalized curriculum standard offers the teacher the freedom to choose from a variety of examples to use for teaching the process. The community of the school is rural and many of the children are familiar with small farms. The children drink milk everyday at school and, therefore, have personal experiences with the beverage. Because of these factors, the teacher decides to focus on milk production.

Behaviorist Learning Theories

Behaviorism defines learning as a change in observable behaviors due to environmental stimuli. Using behaviorist learning theories, a teacher begins a lesson on milk production by having the children gather during group time on a large carpet. As the children sit on the carpet facing the teacher only, he or she presents the book, The Milk Makers, by Gail Gibbons. The children face only the teacher to avoid undesirable reinforcement that could distract from the goal of the lesson. The teacher uses the picture book to explain the topic because the children are engaged with the visual material as the teacher narrates the pictures. As the children listen to the story, they receive a summary of the information they are expected to learn.

When the teacher is finished reading the story, he or she re-explains the four stages of milk production. As she summarizes the information, she introduces four pictures that illustrate each stage. After the summary, the teacher passes each child a set of pictures to view. The teacher tests the children on their understanding by having them hold up the pictures in sequential order.

The assessment is based on both classical and operant conditioning. Each child will hold up a picture, the unconditioned response, when the teacher asks for a certain card, the unconditioned stimulus. The teacher's positive feedback, a conditioned stimulus, will prompt the correct choice, the conditioned response, according to the lesson. Operant conditioning is utilized as the children are reinforced with stickers and chosen activities.

During the teacher's assessment the children hold up one picture at a time. The children face the teacher so each child is focusing on the appropriate picture and the teacher's feedback. Each child who holds up the appropriate picture receives a star. When a child has received four stars in a row, he or she may leave the group area for a chosen activity. The teacher retests the remaining children until each has mastered the material.

Behaviorist learning theories simplify lessons so that the child's focused attention and the teacher's curriculum goals remain specific. Because of the efficiency of a behaviorist lesson plan in terms of planning, execution, and assessment, the teacher has more time for alternate classroom tasks. The clear structure of a behaviorist lesson can be especially beneficial for children who are easily distracted or over-stimulated. However, the categorical focus of behaviorism can be wearisome for children in need of variety and stimulation.

Social Cognitive Learning Theories

Using social learning methods, the teacher has the children sit in a circle on a large carpet for group time. The children are arranged so that every person is visible. The teacher sits at the head of the circle and reads The Milk Makers, by Gail Gibbons. After the story, the teacher distributes four cards to each child displaying four stages of milk production.

After reading the story, the teacher explains the pictures before explicitly demonstrating how to present the pictures in sequential order. The teacher passes the four pictures to each child and begins the assessment. The children are asked to show the first card in the process of milk production. The teacher calls on each child who displays the appropriate picture. A model child is asked to describe the picture. The teacher then asks for the same picture again, waiting for each child to present the correct answer as demonstrated by the model. Based on social cognitive learning theories, the children expect to receive recognition for selecting the appropriate picture.

Once the teacher begins to assess the children's understanding, the children use each other's responses to evaluate their individual progress as compared to others. The final assessment utilizes modelling, reinforcement, and feedback as described by social cognitive theories.

The group approaches each picture in the same manner. After every picture has been discussed, the teacher quickly calls for the pictures again, giving the children less time to present the appropriate answer. Children who choose the correct pictures are recognized by the teacher and are reinforced with praise. Using vicarious reinforcement, these children serve as models for the ignored children who have selected incorrectly.

At the end of the lesson the children place their cards in correct order and hand them back to the teacher. The teacher uses the order of each set to assess individual learning.

Social cognitive theories reflect the natural tendencies of individuals to alter personal behaviors based on the observed behaviour of others. They are effective because they are natural. In classroom groups, children often rely on each other for support and guidance in both explicit and implicit ways. However, teachers should be wary of the essence of motivation as defined by classroom competition. Excessive use of modelling to influence children can lead to unnecessary competition. Unnecessary competition can affect the inherent motivation of children in a variety of ways.

Cognitive Learning Theories

A lesson about milk production using cognitive learning methods begins with a group discussion about milk. The teacher asks the children if they drink milk, where they buy it, and where the milk comes from. The children are encouraged to hypothesize about the process of transferring milk from the cow to the grocery store. As the children make guesses, the teacher transcribes ideas so the children can view the words. After the children are finished hypothesizing, the group votes on which idea makes the most sense. As children discuss ideas related to milk production, personal experiences are encouraged and evaluated. The teacher listens to discover each child's level of understanding.

When the topic seems exhausted the teacher reads the book, The Milk Makers, by Gail Gibbons. The children are encouraged to interrupt the story for questions related to the previous hypotheses. As the children interact with the story they are asked to edit their earlier ideas.

After the story, the teacher asks the group to review the new ideas. Pictures illustrating the main ideas of the story are introduced to focus the children on the most distinct stages of milk production. After discussing the story, materials are removed and a numbered board is introduced. The group is asked to assign the four stages in order without seeing the pictures. As the group discusses the appropriate order, the pictures are re-introduced and attached to the board. As the children finish, the teacher summarizes the information. The book and board is left in the room so the children can revisit the lesson autonomously.

The basic principles underlying cognitive learning theories include thought as an active pursuit, a foundation of experience used to organize new information, a personal perspective regarding new information, a social environment to acquire new knowledge, and the use of practice to further differentiate between experience and new information. When children think, they use all of their senses. The process of sensing is a highly involved network of stimuli, as described by neuroscience. As children contemplate using their senses, they incorporate Piaget's notions of assimilation and accommodation to regain equilibrium. By placing learning in a social environment, children expand their repertoire of experiences by contemplating the experiences of others. The process of learning is enhanced with reconsiderations of past experiences and new details. By using these ideas to form a learning environment rather than a lesson plan, the teacher makes the "lesson," or learning environment, more naturally motivated.

Using cognitive learning theories, the teacher offers a variety of experiences to approach information, assess understanding and summarize the combination of information and understanding. The children are active in the exploration using social interaction and feedback to stimulate individual thinking processes. Even during the physically passive activity of listening to the picture book, the children are encouraged to converse with the story, allowing new information to clarify previous understanding. When the teacher writes down the children's hypotheses, the class is able to revisit a solidified idea during the dynamic process of differentiating experience. This is perhaps the defining characteristic of the lesson because this solidification provides the framework for the children's processes of thought. The children see simultaneously the journey of their thinking and the highly varying nature of contemplation as sense becomes knowledge.

Cognitive learning theories infuse the classroom curriculum with meaningful interaction. Children grow together in intricate ways. Not all experiences can be measured equally, because everyone's experience is utterly unique. By collecting individual experiences the classroom builds a learning environment that is both deep and authentic. The assessment of such an environment may seem difficult at first glance, because the philosophy collides with standardized assessment practices. However, with practice, the teacher can realize a more artistic approach to assessment that values depth of understanding rather than test measures.

Constructivist Learning Theories

To prepare for the topic of milk production in a constructivist environment, the teacher organizes a field trip to the local dairy. He or she coordinates the field trip with the cafeteria milk delivery so the children can visit the delivery truck the following morning. The day before the field trip, the children and teacher discuss milk production. Personal experiences are collected and hypotheses are formulated regarding the field trip. The children make a list of items to find in the dairy and draw pictures of farmers and their cows.

The children spend the following day visiting the dairy. Each child carries a clipboard to record information. The teachers photograph the tour and write down the children's verbal reflections.

During the following morning, the children visit the cafeteria to meet the milk delivery man. The children tour the truck and watch him refill the cafeteria refrigerators. Some children draw pictures of the truck while others tally the number of carts carried by the delivery man. The children and teacher gather during the afternoon to discuss their experiences. The teacher records personal observations related by the children. As the children discuss their favourite experiences, teachers encourage the children to explore significant elements. As the children relate to the group, the teachers discover which topics are most exciting to the children.

The following week the room is transformed into a dairy. The water table is equipped with milk jugs and funnels. The writing area is prepared with clipboards holding inventory charts. The block area contains farm animals and semi-trucks. The dramatic play area is decorated according to farm themes. The reading area includes books about cows, dairies, and nutrition.

During the morning, the children gather on a large carpet to prepare for the day and discuss the current activities. Based on the children's interests, the teachers divide the children in two groups. One group discusses the trip to the dairy and reviews pictures and observations recorded by the students and teachers. The other group discusses the morning visit with the delivery man. Each group defines favourite moments and illustrates these moments by drawing pictures.

After the separate groups have finished their illustrations, they share with the class. Each group discusses the events as recounted by students according to their illustrations. To conclude, the children create a milk production timeline using their pictures. As the children work together to create the timeline, they discuss the different stages involved in milk production.

The principles of constructivist learning require that teachers ask the children many questions about a variety of examples, which occur within the learning environment. The constructivist learning environment must be authentic and learning experiences must be relevant. Based on both Piaget and Vygotsky, learning experiences must be social in context to augment individual development. Learning should never be forced, but should be appreciated as it occurs naturally. By keeping the learning environment authentic and the children's natural perceptions worthy, motivation exists as an element of the environment. The teacher is an observer of perception rather than a presenter of information. The teacher provides for the learner rather than imposing on the learner.

During the constructivist process of studying milk production, the children use natural thinking methods to survey an authentic environment. As the children become more experienced, play experiences are provided to elaborate on those experiences. To access higher order reasoning, the children are expected to illustrate with both drawings and conversations. "For Vygotsky, this symbolic use of objects, actions, words, and people prepares the way for the learning of literacies based on the use of symbols like reading, writing, and drawing." As children explore their new knowledge, they summarize and reassess the information in small groups. The structured format as practiced in small groups allows children to take their learning to the next level. As children discuss their learning, the imagination is fortified for new experiences.

Constructivist learning theories are most problematic in areas of special education. The experiences of constructivist education necessitate a more coercive mediator for special learners than is necessary for children of typical development. In this situation, the teacher must regard focused attention as the most important relationship between the teacher and the student. What detail the child focuses on is less important than the process of focusing on a detail. This detail can take on an infinite number of shapes and sizes in the mind of the teacher, but can become quite specific and permanent to the child. While other students may be capable of observing intricate relationships between a variety of details, the special learner may be satisfied with a sole element for contemplation. This element could provide the path for the teacher to mediate focused attention without losing inherent motivation. Constructivist learning in special education can be effective, but it requires more patience, acceptance, and focus by the teacher without being absolute in areas of control. The most obscure observation of a lesson as provided by the special learner, can be the most enlightening if given a direction.

Safety Measures

Accessible School Facilities and Programs

Ensure that school-sponsored programs both on-site and off-site (such as field trips, vocational education work experiences, extra-curricular activities, and sporting events) are accessible to all students and staff.

Accessibility to facilities for those with disabilities requires planning for new and renovated buildings and grounds and may require retrofitting of existing facilities. Children's height and other dimensions must be taken into account when designing or purchasing drinking fountains, toilet stalls, lavatories, sinks, and fixed or built-seats and tables. Include accessible routes for persons to reach buildings and other spaces. Ground surfaces along accessible routes, transportation (drop-off and pick-up sites), getting from one floor to another in multiple-story buildings, and parking spaces must be considered as part of facility planning. Apply these designs to both temporary and permanent facilities—any building that is used for the public.

Communicating Safety Policies

Communicate all safety policies to staff, students, and families. Notify parents and staff in advance of physical plant projects and other changes that might affect the health, safety, and well-being of students and staff. Inform staff, students, and families about unplanned incidents such as a chemical and biological exposure or exposure to certain communicable diseases.

Knowledge of safety policies, such as student drop-off and pick-up areas or prohibition of weapons in school, is essential to compliance. Warning parents, students, and staff about projects that affect the physical environment (e.g., painting, pesticide spraying) allows persons with unusual sensitivities to be protected from harm. Having a plan to deal with an unforeseen environmental exposure reduces unnecessary delay between exposure and treatment, thereby optimizing health outcomes.

Involve staff, students, and families in the development and revision of safety policies. Policies without clear parameters may be open to varying interpretation. Policies must be explicit, well-disseminated and explained to all those expected to abide by them. The existence of school health and safety teams with well-defined roles and clear reporting mechanisms can help clarify communication and improve the accuracy, approval, and acceptance of messages.

Projects that benefit from advanced notification include painting, renovation, pesticide application, and removal of mold or asbestos. Schools have a responsibility not only to minimize students' exposure but also to alert their families to the potential for exposure. Students with special health needs such as allergy or asthma who might be unusually susceptible can receive additional protection. When a school cannot predict an unusual environmental event, such as a chemical spill on a nearby highway, the school should consult with emergency personnel about the best ways to protect students. School staff should notify students' families and health professionals of any such exposure and report the substance involved, signs and symptoms to watch for, and how to seek any necessary health care.

Adoption of a plan that addresses environmental concerns will assist the district in responding to them quickly and appropriately. Principles and goals of "risk communication" should be considered when designing a notification mechanism. This helps ensure that heath and safety messages are accurate and clearly understood by families, students, and staff. Parents with limited literacy or limited understanding of the English language must also be considered in this plan. The district should have knowledgeable personnel and/or consultants available to assist with investigations and to assist district personnel in developing the plan.

Buildings: Construction and Renovation

Designing and building schools as well as improving existing systems and buildings so that they provide a healthy and safe indoor and outdoor environment can prevent health and safety problems for occupants. Schools that are appropriately designed, constructed, and maintained can reduce operations and maintenance costs. Construction and renovation often disturb existing materials or introduce new materials thereby generating unsafe quantities of particulates, gases, and vapors, which result in poor indoor air quality.

Safety of a school environment must consider fire, earthquake and other safety codes (e.g., adequate stairways and exits, safety glass), thermal comfort controls, humidification and dehumidification systems, moisture protection measures, and building commissioning. Opt for energy efficiency and environmentally friendly materials and consider the energy absorbing properties of chosen materials. The design and construction of a healthy and safe school environment must also specifically consider school-site selection (based on transportation needs such as walking and biking paths), accessibility standards (i.e., accommodating disabilities), safe surfacing (e.g., playgrounds, hypoallergenic indoor flooring), and source control measures in areas such as science laboratories and vocational technical areas. Supplies of hot and cold water sources for sinks and toilets should be adequate and located strategically to promote hygiene (e.g., near food preparation areas, in rooms where students receive medical procedures, in toileting areas, in classrooms where chemical exposure may require flushing with water). Drinking fountain locations should promote water drinking but be protected from traffic to avoid oral injuries. Design classrooms, media centres, and libraries with good lighting and acoustics. Stairways, hallways, and restrooms should also be well-lit.

In the design stage of a construction and renovation project, strategic plans should be implemented to minimize and eliminate potential exposures to various environmental hazards to workers and occupants. These strategies include but are not limited to: work site isolation, safety practices, indoor air quality-friendly products and materials selection, construction methods, activities scheduling, good housekeeping practices, and project updates and communications. Federal and state regulatory requirements apply to renovations that disturb certain highly regulated substances, such as asbestos-containing materials and lead paint. Renovations in occupied buildings should only be undertaken after the strategic plans have been agreed to by all parties including the school administration, contract administrators, contractors, parents, students, and other interested parties, and after obtaining necessary regulatory approval.

Buildings and Grounds: Maintenance

Develop and implement comprehensive preventive maintenance procedures to ensure a healthy and safe environment within the building and on school grounds. Include staff training and have procedures that include playgrounds, sports areas, and bathroom facilities.

A comprehensive preventive maintenance program can avert significant and premature deterioration of the building, its systems, and its playgrounds that could lead to compromised health and safety of students and staff.

An environmental safety review of buildings and grounds should be done at least annually. Proper attention to the maintenance of the heating, ventilating, and air-conditioning systems, building envelope (roofs, walls, windows, flooring, subflooring), and housekeeping will improve indoor air quality and energy efficiency and will reduce costs and level of custodial effort to keep the building clean. The maintenance plan should include consideration of weather related problems, such as water on floors in rainy/snowy weather. Maintenance should also include procedures for maintaining safety on school grounds, including playground surfaces and equipment.

Cover trash containers to keep out rainwater and remove waste on a regular schedule to prevent noxious odors and environmental reservoirs for disease. Open trash containers with decaying organic materials (scraps of food, for example) attract flies and other vermin that can carry bacteria and viruses to food sources and to humans directly. Cockroaches and rodents can also be vectors of disease.

Toilet facilities must be maintained to be both hygienic and safe. Areas of privacy must be provided (e.g., stall doors that are intact and operational). Adequate supplies of soap, toilet tissue, and paper towels must be maintained. Students should not be discouraged from utilizing toilet facilities for reasons of cleanliness or safety. Require that an experienced maintenance supervisor develop inspection and maintenance procedures, including a detailed preventive maintenance schedule for all equipment, grounds, and facilities. School administrators must be aware of estimated labour-hours to complete all preventive maintenance activities and have a budget to meet those needs.

Classroom Safety: Equipment, Facilities, Student Conduct

Teach students safety practices, ensure safe conduct, and enforce use of applicable safety guards and protection devices in classrooms. Provide appropriate supervision, safe equipment, and safe facilities. Apply these principles to vocational education settings, to youth employment situations, and to all art, science, food preparation, industrial arts, and shop classes.

Safety education, safe practices, and supervision, when enforced through school policy in science and shop classes, art courses, classes where there is food preparation, and vocational education classes, will prevent serious injuries to staff and students.

A coordinated effort to review safety needs as well as to revise and maintain safety protocols in these classes should be implemented through representatives from vocational education, science, and art. Class safety rules should be developed and taught to students. Students should sign a contract at the beginning of the term agreeing to follow the rules. Provide adequate supervision. Inspection checklists should be used in shop and vocational education classes.

Chemicals are of particular concern in classrooms. It is recommended that chemicals be stored by their chemical family rather than alphabetically to minimize dangerous interactions. Dispose of chemicals that are on the banned substance list, are out of date, or are in unlabelled containers. Material safety data sheets (MSDS) should be available to staff and students for each chemical stored and/or used in the school setting.

Certification programs, continuing education, and educational supplies that pertain to the prevention of injuries in these classes are available. A publication of the American Chemical Society and an Internet site called "The Catalyst" (a resource for science teachers) provide detailed safety information pertaining to chemistry, biology, and physics in the school classroom. Guidelines on work space per student, eye protection, fire prevention, and protection from injuries in physics experiments that involve electricity, motion, energy, heat, and sound are available at this website. Inspections by the US Occupational Safety and Health Administration may be considered in order to verify compliance with meeting safety standards for staff.

Youth who are employed, particularly those who work as part of school-to-work programs or vocational training, require knowledge of safety practices and the skills to recognize and avoid unsafe work-site situations.

Safety on out-of-school Trips

Develop and implement plans to address the safety of students on school-sponsored, out-of-school trips (field trips). Policy should address: supervision of students, transportation to sites, student-specific health information, equipment and expertise required to implement students' individualized health service plans (including administration of medication), and behavioural expectations of students and supervisors.

Schools are responsible for students and their safety at any school-sponsored event, on or off school grounds.

Adequate supervision of students must be planned in advance of each trip and must take into consideration students' health, mental health, and safety needs. This includes having students accompanied by staff who are trained to administer medications, perform first-aid, and observe for health problems (for example, recognizing symptoms of asthma or observing that a student with diabetes has eaten lunch). Arrangements to transport health-related equipment must be made. A responsible adult on the trip should have a copy of each student's emergency information card. Information must include emergency contact information and key health information that will be needed in an emergency.

Encourage the use of school vehicles driven by appropriately trained and licensed school employees, not private vehicles, when the school district provides transportation to school-sponsored events. When private vehicles must be used, require operators to be licensed drivers of the type of vehicle driven, carry insurance for occupants of their vehicles, require occupants to wear safety belts, and follow state regulations for inspection and registration for the vehicle.

Behavioural expectations may include, for example, making one's location known at all times; avoidance of tobacco, alcohol, and illicit drugs; and housing males and females in separate sleeping quarters.

Safe Pedestrian and Vehicle Traffic Areas: Establish and enforce a plan that is designed to provide safe movement of motorized vehicles, non-motorized vehicles, and pedestrian traffic on school property. Include all parking, pedestrian, and vehicle traffic areas, bicycle lanes, and student drop-off/pick-up areas. Apply the policy to staff and students driving on campus and to recreational and commercial service vehicles. The plan should encourage walking and/ or bicycling to school and include the establishment of safe routes to school.

Multiple modes of transportation at school as well as transportation to and from school and school-sponsored activities put students and staff at some risk for collision. Proper planning, development and enforcement of standards, and education can decrease risk of collision and injury.

Route vehicular traffic onto schools' driveways and parking lots to minimize danger to pedestrians. Protect pedestrian paths from bicyclists and students using skates, skate boards, and scooters (e.g., separate lanes). Protect users of these non-motorized recreational vehicles from motorized vehicle traffic. Playgrounds should be located away from traffic. Have clearly marked and separate drop-off and pickup areas for pedestrians, school bus riders, and private vehicle users. Situate them so as to reduce student and staff exposure to vehicle exhaust fumes. Pickup and drop-off points for students should be limited to the curb and preferably at an off-street location that is protected from traffic. Assure adequate supervision while students are boarding and exiting vehicles. Be certain that crossing guards and members of safety patrols are trained for these roles. Discourage the playing of car radios and public announcement systems in vehicles used to transport students. Communicate all policies to staff, students, and their families.

Conduct a school transportation safety assessment when considering where to build new schools. Assess whether areas have adequate road capacity to handle increased traffic, adequate sidewalks, bicycle lanes, places for school bus stops, and low crime rates that make walking safe. Efforts should be coordinated with appropriate jurisdictional authority to provide well-posted and enforced reduced-speed school zones around campuses.

Playground Safety

Use and monitor the use of the most updated US Consumer Product Safety Commission (CPSC) and ASTM International guidelines for playground safety. Use the guidelines to address playground surfacing, the use and maintenance of equipment, and supervision.

Research has shown that many playgrounds fail to meet CPSC and other safety guidelines and standards. Following guidelines greatly reduces risks of injury to students and others who use the facilities.

Students must be taught to play safely. Falling from playground structures and colliding with equipment or other students can result in head, face, oral, and other musculoskeletal injuries. More than 200,000 playground injuries are reported each year in the United States. Approximately 75 percent of these injuries are attributable to falls, mostly from slides, jungle gyms, and other climbing equipment. Other causes of injury include running into equipment, various collisions, burns from hot surfaces or equipment, and strangulation. Student conduct related to playground safety must be also be addressed.

Schools should follow CPSC and ASTM International safety guidelines to prevent these types of injuries to students. ASTM International was formerly known as American Society for Testing and Materials. Guidelines are fairly specific (e.g., do not wear bicycle helmets on play equipment, details on equipment hardware, inspections for sharp edges) and there are multiple ways to retrieve this information (e.g., videos, checklists, brochures, instruction books). Major focus areas include separation of playground areas for different age groups, installation and maintenance of safe and developmentally appropriate equipment, use of appropriate surface materials, appropriate fall zone areas, and adequate supervision at all times. Playground equipment and play surfaces should be inspected and maintained. Records should be kept of all playground injuries and reviewed. Injury data should be carefully analyzed and used to guide preventive, intervention, and education strategies. Inspections should take place on at least an annual basis (more often depending on life of equipment and surfaces, such as plastic equipment) and adjustments should be made on the basis of injury cause data, updated guidelines, and repair records.

Exposure to Toxic/poisonous Substances in Classrooms

Prohibit the use of toxic and poisonous substances as part of classroom or vocational education unless there is a clearly documented need that cannot be otherwise met and there are protocols and procedures in place to protect students and staff from toxin exposure. Communicate policies on acceptable and unacceptable substances to students, staff, and families.

Ingestion, inhalation, or other misuse of potentially toxic substances, whether intentional or unintentional, can be prevented. By adopting policies that reduce access, schools and districts can avoid harmful consequences, such as poisoning and burns.

Art, Theater, Shop, Vocation

Ceramic kilns can be used if they are vented sufficiently and only a teacher or other trained adult is potentially exposed to the heat, kiln wash, etc. Ceramic glazes, either leaded or lead-free, and processes or chemicals requiring ventilation should not be used in elementary schools. For older students in classes such as Chemistry, substances should be properly stored and used with supervision. In areas in which students through age eight may have access, potentially toxic substances should be stored in a locked cabinet.

Poison Control and emergency assistance numbers should be clearly posted by all telephones. Poison control and emergency assistance numbers are 800-222-1222 and 911, respectively. Staff and students should be trained in proper response to poisonings and toxic exposures.

Live Animals in School Environment

Limit exposure to live animals in order to protect the health and safety of students and staff.

Students in schools should not have access to live animals that may pose a threat to safety and health.

Exposure to live animals places students at risk for animal bites, allergic reactions, and infection from animal vectors. Furred and feathered animals are common triggers for students with allergies and asthma. Reptiles are frequent carriers of infectious diseases. Access to all animals on school property should be limited, so that no animal roams freely.

Animals should be eliminated from regular classrooms. Animals necessary for certain curricula, such as biology or animal husbandry/vocational-agricultural programs, should be carefully confined in suitable, sanitary, self-contained enclosures appropriate to the size of the animal. Staff must be responsible for ensuring that enclosures are kept in a sanitary condition. Prior to introducing any animals into the classroom, school staff must verify that students and school personnel have no known allergy to that animal and that animals are free from any diseases or parasites. Animals must present no physical danger to students and contact should be limited to instructional purposes. Students must be fully supervised during all points of animal contact.

Tobacco Use Policy

Develop and enforce policies that prohibit tobacco use on school property by all students, school staff, families, and visitors. This policy should include school vehicles and any school-sponsored indoor or outdoor event.

Environmental tobacco smoke exposure is a well-recognized health hazard for children and adolescents. Tobacco smoke is associated with serious adverse health effects, including bronchitis, emphysema, exacerbation of asthma, lung cancer, heart disease, and many other illnesses.

States and/or school districts typically ban smoking inside schools as well as on school grounds for teachers, staff, and students to minimize students' opportunities to smoke and their exposure to environmental smoke. Studies show that restrictions on smoking may help young persons refrain from starting to smoke. Pipes, cigars, chewing tobacco, and any tobacco product should be included in this policy. Tobacco cessation programs should be offered to all who use tobacco.

Drug/alcohol-free School Policy

Develop and enforce alcohol-free and drug-free policies for all school staff, families, students, and visitors at indoor and outdoor school-sponsored events.

Substances that can impair function and compromise the safety of students and staff must not be allowed on school property or at school-sponsored events. It is illegal for students to purchase, possess, and utilize such substances.

An alcohol and drug-free policy still permits staff and students to use prescribed medications during the school day in order to maintain their health. Illicit use of drugs, including tobacco and alcoholic beverages, cannot be tolerated on school property. Failure to comply with these policies should result in disciplinary action and referral to appropriate treatment programs. While expulsion from school may seem to be appropriate, it may aggravate the student's problem rather than help move towards a solution.

Alternate education and therapeutic intervention programs can provide a more acceptable solution and ensure that students receive necessary treatment.

A policy addressing staff using alcohol or other drugs while driving vehicles used to transport students must be in place to ensure the safety of all. Employees found to be using alcohol and illicit drugs must be immediately removed from such duty and appropriate referrals for evaluation and treatment should be made.

Indoor/outdoor Allergens, Irritants, air Quality

Develop and enforce policies that minimize exposure to indoor and outdoor allergens and irritants for students and staff.

Reducing exposure to allergic triggers is a school's responsibility. Enforcing policies helps to prevent life threatening events and to keep students and staff with sensitivities free of symptoms and better able to carry out their academic functions.

Allergies to foods, insect stings, medications and latex puts approximately 3% of students at risk for severe allergic reactions. Dust mites, pollen, cockroach droppings, molds, animal saliva, urine, and dander are common allergic triggers that cause less severe reactions. Asthma can be exacerbated by these allergens, by tobacco smoke, and by strong odors. Include specific environmental precautions in allergic students' individualized health services plans. On days with high pollen counts and/or pollution levels (e.g., smog, ozone), physical activities for sensitive individuals may need to be conducted in a controlled indoor environment. Retrofit buses and reduce idling to minimize students' exposure to vehicle emissions. Use vinyl or nitrile gloves, rather than latex, in handling food, in laboratories, and in caring for special-needs children.

To decrease fungal and pollen exposure in mechanically ventilated buildings, keep windows closed and use efficient filters. Periodically disinfect locker rooms because fungi often grow in moist environments. Regulate the relative humidity of the air (e.g., via insulation, dehumidification, source control, temperature control). Unless carpeting is necessary and unless its composition and schedule of maintenance minimize dust, mold, and chemical irritants, consider hard surfaces instead of carpets. Avoid unnecessary accumulation of materials in classrooms and hallways that collect dust and harbor molds.

Limit exposure to animal allergens by minimizing animal presence in classrooms. Weigh risk of allergen exposure against risk of pesticide exposure. Implement pest control strategies (e.g., rats, mice, cockroaches, flies mosquitoes) by controlling food sources and moisture and by using specific pesticides or other "integrated pest management" methods. Recognize that many staff and students are in contact with animals and carry allergens on their clothing to school. Do not require students with certain animal allergies to take field trips to zoos or farms or to be exposed to animals (e.g., science projects). Because school renovations that produce dust can aggravate asthma, schedule renovations when students are not present.

Some districts prohibit all students from bringing a food item to school (e.g., nuts) when a fellow student is allergic. Although this is one management strategy and proves useful on celebratory occasions when food is brought from homes, it is difficult to enforce, often provides a false sense of security, and is not recommended by the Food Allergy and Anaphylaxis Network. Setting aside a meal table for selected food allergic students is more restrictive but generally safer than relying on all students' parents to read food labels for hidden allergic ingredients. In addition to the allergic child, educate all students, lunch monitors, and other staff on ingredient avoidance. Prohibit sharing of foods and eating on buses. Keep potential allergic foods, such as those with nuts as an ingredient, off of school food service menus and out of vending machines.

Reservoirs of Infectious Agents in Physical Environment

Control the indoor and outdoor school environment to prevent potential reservoirs for infectious agents from becoming a source of disease (e.g., standing water and animal droppings).

Diseases caused by environmental source infectious agents can be life threatening. Preventive maintenance and control of the environment are relatively straightforward, effective and essential.

Infectious agents (e.g., bacteria, fungi) are always present in the air, on environmental surfaces, and as part of contact with other persons. Bioaerosols are microscopic organisms in the air we breathe, are always present in the environment, and pose no problems when kept within reasonable limits. Although bacteria cause many odors in indoor environments (e.g., human body odor, locker room odors, sour milk), exposure to such bacteria is rarely harmful.

Rarely, specific infectious agents can become so populous that they pose a particular health risk. When excessively concentrated bioaerosols are inhaled, they can cause disease. The most serious risks are to immunologically compromised individuals. There are many examples: humidifiers may harbor bacteria and cause pneumonia, rhinitis (i.e., runny nose), and other respiratory infections; accumulation of bird droppings (feces) can carry infectious fungi (e.g., Histoplasmosis, Cryptococcosis); human contact with rodent droppings can lead to hantavirus infection; human contact with parasites and bacteria in feces of cats, dogs, fowl, and reptiles can cause diseases such as toxoplasmosis and salmonella. Untreated water reservoirs can release bioaerosols or attract disease-transmitting insects (e.g., mosquitoes), which may increase the risk for West Nile virus, Legionella disease, and malaria.

Birds, mice, rats and bats should not be allowed to colonize in attics, air intakes, or other areas near schools where people are likely to be exposed to fecal aerosols. Utilize methods to discourage migrating birds from congregating on school grounds. Any accumulated bird or rodent droppings should be treated to kill disease-causing organisms and then removed when the building is unoccupied.

Regularly clean ventilation systems and carpets. Prevent build-up of dirt and moisture. Immediately attend to unusual situations that could result in bioaerosol problems (e.g., wet carpets). Stagnant water should not be allowed to collect in ventilation system drain pans. Aerosol humidifiers should not be used in schools unless specific cleaning protocols are followed for preventing growth of infectious agents. Keep trash cans tightly covered and keep rain gutters clear of obstruction to prevent accumulation of standing water, a breeding ground for mosquitoes.

Universal Precautions; Blood-borne Pathogens

Provide school staff with education on the safe handling of blood, vomit, urine, other body fluids, and fecal material. Provide ample and convenient supplies of gloves, containers for proper disposal of needles and other sharp objects, disinfectants (including bleach), and other equipment in identified, predetermined locations, including classrooms.

Staff trained in procedures to handle potential exposure to blood-borne pathogens and other infectious agents minimizes risk to students and other staff and alleviates unnecessary anxiety. Hepatitis B, hepatitis C, human immunodeficiency virus (HIV), cytomegalovirus, and other viral infections are readily preventable through the use of basic protocols. A blood-borne pathogen exposure control plan for schools is mandated by the Occupational Safety and Health Administration.

Sport and playground injuries, severe bites, used needles, and many other occurrences in school can expose students and staff to blood-borne pathogens. "Universal precautions" refers to a set of protocols for handling body fluids properly (i.e., blood, saliva, urine, vomit). Body Substance Isolation (BSI) is an acceptable and alternative set of procedures to universal precautions and differs primarily in that this includes handling of all body fluids and substances.

Universal precautions include: hand washing, avoiding punctures, utilizing gloves when handling body fluids, using containers with plastic liners to dispose of contaminated tissues, having special containers for disposing of contaminated sharp objects, promptly washing blood and other human fluids from skin, and cleaning hard surfaces with a disinfectant (e.g., diluted household bleach).

Gloves, disinfectants, and containers to dispose of contaminated materials should be made available throughout the school for easy access. Vinyl and nitril (or nitrile) gloves have less risk than latex for allergic reaction. Nitril gloves have been shown to provide comparable pathogen protection to latex gloves. Masks are required for procedures where splattering to the face is a risk. Good hand washing technique is essential for preventing the spread of disease and should be taught to all staff and students. Adequate facilities for hand washing that should be available throughout all school facilities include warm water, soap or detergent, towels, waste receptacles and posted signs to instruct on hand washing technique.

Hand Washing

Encourage frequent hand washing with warm water and soap for students and staff in order to prevent or reduce the spread of communicable diseases.

Thorough hand washing with warm water and soap is the most effective way to prevent and avoid communicable disease. Students and staff should be encouraged to wash their hands with soap and warm water before consuming any food and after the use of the toilet or assisting others with toilet needs. To help prevent disease transmission, health services staff should educate students and staff on the importance of hand washing after nose-wiping, before preparing foods, before eating, and after using the toilet.

Schools should be equipped with adequate facilities and supplies. Adequate facilities for hand washing include warm water, soap, waste receptacles, and posted signs to instruct on hand washing technique. Schools with automatic shutoff water faucets should ensure that water runs for at least 30 seconds to provide adequate time for effective hand washing. Soap dispensers and towel dispensers should be checked daily or more often to be certain they are replenished and functioning.

Waterless hand cleaner should be used when running water is not available, but not to replace soap and water when running water is available.

A Plan for Safe School bus Transportation

Develop and implement a plan that promotes safety for bus transportation. Include driver qualifications, student and bus driver transportation equipment, emergency provisions and plans, loading/ unloading procedures, staff-child ratios, vehicle maintenance schedules and provisions for special events, special routes, and for children with special needs. Follow legal guidelines as well as local and state regulations and laws.

A transportation plan provides a process for schools to determine needs of students and drivers. Adherence to a transportation plan that is designed to optimize safety will protect staff and students from harm, prevent injuries and help to avoid delays.

Federal, state, and local regulations and policies must be implemented, enforced, and augmented by best practices to ensure optimal safety. For loading and unloading, have students do the following: stand at least 10 feet from the edge of the road, wait for driver's permission to load, take caution against catching clothing and drawstrings on bus handrails when exiting, and cross in front of bus where they can be seen by the driver.

Drivers need communication devices so they can communicate to a central dispatcher in the event of an emergency or atypical situation. Provide equipment for students with special health care needs. Safety seats and restraints, wheelchairs, and wheelchair tie down systems must meet the specific safety needs of students of various heights, weights and positional needs. Inspect these regularly and make needed repairs.

Ensure that transportation needs specified in students' individualized plans are met. Train personnel and familiarize them with procedures necessary to evacuate students in wheelchairs and child restraints as well as students with a range of behavioural and communication problems. School districts should involve police, fire, and emergency medical services personnel in evacuation training exercises. Bus routing schedules should minimize transportation time as excessive hours on a school bus can compromise sleep, study hours, and extra-curricular activities. Students picked up first in the morning could be dropped off first in the afternoon.

Use only well-maintained vehicles that have passed regular and consistent inspection and comply with "National School Transportation Specifications and Procedures". Train transportation staff to address child passenger safety precautions, including use of safety restraints, handling of emergency situations, defensive driving, child supervision responsibilities, and education of students.

Health Information for Transportation

Provide the transportation department and drivers with access to all health and safety information about students with special health care needs that is relevant to safe transportation, without compromising students' confidentiality. Bus drivers spend large amounts of time with and have great responsibility for students with special health care needs, and they must be adequately prepared to meet these needs. Understanding what students with special health care needs may require, including information about their health care and equipment, can reduce staff anxiety and produce a safer environment for the student.

Personnel on school buses should be trained in first aid and cardiopulmonary resuscitation (CPR). Health and safety information should be conveyed to the driver by the school nurse who has developed the health services plan for the student with input from the student's family School personnel who transport students with special health care needs must also know if certain seating and placement choices within the bus pose a health or safety risk. For example, some students will require a specific type of seat or should not be near an air conditioning vent. Staff requires access to information on management of students' particular behavioural problems.

School personnel who transport students must have the ability to communicate with them in a manner that is comfortable, familiar, and appropriate to the student. Guidelines for staff must be specific to students' language, speech, and hearing-related communication needs so that student and transportation staff can convey relevant health and safety information to each other.

Bicycles, Skateboards, Skates, Scooters on Campus

Establish and enforce policies for the safe use of all non-motorized wheeled recreational devices on school property, including appropriate use of protective gear.

Safety precautions prevent and reduce injury. Head injuries are the most serious type of injury sustained by cyclists of all ages. Approved helmets, when worn properly, save lives and prevent traumatic brain injuries.

Many families and schools encourage students to bicycle to school because of the benefits of regular exercise. Non-motorized wheeled devices that students (and staff) use for transportation or recreation include bicycles, tricycles, skateboards, skates, and scooters. Safety policies need to be communicated to families, staff, and students. Policies must include the required use of properly fitted, approved helmets and prohibitions on the carrying of passengers. In addition to helmets, require the use of other personal protection equipment such as wrist guards and knee and elbow pads. Helmets and other protective gear must be worn properly to prevent injuries.

Allow the use of wheeled non-motorized devices on specific areas of campus and on crosswalks leading to and from the facility. Avoid use in loading and unloading zones during school hours. Wheeled non-motorized devices should be walked, not ridden, in areas of heavy pedestrian traffic. School staff should help establish the safest routes for staff and students on bicycles (and other such vehicles) to get to school. Secure storage space should be provided for these non-motorized wheeled devices and for helmets.

Safe Student Conduct During Transportation

Establish and implement comprehensive training programs for staff and for students so that students demonstrate acceptable behaviour during transportation and during drop-off and pickup.

Training transportation staff to manage student behaviour can prevent serious injuries that originate with or are exacerbated by poor student conduct. Behaviour management techniques, interaction with students' families and collaboration with students' regular school programs can enhance transportation safety.

Managing student behaviour and having appropriate discipline are unusually challenging when students are being transported. Poor conduct can lead to vandalism, injury, and death. Transportation staff must address behaviour management issues of all students who share the same vehicle, including those with special needs. Students and families must understand the rules and expectations. Safety should be the focus of student conduct, which includes: keeping passengers seated, using safety belts when available, and keeping arms and heads inside windows. Excessive noise and unsafe student behaviour can distract or harm the driver, increasing the risk of a crash.

One way to enforce safe student conduct on school buses is to have additional staffing on the bus. Teach school transportation staff basic behaviour management techniques (e.g., how to give positive reinforcement for good behaviour and discourage bad behaviour). Transportation staff should have rules that are simple, realistic, and enforced fairly. Transportation staff should monitor student behaviour, be consistent with their responses, and take a positive attitude and approach with students. Strong and consistent enforcement of discipline in accordance with district policy must be maintained.

Students with special health, mental health, and educational needs (including but not limited to students with primarily mental and emotional disabilities) can have individualized transportation behaviour protocols written into their Individualized Education Program. Arrange this if behaviour problems are anticipated when the student's Individualized Education Program is developed or as they arise. Individualized behavioural protocols designed to promote acceptable conduct during transportation should be developed together with students' families and with the multidisciplinary teams that are involved with students' on-site education and support. School personnel who transport students with special health care needs and behaviour management problems must follow all federal regulations and school district policies related to students with special needs.

Bus Drivers and Alcohol/drug use

Adopt and enforce a zero tolerance, alcohol-free, and other drug-free policy for school bus drivers.

High rates of motor vehicle crashes are associated with alcohol and other drug impairment. School bus drivers must not be impaired by alcohol or other drugs that can affect their driving abilities and compromise the safety of students.

More than fifty percent of all motor vehicle crashes involve alcohol. School bus drivers should be regularly tested for drugs and alcohol, and if they are found to be under the influence of alcohol or other drugs, they should immediately be fired.

Specific regulations regarding the operation of a school bus when taking medications (e.g., anti-depressant agents, anti-hypertensive agents, antihistamines) are determined at the state level. At the very least, bus drivers should be instructed not to operate school buses if initiating any medication, any new dose of a medication, or initiating any new combination of medications which may result in drowsiness, lightheadedness, or other adverse reaction that could impair ability to safely operate a school bus. If any previous experience with a medication or combination of medications has resulted in such an adverse reaction, it must not be taken within 24 hours of operating a school bus. A bus driver on a medication (over-the-counter and prescribed) should report this immediately to his/her supervisor.

Emergency Supplies and Equipment

Provide and maintain emergency supplies (such as first aid equipment, posted signs, and communication equipment) in identified, predetermined locations, including in all buildings and buses. Emergency supplies should also be available at all indoor and outdoor school-sponsored events. Emergencies can occur at any time or at any place, and supplies need to be available to treat less severe injuries and to stabilize more severe injuries until appropriate help arrives.

Special emergency equipment required for any student with a special health care need must also be accessible and in ample supply (e.g., glucagon for students with diabetes). Schools need to be prepared for emergencies on campus and at all school-sponsored events (e.g., field trips, sporting events, and outdoor education). Therefore, equipment should include some means of communicating rapidly if emergency medical services are needed (e.g., walkie-talkies, telephones). Emergency assistance numbers should be posted in strategic places (e.g., near telephones).

Facility Preparation for Evacuation, Lockdown, Disasters

Establish physical environment and ground security measures that will prepare each school to respond to fire, natural disasters, attacks, and other crises.

Rationale

By preparing the school environment and personnel for crises well in advance, lives can be saved, injuries reduced, and school property preserved.

Schools must have a system for which evacuation, lockdown, and other responses to situations are decided. Establish the safest areas on or near campus to evacuate students and staff for various types of disasters (e.g., hurricanes, flood, earthquake, fire, loss of electricity). Have a plan to safely transport students in cases where hazardous chemical or biological exposure requires evacuation that is distant from the school site. In addition to regular assessments of school buildings and grounds (e.g., for fire hazards), provide opportunities for students and staff to practice evacuations (e.g., fire drills).

Plans need to define how each school will be closed to outsiders and how to secure the campus perimeter and protect the building against vandalism. Methods for effective enforcement must be considered, including the presence of law enforcement on campus. Some schools must also prepare to accept people who are evacuated for disasters that occur elsewhere.

Educate staff and students on disaster plans, make the information known and accessible, and pre-assign tasks to members of the staff. This includes training staff how to use fire extinguishers, use communication equipment, and implement other aspects of disaster plans. Develop a system to report violent incidents; to deal with the media; to reach staff, students and families; and to respond to the aftermath (both physical and emotional). Partnerships with various community agencies (e.g., public utilities, fire, law enforcement, emergency medical services, health, mental health, and social service agencies) and parents are necessary to develop these plans.

Principles of Teaching Technology

Educational technology, sometimes termed EdTech, is the study and ethical practice of facilitating e-learning, which is the learning and improving performance by creating, using and managing appropriate technological processes and resources. The term educational technology is often associated with, and encompasses, instructional theory and learning theory. While instructional technology is "the theory and practice of design, development, utilization, management, and evaluation of processes and resources for learning," according to the Association for Educational Communications and

Technology (AECT) Definitions and Terminology Committee, educational technology includes other systems used in the process of developing human capability. Educational technology includes, but is not limited to, software, hardware, as well as Internet applications, such as wikis and blogs, and activities. But there is still debate on what these terms mean.

Technology in education is most simply and comfortably defined as an array of tools that might prove helpful in advancing student learning and may be measured in how and why individuals behave. Educational Technology relies on a broad definition of the word "technology." Technology can refer to material objects of use to humanity, such as machines or hardware, but it can also encompass broader themes, including systems, methods of organization, and techniques. Some modern tools include but are not limited to overhead projectors, laptop computers, and calculators. Newer tools such as smartphones and games (both online and offline) are beginning to draw serious attention for their learning potential. Media psychology is the field of study that applies theories of human behaviour to educational technology.

Consider the *Handbook of Human Performance Technology*. The word technology for the sister fields of Educational and Human Performance Technology means "applied science." In other words, any valid and reliable process or procedure that is derived from basic research using the "scientific method" is considered a "technology." Educational or Human Performance Technology may be based purely on algorithmic or heuristic processes, but neither necessarily implies physical technology. The word technology comes from the Greek "techne" which means craft or art. Another word, "technique," with the same origin, also may be used when considering the field Educational Technology. So Educational Technology may be extended to include the techniques of the educator.

A classic example of an Educational Psychology text is Bloom's 1956 book, *Taxonomy of Educational Objectives*. Bloom's Taxonomy is helpful when designing learning activities to keep in mind what is expected of—and what are the learning goals for—learners. However, Bloom's work does not explicitly deal with educational technology *per se* and is more concerned with pedagogical strategies.

According to some, an Educational Technologist is someone who transforms basic educational and psychological research into an evidence-based applied science (or a technology) of learning or instruction. Educational Technologists typically have a graduate degree (Master's, Doctorate, Ph.D., or D.Phil.) in a field related to educational psychology, educational media, experimental psychology, cognitive psychology or, more purely, in the fields of Educational, Instructional or Human Performance Technology or Instructional Systems Design. But few of those listed below as theorists would ever use the term "educational technologist" as a term to describe themselves, preferring terms such as "educator." The transformation of educational technology from a cottage industry to a profession is discussed by Shurville, Browne, and Whitaker.

History

Educational technology could be traced back to the emergence of very early tools, e.g., paintings on cave walls. But usually its history starts with the introduction of educational films (1900s) or Sidney Pressey's mechanical teaching machines in the 1920s.

The first large scale usage of new technologies can be traced to US WWII training of soldiers through training films and other mediated materials. Today, presentation-based technology, based on the idea that people can learn through aural and visual reception, exists in many forms, e.g., streaming audio and video, or PowerPoint presentations with voice-over. The 1950s led to two major, still popular designs. Skinners work led to "programmed instruction" focusing on the formulation of behavioural objectives, breaking instructional content into small units and rewarding correct responses early and often. Advocating a mastery approach to learning based on his taxonomy of intellectual behaviors, Bloom endorsed instructional techniques that varied both instruction and time according to learner requirements. Models based on these designs were usually referred to as computer-based training" (CBT), Computer-aided instruction or computer-assisted instruction (CAI) in the 1970s through the 1990s. In a more simplified form they correspond to today's "e-contents" that often form the core of "e-learning" set-ups, sometimes also referred to as web-based training (WBT) or e-instruction. The course designer divides learning contents into smaller chunks of text augmented with graphics and multimedia presentation. Frequent Multiple Choice questions with immediate feedback are added for self-assessment and guidance. Such e-contents can rely on standards defined by IMS, ADL/SCORM and IEEE.

The 1980s and 1990s produced a variety of schools that can be put under the umbrella of the label Computer-based learning (CBL).

Frequently based on constructivist and cognitivist learning theories, these environments focused on teaching both abstract and domain-specific problem solving. Preferred technologies were micro-worlds (computer environments where learners could explore and build), simulations (computer environments where learner can play with parameters of dynamic systems) and hypertext.

Digitized communication and networking in education started in the mid 80s and became popular by the mid-90's, in particular through the World-Wide Web (WWW), eMail and Forums. There is a difference between two major forms of online learning. The earlier type, based on either Computer Based Training (CBT) or Computer-based learning (CBL), focused on the interaction between the student and computer drills plus tutorials on one hand or micro-worlds and simulations on the other. Both can be delivered today over the WWW.

Today, the prevailing paradigm in the regular school system is Computer-mediated communication (CMC), where the primary form of interaction is between students and instructors, mediated by the computer. CBT/CBL usually means individualized (self-study) learning, while CMC involves teacher/tutor facilitation and requires scenarization of flexible learning activities. In addition, modern ICT provides education with tools for sustaining learning communities and associated knowledge management tasks. It also provides tools for student and curriculum management.

In addition to classroom enhancement, learning technologies also play a major role in full-time distance teaching. While most quality offers still rely on paper, videos and occasional CBT/CBL materials, there is increased use of e-tutoring through forums, instant messaging, video-conferencing etc. Courses addressed to smaller groups frequently use blended or hybrid designs that mix presence courses (usually in the beginning and at the end of a module) with distance activities and use various pedagogical styles (e.g., drill & practise, exercises, projects, etc.).

The 2000s emergence of multiple mobile and ubiquitous technologies gave a new impulse to situated learning theories favouring learning-in-context scenarios. Some literature uses the concept of integrated learning to describe blended learning scenarios that integrate both school and authentic (e.g., workplace) settings.

Students are now growing up in a digital age where they have constant exposure to a variety of media.

Theories and Practices

Three main theoretical schools or philosophical frameworks have been present in the educational technology literature. These are Behaviorism, Cognitivism and Constructivism. Each of these schools of thought are still present in today's literature but have evolved as the Psychology literature has evolved.

Behaviorism

This theoretical framework was developed in the early 20th century with the animal learning experiments of Ivan Pavlov, Edward Thorndike, Edward C. Tolman, Clark L. Hull, B.F. Skinner and many others. Many psychologists used these theories to describe and experiment that is parallel to human learning. While still very useful this philosophy of learning has lost favor with many educators.

Skinner's Contribution

B.F. Skinner wrote extensively on improvements of teaching based on his functional analysis of Verbal Behaviour and wrote "The Technology of Teaching", an attempt to dispel the myths underlying contemporary education as well as promote his system he called programmed instruction. Ogden Lindsley also developed the Celeration learning system similarly based on behaviour analysis but quite different from Keller's and Skinner's models.

Cognitivism

Cognitive science has changed the way educators view learning. Since the very early beginning of the Cognitive Revolution of the 1960s and 1970s, learning theory has undergone a great deal of change. Much of the empirical framework of Behaviorism was retained even though a new paradigm had begun. Cognitive theories look beyond behaviour to explain brain-based learning. Cognitivists consider how human memory works to promote learning.

After memory theories like the Atkinson-Shiffrin memory model and Baddeley's Working memory model were established as a theoretical framework in Cognitive Psychology, new cognitive frameworks of learning began to emerge during the 1970s, 1980s, and 1990s. It is important to note that Computer Science and Information Technology have had a major influence on Cognitive Science theory. The Cognitive concepts of working memory (formerly known as short term memory) and long term memory have been facilitated by research and technology from the field of Computer Science. Another major influence on the field of Cognitive Science is Noam Chomsky. Today researchers are concentrating on topics like Cognitive load and Information Processing Theory. In addition, psychology as applied to media is easily measured in studying behaviour. The area of media psychology is both cognative and affective and is central to understanding educational technology.

Constructivism

Constructivism is a learning theory of educational philosophy that many educators began to consider in the 1990s. One of the primary tenets of this philosophy is that learners construct their own meaning from new information, as they interact with reality or others with different perspectives. Constructivist learning environments require students to use their prior knowledge and experiences to formulate new, related, and/or adaptive concepts in learning. Under this framework the role of the teacher becomes that of a facilitator, providing guidance so that learners can construct their own knowledge. Constructivist educators must make sure that the prior learning experiences are appropriate and related to the concepts being taught. Jonassen (1997) suggests "well-structured" learning environments are useful for novice learners and that "ill-structured" environments are only useful for more advanced learners. Educators utilizing technology when teaching with a constructivist perspective should choose technologies that reinforce prior learning perhaps in a problem-solving environment.

Instructional Technique and Technologies

"Children and adult people are growing up in a vastly changing context. No aspect of their lives is untouched by the digital era which is transforming how they live, relate and learn" Some examples of these changes in the classroom include: Problem Based Learning, Project-based Learning, and Inquiry-based learning. Together they are active learning educational technologies used to facilitate learning. Technology which includes physical and process applied science can be incorporated into project, problem, inquiry-based learning as they all have a similar educational philosophy. All three are student centred, ideally involving real-world scenarios in which students are actively engaged in critical thinking activities. The process that students are encouraged to employ (as long as it is based on empirical research) is considered to be a technology. Classic examples of technologies used by teachers and Educational Technologists include Bloom's Taxonomy and Instructional Design.

Theorists

This is an area where new thinkers are coming to the forefront everyday. Many of the ideas spread from theorists, researchers, and experts through their blogs. Extensive lists of educational bloggers by area of interest are available at Steve Hargadon's "SupportBloggers" site or at the "movingforward" wiki started by Scott McLeod. Many of these blogs are recognized by their peers each year through the edublogger awards. Web 2.0 technologies have led to a huge increase in the amount of information available on this topic and the number of educators formally and informally discussing it. Most listed below have been around for more than a decade, however, and few new thinkers mentioned above are listed here.

- Alan November
- Seymour Papert
- Will Richardson
- John Sweller
- Don Krug
  Alex Jones
- Russell Long (EdTech Practitioner)
- George Siemens
- David Wiley
- David Wilson
- Bernard Luskin

Benefits

Educational technology is intended to improve education for the 21st century learner. Students today are considered "Digital Natives" who were born and raised in a digital environment and inherently think different because of this exposure to technology. Some of the claimed benefits of incorporating technology into the classroom are listed below:

- Easy-to-access course materials. Instructors can post their course material or important information on a course website, which means students can study at a time and location they prefer and can obtain the study material very quickly.
- Student motivation. According to James Kulik, who studies the effectiveness of computers used for instruction, students usually learn more in less time when receiving computer-based instruction and they like classes more and develop more

positive attitudes toward computers in computer-based classes. Teachers must be aware of their students' motivators in order to successfully implement technology into the classroom . Students are more motivated to learn when they are interested in the subject matter, which can be enhanced by using technologies in the classroom and targeting the need for screens and digital material that they have been stimulated by outside of the classroom.

- More opportunities for extended learning. According to study completed in 2010, 70.3% of American family households have access to the internet . According to Canadian Radio Television and Telecommunications Commission Canada, 79% of homes have access to the internet. This allows students to access course material at home and engage with the numerous online resources available to them. Students can use their home computers and internet to conduct research, participate in social media, email, play educational games and stream videos.

—> Using online resources such as Khan Academy or TED Talks can help students spend more time on specific aspects of what they may be learning in school, but at home. These online resources have added the opportunity to take learning outside of the classroom and into any atmosphere that has an internet connection. These online lessons allow for students who might need extra help to understand materials outside of the classroom. These tutorials can focus on small concepts of large ideas taught in class, or the other way around. Schools like MIT have even made their course materials free online so that anybody can access them. Although there are still some aspects of a classroom setting that are missed by using these resources, they are still helpful tools to add additional support to the already existing educational system.

- Wide participation. Learning material can be used for long distance learning and are accessible to a wider audience.
- Improved student writing. It is convenient for students to edit their written work on word processors, which can, in turn, improve the quality of their writing. According to some studies, the students are better at critiquing and editing written work that is exchanged over a computer network with students they know.
- Differentiated Instruction. Educational technology provides the means to focus on active student participation and to

present differentiated questioning strategies. It broadens individualized instruction and promotes the development of personalized learning plans in some computer programs available to teachers.

Students are encouraged to use multimedia components and to incorporate the knowledge they gained in creative ways.. This allows some students to individually progress from using low ordered skills gained from drill and practice activities, to higher level thinking through applying concepts creatively and creating simulations . In some cases, the ability to make educational technology individualized may aid in targeting and accommodating different learning styles and levels.

Overall, the use of internet in education has had a positive impact on students, educators, as well as the educational system as a whole. Effective technologies use many evidence-based strategies (e.g., adaptive content, frequent testing, immediate feedback, etc.), as do effective teachers. It is important for teachers to embrace technology in order to gain these benefits so they can address the needs of their digital natives

- "Additional Benefits":
- The Internet itself has unlocked a world of opportunity for students. Information and ideas that were previously out of reach are a click away. Students of all ages can connect, share, and learn on a global scale.
- Using computers or other forms of technology can give students practice on core content and skills while the teacher can work with others, conduct assessments, or perform other tasks.
- Using technology in the classroom can allow teachers' to effectively organize and present lessons. Multimedia presentations can make the material more meaningful and engaging.
- *""Technology's impact in schools has been significant, advancing how students learn, how teachers teach and how efficiently and effectively educational services can be delivered," said Carolyn April, director, industry analysis, CompTIA." With emerging technologies such as tablets and netbooks, interactive whiteboards and wireless solutions gaining ground in the classroom, the reliance on IT by the education market will only grow in the years ahead."*

- Studies completed in "computer intensive" settings found increases in student centre, cooperative and higher order learning, students writing skills, problem solving, and using technology. In addition, positive attitudes toward technology as a learning tool by parents, students and teachers are also improved.

Social Networking

Social networking sites are virtual communities for people interested in a particular subject or just to "hang out" together. Members communicate by voice, chat, instant message, video conference, and blogs, and the service typically provides a way for members to contact friends of other members.

In a study conducted by the National School Boards Association (2007), it was reported that 96% of students with online access have used social networking technologies, and more than 50% talk online specifically about schoolwork. These statistics support the likelihood of being able to bring these technologies into our classrooms and find successful teaching methods to employ their use in an educational setting. Social networking inherently encourages collaboration and engagement. This is meaningful to teachers who are trying to find ways to involve every student in something that is personally engaging. For the teacher, social networking provides professional development by introducing them a discovery of the learning potential for themselves, finding other educators who are using such technologies in their classrooms, and then connecting with those educators who automatically provide a virtual support community.

Social networking can also be used as a motivational tool to promote self-efficacy amongst students. In a study by Bowers-Campbell (2008) Facebook was used as an academic motivation tool for students in a developmental reading course. The connection between SNSs and higher education is strong, particularly with Facebook. Initially introduced only for users who had a college or university e-mail address, Facebook expanded later to the general public (Junco and Mastrodicasa, 2007), and traditional-aged college students (ages eighteen to twenty-four) specifically use Facebook more than MySpace or other SNSs (Salaway and others, 2007). We live in an age of digital technology where information is available at any time. The rationale behind the use of social networks as a tool for professional learning includes the idea that the Internet is this generation's defining technology for literacy (Coiro & Dobler,2007), and preservice and inservice teachers will utilize popular media such as Facebook. Facebook provides one link where multiple organizations can be accessed simultaneously. As professional information is posted through feeds on Facebook, group members may respond and interact with other members, just as users can socially interact with their friends on Facebook.

Student interaction is at the core of constructivist learning environments and Social Net-working Sites provide a platform for building collaborative learning communities. By their very nature they are relationship-centred and promote shared experiences. With the emphasis on user-generated-content, some experts are concerned about the traditional roles of scholarly expertise and the reliability of digital content. Students still have to be educated and assessed within a framework that adheres to strict guidelines of quality. Every student has his or her own learning requirements, and a Web 2.0 educational framework provides enough resources, learning styles, communication tools and flexibility to accommodate this diversity.

Criticism

Although technology in the classroom does have many benefits, there are clear drawbacks as well. Limited access to sufficient quantities of a technology, lack of training, the extra time required for the implementations of technology, and the apprehension associated with assessing the effectiveness of technology in the classroom are just a few of the reasons that technology is often not used extensively in the classroom. To understand educational technology one must also understand theories in human behaviour as behaviour is affected by technology. Media Psychology is the study of media, technology and how and why individuals, groups and societies behave the way they do. The first Ph.D program with a concentration in media psychology was started in 2002 at Fielding Graduate University by Bernard Luskin. The Media Psychology division of APA, division 46 has a focus on media psychology. Media and the family is another emerging area affected by rapidly changing educational technology. There are many benefits of using technology in the education system, however there are also negative aspects.

Technology base educational videos and games are being integrated into the lives and classrooms of new generations. These videos and games are meant to be used as tools to help growing minds develop, and to increase knowledge and awareness. Videos such as Baby Einsteins line of infant DVDs are a topic of conflicting interest, according to the University of Washington study of infant vocabulary is slipping due to educational baby DVDs.

Published in the Journal of Pediatrics, a 2007 University of Washington study on the vocabulary of babies surveyed over 1,000 parents in Washington and Minnesota. The study found that for every one hour that babies 8–16 months of age watched DVDs and Videos they knew 6-8 fewer of 90 common baby words than the babies that did not watch them. Andrew Meltzoff, Ph.D, a surveyor in this study states that the result makes sense, that if the baby's 'alert time' is spent in front of DVDs and TV, instead of with people speaking, the babies are not going to get the same linguistic experience. Dr. Dimitri Chistakis, another surveyor reported that the evidence is mounting that baby DVDs are of no value and may be harmful.

Electronic devices such as cellphones and computers facilitate rapid access to a constant stream of sources, each of which may receive cursory attention. Michel Rich, an associate professor at Harvard Medical School and executive director of the centre on Media and Child Health in Boston, said of the digital generation, "Their brains are rewarded not for staying on task, but for jumping to the next thing, and the side effects could linger: the worry is we're raising a generation of kids in front of screens whose brains are going to be wired differently." In addition, poorly designed technologies tend to produce low test scores and negative reactions from students.

Many students who are at high risk for school failure have the potential to learn; but their academic achievement in the core areas of reading, mathematics and writing falls far short of their potential. There is growing evidence that the academic difficulties experienced by these students is cumulative in nature, and the gap between achievement and potential grows from childhood into adolescence. These young adults tend to drop out of school more frequently than do students without these difficulties, and they experience higher levels of unemployment and underemployment.

As a group, they face a significant risk for lifelong problems. ccc "*Students have always faced distractions and time-wasters. But computers and cellphones, and the they offer, pose a profound new challenge to focusing and learning. Researchers say the lure of these s , while it affects adults too, is particularly powerful for young people. The risk, they say, is that developing brains can become more easily habituated than adult brains to constantly switching tasks — and less able to sustain attention.*"

Digital Divide

One of the greatest barriers of integrating technology into the school system deals with the digital divide. The concept of the digital divide was originally defined as a gap between those who have access to digital technologies and those who do not. This access is associated with age, gender, education, income, ethnicity, and geography. The first deals with the onset of integrating technology into the curriculum and the gap between the digital haves and have nots. In most cases, this form of the digital divide means that those who have access to a computer and the Internet are considered a digital have, while on the other hand, those who do not are considered a digital have not. In today's society, this is still a significant barrier to implementing technology into the curriculum because the socio-economic status of a school, and its students, will impact whether resources can be purchased and implemented in the school system. Schools that are able to provide technology within the classroom are able to expose their students to a new means of learning, while the students in lower socio-economic schools may miss out on these experiences.

As more and more people have gone online and started using the Internet for an increasing number of activities, researchers have begun to reconsider the notion of the digital divide. Some scholars offered a redefined understanding by seeing the digital divide as a complex and dynamic phenomenon that is essentially multifaced and includes technical access (the physical availability of technology) and social access (the mix of professional knowledge, economic resources, and technical skills required for effectual use of technology). This means that even if schools and students have access to technology, the ways in which teachers use and introduce it is significant to consider. This form of the digital divide is yet another barrier because it also goes hand-in-hand with the resources the schools have and the training teachers receive. If a teacher, for example, is not well equipped and confident in utilizing a form of technology, those students will miss out on gaining the valuable skills required for today's society.

Another factor that plays into the digital divide, which makes it difficult to implement technology into the curriculum, is the generational digital divide. Herrington recognizes that the generational divide is interpreted to mean that people on one side of the gap, including the youth, have more access and a greater ability to use new technologies than those on the other side like the adults who were born before the advent of the Internet. The generational digital divide is a common barrier because it challenges teachers to keep up with the ever-changing technology in the classroom. Even extending beyond the classroom, by the time an individual "adopts a technology, a new one is developed, marketed, and requires a new adoption cycle". Students, who have grown up in a digital environment, may be well acquainted with the on-going process of new technological innovation but may be lacking the guidance they need in order to use these technologies effectively. From the teacher's perspective, this process could be an intimidating experience because something as foreign as the computer and Internet must first be learned and then taught to the students in a classroom setting. It is difficult to formulate a curriculum, which aims to integrate technology into the classroom, when the decision-makers are still in the process of learning about it themselves.

Teacher Training

In a study to investigate how teacher preparation programs are preparing future K-12 educators to effectively use technology to enhance learning, the results demonstrated a gap in understanding the appropriate uses of technology in a learning environment. Similar to learning a new task or trade, special training is vital to ensuring the effective integration of classroom technology. The current school curriculum tends to guide teachers in training students to be autonomous problem solvers. This has become a significant barrier to effective training because the traditional methods of teaching have clashed with what is now expected in the present workplace. Today's students in the workplace are increasingly being asked to work in teams, drawing on different sets of expertise, and collaborating to solve problem.

These experiences are not highly centred on in the traditional classroom, but are twenty-first century skills that can be attained through the incorporation and engagement with technology. Changes in instruction and use of technology can also promote a higher level of learning among students with different types of intelligence. Please see the presentation by Ted Robinson where he discusses the ways in which schools kill creativity. Therefore since technology is not the end goal of education, but rather a means by which it can be accomplished, educators must have a good grasp of the technology being used and its advantages over more traditional methods. If there is a lack in either of these areas, technology will be seen as a hindrance and not a benefit to the goals of teaching.

Another major issue arises because of the evolving nature of technology. Teachers may find themselves acting as perpetual novices when it comes to learning about technology. This is because technology, including the Internet and its range of applications, is always in a state of change and teachers must attempt to keep current. Marc Prensky discusses the idea that teachers are digital immigrants, and students are digital natives. Teachers must continuously work at learning this new technological language, whereas students were born into retrieving information, problem solving, and communicating with this technology.

The ways in which teachers are taught to use technology is also outdated because the primary focus of training is on computer literacy, rather than the deeper, more essential understanding and mastery of technology for information processing, communication, and problem solving. New resources have to be designed and distributed whenever the technological platform has been changed. However, finding quality materials to support classroom objectives after such changes is often difficult even after they exist in sufficient quantity and teachers must design these resources on their own. The study by Harris notes that the use of random Professional Development days is not adequate enough in order to foster the much-needed skills required to teach and apply technology in the classroom. "We are currently preparing students for jobs that don't yet exist..using technologies that haven't been invented...in order to solve problems we don't even know are problems yet". Learning, therefore, becomes and on-going process, which takes time and a strong commitment among the community of educators.

Teacher training faces another drawback when it comes to one's mindset on the integration of technology into the curriculum. The generational divide might also lead to a generational bias, whereby teachers do not feel the need to change the traditional education system because it has been successful in the past. This does not necessarily mean it is the right way to teach for the current and future generations. Considering the fact that today's students are constantly exposed to the impacts of the digital era, learning styles, and the methods of collecting information has evolved. To illustrate this concept Jenkins states, "students often feel locked out of the worlds described in their textbooks through the depersonalized and abstract prose used to describe them," whereas games can construct worlds for players to move through and have some stake in the events unfolding. Even though technology can provide a more personalized, yet collaborative, and creative, yet informative, approach to learning, it may be difficult to motivate the use of these contemporary approaches among teachers who have been in the field for a number of years.

Assessment

Research has shown that there is a great deal of apprehension associated with assessing the effectiveness of technology in the classroom and its development of information-age skills. This is because information-age skills, also commonly referred to as twenty-first century literacies, are relatively new to the field of education. According to the New Media Consortium, these include "the set of abilities and skills where aural, visual, and digital literacy overlap". Jenkins modifies this definition by acknowledging them as building on the foundation of traditional literacy, research skills, technical skills and critical-analysis skills taught in the classroom.

Current school assessments are based on standardized tests and the ability to complete these uniform tests, regardless of one's preferred learning style. Many factors play into this observation including the strong impact of time. By using technology and learning through discovery, teachers may feel that they are not able to cover the material needed to meet the requirements of the curriculum. Therefore, the traditional style of teaching, including the lecturing in front of the class, and a "one-size-fits-all" approach to testing is common in today's classrooms. This is a barrier because it prevents the full integration of technology into the curriculum, the ability to learn through inquiry, and the collaborative problem-solving skills, which prove to be essential traits needed in the twenty-first century.

Educational Technology and the Humanities

Research from the Alberta Initiative for School Improvement (AISI) indicates that inquiry and project-based approaches, combined with a focus on curriculum, effectively supports the infusion of educational technologies into the learning and teaching process.

The Advancement of Education Through Technology

Open Course Ware: In recent years, OpenCourseWare (OCW), an academic initiative that gives the public access to much of the same information used in undergraduate and graduate programs at institutions of higher education, has greatly improved the quality of educational material available for free on the Internet. The idea of OpenCourseWare gained prevalence in 2002 when MIT began distributing academic material from courses to the public for free.

Through the early 2000s, this idea began to gain popularity with other colleges and universities. As of 2008, there were close to 150 collegiate institutions that had operational OpenCourseWare programs, or were in the process of planning such programs. These institutions include Harvard, Princeton, Stanford, University of Pennsylvania, and University of Michigan. Such programs are an example of how technology can allow more people to have access to information and resources that have originally only been accessible to students at prestigious universities.

Over-the-Counter Data

Advancements in the design of education technology tools that present data to education stakeholders, such as the student data system, have had a significant impact on education and students. For example, data systems' capacity to assist data analysis is unprecedented and it is inadvisable to use data without the assistance of a data system. To improve the accuracy of data analyses performed with the use of edtech, it is recommended these edtech tools adhere to a design approach called over-the-counter data (OTCD), which involves embedding labels, supplemental documentation, and a help system and making key package/display and content decisions.

Technology in the Classroom

There are various types of technologies currently used in traditional classrooms. Among these are:

- Computer in the classroom: Having a computer in the classroom is an asset to any teacher. With a computer in the classroom, teachers are able to demonstrate a new lesson, present new material, illustrate how to use new programs, and show new websites.
- Class website: An easy way to display your student's work is to create a web page designed for your class. Once a web page is designed, teachers can post homework assignments, student work, famous quotes, trivia games, and so much more. In today's society, children should know how to use the computer to navigate their way through a website, so why not give them one where they can be a published author? Just be careful, as most districts maintain strong policies to manage official websites for a school or classroom. Also, most school districts provide teacher webpages that can easily be viewed through the school district's website.

- Class blogs and wikis: There are a variety of Web 2.0 tools that are currently being implemented in the classroom. Blogs allow for students to maintain a running dialogue. They work a tool for maintaining a journal of thoughts, ideas, and assignments, as well as encourage student comment and reflection. Wikis are more group focused to allow multiple members of the group to edit a single document and create a truly collaborative and carefully edited finished product.

Blogs allow the student to express their knowledge of the information learned in a way that they like. Blogging is something that students do for fun sometimes, so when they are assigned an assignment to do a blog they are eager to do it! If you are a teacher and need to find a way to get your students eager to learn, create, and inspire assign them a blog. They will love it.

- Wireless classroom microphones: Noisy classrooms are a daily occurrence, and with the help of microphones, students are able to hear their teachers more clearly. Children learn better when they hear the teacher clearly. The benefit for teachers is that they no longer lose their voices at the end of the day.
- Mobile devices: Mobile devices such as clickers or smartphone can be used to enhance the experience in the classroom by providing the possibility for professors to get feedback.
- Interactive Whiteboards: An interactive whiteboard that provides touch control of computer applications. These enhance the experience in the classroom by showing anything that can be on a computer screen. This not only aids in visual learning, but it is interactive so the students can draw, write, or manipulate images on the interactive whiteboard.
- Digital video-on-demand: Replacement of hard copy videos (DVD, VHS) with digital video accessed from a central server (e.g. SAFARI Montage). Digital video eliminates the need for in-classroom hardware (players) and allows teachers and students to access video clips immediately by not utilizing the public Internet.
- Online media: Streamed video websites can be used to enhance a classroom lesson (e.g. United Streaming, Teacher Tube, etc.)
- Online study tools: Tools that motivate studying by making studying more fun or individualized for the student (e.g. Study Cocoa)

- Digital Games: The field of educational games and serious games has been growing significantly over the last few years. The digital games are being provided as tools for the classroom and have a lot of positive feedback including higher motivation for students.

There are many other tools being used depending on the local school board and funds available. These may include: digital cameras, video cameras, interactive whiteboard tools, document cameras, or LCD projectors.

- Podcasts: Pod-casting is a relatively new invention that allows anybody to publish files to the Internet where individuals can subscribe and receive new files from people by a subscription. The primary benefit of pod-casting for educators is quite simple. It enables teachers to reach students through a medium that is both "cool" and a part of their daily lives. For a technology that only requires a computer, microphone and internet connection, pod-casting has the capacity of advancing a student's education beyond the classroom. When students listen to the pod-casts of other students as well as their own, they can quickly demonstrate their capacities to identify and define "quality." This can be a great tool for learning and developing literacy inside and outside the classroom. Pod-casting can help sharpen students' vocabulary, writing, editing, public speaking, and presentation skills. Students will also learn skills that will be valuable in the working world, such as communication, time management, and problem-solving.

Although pod-casts are a new phenomenon in classrooms, especially on college campuses, studies have shown the differences in effectiveness between a live lecture versus podcast are minor in terms of the education of the student.

2

Objectives and Differential Aspirations

The objectives of Vocational Education System in the context of fulfillment of national goal are to train the students for employment in the growing sectors of economy both organized and unorganized, to provide an alternative channel for higher education and to prepare students for self-reliance and gainful employment. There has been a great improvement in the demand for computer professionals during the past few years. To cater to certain computer oriented requirements of the business sector the Computer science course syllabus has been drafted.

Life is very complex and complicated. But an aim in life can make the complex life simple and purposeful. Aims give us direction to work and without aim, destination, or objective life becomes incomplete and haphazard. Individual has different interests, attitudes and needs. Every individual wants to achieve certain goals in life. But a clear-cut aim makes the road of life easy. Educational aims are varied. They have their different role in different fields.

Some Specific Aims

Some specific aims are listed below:

Knowledge Aim

The aim of education is the acquisition of knowledge, skills and attitudes. It helps to adjust properly in one's own environment. Knowledge helps the man to overcome the nature and satisfy human wants. It links the teacher and taught with social situation. It helps with certain skills to live in a society as human being and civilized one. Philosophers and educationists of the world believe in knowledge. It is the valuable asset of life, which helps the individual to overcome misery and problems of life.

Vocational Aim

Knowledge aim of education is narrow by nature. The theoretical knowledge will never meet our basic needs of life. We need bread and butter to fill up our belly. We can get it if education is vocationalised. Gandhiji realized it in 1937 when he introduced Basic Education. Vocational aim develops the social efficiency of the individual. It reduces mental tension after completion of education. Those who are lower, intelligence in vocational education or training are a blessing for them. Realizing this aspect. Indian Education Commission (1964-66) introduces work-experience in the curriculum.

Character Building Aim

The Indian concept of education believes in self-realization. Self-realization is possible through moral education. So the individual should cultivate moral virtues or values which constitute character. Swami Vivekananda said, "We want that education by which character is formed, strength of mind is increased, the intellect is expanded and by which one can stand on one's own feet."

Complete-Living Aim

The individual has various aspects to be developed. Every aspect of the personality is reflected in various activities to be performed. Education should help the individual to fulfill the various needs and necessities of life like self-preservation, fulfilling necessities of life, rearing and bearing of children, performing civic responsibilities and utilizing his leisure time properly.

Firstly, the individual must know the art of self-preservation. Secondly, education should enable to him to earn his living. Thirdly, he should know how to take care of his own children. Lastly, he must have the idea how to utilize the leisure hours properly in a profiting manner.

Harmonious: Development of the personality aim- Gandhiji said, "By education, I mean an all-round drawing out of the best in the child and man-body, mind and spirit." The meaning itself indicates to develop all-round aspects of individual-physical, intellectual, social and spiritual. All these aspects of the individual should be harmoniously developed. True education is development of 3H's instead of 3R's.

The development of Head, Heart and hand of an individual makes him happy.

Democratic Aim of Education

One of the important aims and objective of education suggested by Secondary Education Commission (1952-54) is to develop the democratic citizenship. India is a democratic country. Even citizen must have to realize the duties and responsibilities carefully. So the aim of education is to train carefully the future citizens. Training should be provided to develop the following qualities of the individual.

(i) Capacity for clear thinking

(ii) Receptivity of new idea

(iii) Clarity in speech and writing

(iv) True patriotism

Further the democratic aim of education develop vocational efficiency, personality and leadership quality.

Indian Education Commission (1964-66) under the chairmanship of Dr. D.S. Kothari suggested the following as the aims of education in a democratic set-up.

(i) Increasing productivity

(ii) Developing social and national integrity

(iii) Making education modernized and

(iv) Cultivating of social, moral and spiritual values.

Socioeconomic Aspirations and Rewards

Several researchers have long recognized that occupational aspiration is influenced by socioeconomic status (SES) and that for high school students in particular, the background of their families is especially important. McLaughlin, Hunt, and Montgomery (1976) found that SES affects the occupational and educational aspirations of female high school seniors, a finding in agreement with Empey's (1956) study on males. Krippner (1963) studied students' occupational preferences and their parents' occupational levels using Roe's (1956) occupational scale and found that the occupations students liked to enter were related to the status of their parents' occupational level.

Bogie (1976), working with high school seniors, found that SES was a strong predictor of the discrepancy between an individual's occupational aspirations and selection; that is, the higher an individual's

SES was, the less discrepancy one foresaw between occupational aspirations and attain-ment. Rosen (1956), in her study of social class and occupational choice, found that mothers' occupational aspirations for their sons indicated that class was of paramount importance in both Black and White populations and that racial ethnicity was a less potent factor in explaining variance in aspirations than was SES.

Socioeconomic attainment is strongly linked to educational attainment . Trajectory through an educational system might be one of the key issues to understanding the pathways by which social and economic background lead to future inequalities in health. Institutionalized cultural capital, e.g. formal education, plays a crucial role, but appears to be strongly dependent on the availability of sufficient incorporated cultural capital (an affinity for higher education, the motivation to invest in educational degrees), which is provided by parents via transmitting the attitudes and knowledge needed to succeed in the existing educational system. Educational aspirations or educational expectations might be a good proxy measure of a more hidden element of cultural capital. Therefore understanding the role of educational aspirations in the social reproduction of health inequalities might be an important clue for strategies aiming to reduce inequalities in health. Evidence on the association between socioeconomic background and educational aspirations of offspring are somewhat conflicting, indicating direct as well as indirect pathways.

Adverse childhood conditions might affect educational chances, job opportunities and life chances in general, but this process might be ameliorated via available social sources (supportive family and school environment) and individual sources (sense of coherence). A supportive family and school environment contribute to the development of educational aspirations. However, while parental support seems to be more influential within lower and middle SEP adolescents, school attitudes had a stronger effect on educational expectations for upper SEP adolescents in a study of Australian adolescents. A sense of coherence correlated significantly with school performance, but not with the selection of educational tracks in a study of Swedish adolescents.

Based on the theory of health selection, health disadvantage represented by frequent health complaints, worse well-being as well as more frequent school absence, might distort the development of educational aspirations, lead to underachievement and finally to downward mobility.

Socio-economic Aspiration and Generation Y

Gen Y comprising of those born between 1980 and 2000 would form close to 75% of the global workforce by the year 2025. While it is true that every generation has got smarter and more prosperous than the previous one, millennial men and women born in an environment that has had transformational impact due to digital technologies have developed a significantly different outlook towards various aspects of life. This is the generation which cannot imagine life without internet, computers and mobile. Around 80% of Gen Y is working on two or more devices while simultaneously watching TV! So what does all this mean to the corporates and how do they cope with Gen Y in the organisational context?

At the outset, it would be useful to make a brief comparison of Gen Y with Gen X. Parents of Gen X grew up in times of scarcity and limited resources and hence they were groomed to believe in the values of focus on hard work, investment in education and both men and a significant percentage of women both pursuing their careers albeit mostly in the same location.

Gen Y on the other hand has relatively much better access to larger amount of resources and has grown up in an environment where digital technology has touched every aspect of their lives. Gen Y also values education but has been much better informed and conscious in making decisions regarding the type of programmes and careers they wish to pursue unlike Gen X who have had comparatively limited choices. Gen Y men and women nurture their careers with great care supported by active networking and peer influence with women keen on pursuing their careers of choice even if it means staying away from their families.

It is a fact that most organisations are run by Gen X comprising of a growing number of Gen Y employees. The organisation processes, structure and methods are built to suit the former and have not changed much over the years resulting in conflict with the style and approach required to deal with Gen Y employees. For instance, we often refer to Gen Y as lacking work ethic and not as hardworking as the previous generation. We fail to recognise the fact that Gen Y employees love to mix work with fun. They are as focused and diligent on completing the work at hand but do this in their own way. They are comfortable working from anywhere, any place and hence work does not suffer. They may want to enjoy their weekends but know how to prioritise at times of need and ensure deliverables are met.

Sometimes Gen Y is criticised for their irreverence. This is an interesting theme to delve upon. Firstly because of the exposure they get, Gen Y employees have their opinions firmly in place for most of the things. At the same time, there is a certain expectation in terms of relationship that they have of their seniors. It is a fact that unlike the previous generations where there was a clear distance between the parents and the children and the latter used to look upon their parents with some sort of fear or reverence, in today's times, Gen Y is used to be treated as equals or friends by their parents. Having grown up thus, they expect a similar type of relationship with the adults in the organisation. This psychology needs to be understood and appreciated as it becomes easy to give and take feedback. We need an open and transparent environment that creates room for everyone, valuing contribution from each member of Gen Y or Gen X.

Gen Y gets bored with work that is repetitive in nature and expects to do meaningful and challenging work. It is a fact that every job would have some routine elements and some elements which would be interesting and exciting. Gen Y expects more of the latter, prompted by the exposure and higher awareness they have of their environment as compared to the earlier generations. Therefore managers have to think of ways of making their assignments challenging and set tall goals for the energetic Gen Y.

Another concern often heard is the 'get successful quick' syndrome of Gen Y. Gen Y does not have the patience to slog for years to attain promotions or to afford a luxurious lifestyle. They want to make fast moves and are willing to work hard to get there, including their ability to take risks and even pursue entrepreneurial opportunities to achieve their ambition. Gen Y employees straddle multiple goals while they pursue their careers. In a recently concluded survey among young IT professionals in Pune, it was interesting to note that beyond starting on a job with an IT company and doing an onsite assignment for a few years in the US, what they wish to do is to become a 'rock star' or pursue their real interests which would enable them to get 'recognised' by the media and people far and wide.

It is therefore important for organisations to rethink their structures and compensation frameworks. Allowing young people to don the mantles of responsibilities faster, providing impressive titles and designations, facilitating outcome linked compensation plan rather than years of experience/level based remuneration, enabling quicker promotions feasible and redesigning organisations with flatter structures are some of the measures that would significantly motivate Gen Y employees to stay with the organisation and build their careers instead of looking for frequent changes in order to satisfy their quest for success.

One area where Gen Y employees have undisputedly better skills than others is in the use of technology and their understanding in the smart usage of technology to solve problems or innovate. Gen Y lives, interacts and test their ideas with known and unknown people around the globe with absolute ease. Organisations should encourage them to use these skills and knowledge in the work context and involve them in rethinking the business propositions propelled by the power of technology. Successful relationships, healthy work environments and positive outcomes would emerge by applying the age old principles of engagement, involvement and ownership—principles which continue to be effervescent be they Gen Y or Gen X.

The Teaching Objectives

Teaching includes all the activities of providing education to other. The person who provides education is called teacher. The teacher uses different method for giving best knowledge to his students .He tries his best to make understand students. His duty is to encourage students to learn the subjects.

Teaching means interaction of teacher and students. They participate for their mutual benefits. Both have their own objective and target is to achieve them. Many great teachers of world define teaching in different way and we can say that teaching is just to train the students so that they can stand on their own foot in society .

In teaching, three main aspects comes in our front

1st is teacher

2nd is students

3rd is education

Nature and Characteristics of Teaching

1. The main character of teaching is to provide guidance and training.
2. Teaching is interaction between teacher and students.
3. Teaching is an art to give knowledge to students with effective way.
4. Teaching is a science to educate fact and causes of different topics of different subjects.

5. Teaching is continues process.
6. Teacher can teach effectively, if he has full confidence on the subject.
7. Teaching encourages students to learn more and more.
8. Teaching is formal as well as informal
9. Teaching is communication of information to students. In teaching, teacher imparts information in interesting way so that students can easily understand the information.
10. Teaching is tool to help student to adjust himself in society and its environment.

Objectives

There are many terms used in the field of education that describe what teachers wants to accomplish in their teaching. An aim or goal can be defined as a general objective. They are used to provide a broad outline of disciplinary and interdisciplinary competences that a teacher wants his students to achieve.

In contrast to aims or goals, a (behavioural or instructional) teaching objective describes exactly what a student should be able to do after the lecture. This technical term was developed in the 1950s along with the theory of behaviorism. The basic assumption is that every teaching activity elicits new behavioural responses from the learner. In this definition, learning is regarded as a change in behaviour, and thus it can be measured after the teaching. However, checking the expected outcome requires that the outcome itself first be adequately defined. This is accomplished using "behavioural" teaching objectives. (Note: From here on we shall omit the term "behavioural", opting for the simplified term "teaching objectives").

As posited in Bloom's theory (Bloom, 1956), learning can occur on very different affective, psychomotor, and cognitive levels. It is therefore necessary to relate the teaching objectives to these levels, which are described in "Blooms taxonomy".

Defining aims and objectives in the teaching process is a very important step during the planning process, and helps to select the appropriate content, media and methods.

Effective Teaching

What constitutes effective teaching may be subject to debate it would be simplistic and reductive to insist on a monolithic definition of effective teaching, considering the multiplicity of factors that come into play but most would agree that the basic purpose of teaching is to enable learning. The most effective teaching is that which results in the most effective learning.

Indeed, in a knowledge-driven society where information having increasingly short shelf life, it is important for teachers to focus on the longer-term goal of preparing our students for life, equipping them with more than a finite and rapidly obsolescent body of knowledge, and developing their faculties for understanding, applying and creating knowledge, as well as their ability to constantly refresh and upgrade their knowledge.

A quality graduate is life-skills oriented, learning-enabled and lifelong capable. The aims and desired learning outcomes of effective teaching may thus effect positive changes in the following:

Knowledge

- Discipline/profession-specific knowledge.
- General knowledge: fundamental concepts that an educated person/university graduate should have, regardless of area of specialisation.
- Awareness/familiarity across knowledge domains (i.e. rounded education).

Abilities

- Ability to identify what information is needed and where to find it.
- Evaluation of information and discrimination of what is valid and useful from what is not.
- Application/adaptation of knowledge to problem solving and making of informed judgements.
- Self-directedness in learning and the ability to sustain lifelong learning.
- Capacity for independent research and knowledge.
- Ability to communicate ideas clearly and structure arguments convincingly.

Mindset

- Questioning habit of mind with readiness to seek evidence/support for ideas/concepts presented, and to investigate/challenge established and controversial views including those which are generally taken as knowledge.

- Awareness of the complexity and dynamic nature of human knowledge and the need for evaluation and re-evaluation of knowledge.
- Enjoyment of learning.
- Learning as a lifelong habit.

Lesson Planning and Behavioural Objectives

A lesson plan is a teacher's detailed description of the course of instruction for one class. A daily lesson plan is developed by a teacher to guide class instruction. Details will vary depending on the preference of the teacher, subject being covered, and the need and/or curiosity of students. There may be requirements mandated by the school system regarding the plan.

Developing a Lesson Plan

While there are many formats for a lesson plan, most lesson plans contain some or all of these elements, typically in this order:

- *Title* of the lesson
- *Time* required to complete the lesson
- List of required *materials*
- List of *objectives*, which may be *behavioural objectives* (what the student can *do* at lesson completion) or *knowledge objectives* (what the student *knows* at lesson completion)
- The *set* (or lead-in, or bridge-in) that focuses students on the lesson's skills or concepts—these include showing pictures or models, asking leading questions, or reviewing previous lessons
- An *instructional component* that describes the sequence of events that make up the lesson, including the teacher's instructional input and guided practice the students use to try new skills or work with new ideas
- *Independent practice* that allows students to extend skills or knowledge on their own
- A *summary*, where the teacher wraps up the discussion and answers questions
- An *evaluation* component, a test for mastery of the instructed skills or concepts—such as a set of questions to answer or a set of instructions to follow
- A risk assessment where the lesson's risks and the steps taken to minimize them are documented.

- *Analysis* component the teacher uses to reflect on the lesson itself —such as what worked, what needs improving
- A *continuity* component reviews and reflects on content from the previous lesson

A well-developed Lesson Plan

A well-developed lesson plan reflects the interests and needs of students. It incorporates best practices for the educational field. The lesson plan correlates with the teacher's philosophy of education, which is what the teacher feels is the purpose of educating the students.

Secondary English program lesson plans, for example, usually centre around four topics. They are literary theme, elements of language and composition, literary history, and literary genre. A broad, thematic lesson plan is preferable, because it allows a teacher to create various research, writing, speaking, and reading assignments. It helps an instructor teach different literature genres and incorporate videotapes, films, and television programs. Also, it facilitates teaching literature and English together. Similarly, history lesson plans focus on content (historical accuracy and background information), analytic thinking, scaffolding, and the practicality of lesson structure and meeting of educational goals. School requirements and a teacher's personal tastes, in that order, determine the exact requirements for a lesson plan.

Unit plans follow much the same format as a lesson plan, but cover an entire unit of work, which may span several days or weeks. Modern constructivist teaching styles may not require individual lesson plans. The unit plan may include specific objectives and timelines, but lesson plans can be more fluid as they adapt to student needs and learning styles.

Setting Objectives

The first thing a teacher does is create an objective, a statement of purpose for the whole lesson. An objective statement itself should answer what students will be able to do by the end of the lesson. Harry Wong states that, "Each [objective] must begin with a verb that states the action to be taken to show accomplishment. The most important word to use in an assignment is a verb, because verbs state how to demonstrate if accomplishment has taken place or not." The objective drives the whole lesson, it is the reason the lesson exists. Care is taken when creating the objective for each day's lesson, as it will determine the activities the students engage in. The teacher also ensures that lesson plan goals are compatible with the developmental level of the students. The teacher ensures as well that their student achievement expectations are reasonable.

Selecting Lesson Plan Material

A lesson plan must correlate with the text book the class uses. The school usually selects the text books or provides teachers with a limited text book choice for a particular unit. The teacher must take great care and select the most appropriate book for the students.

Types of Assignments

The instructor must decide whether class assignments are whole-class, small groups, workshops, independent work, peer learning, or contractual:

- Whole-class—the teacher lectures to the class as a whole and has the class collectively participate in classroom discussions.
- Small groups—students work on assignments in groups of three or four.
- Workshops—students perform various tasks simultaneously. Workshop activities must be tailored to the lesson plan.
- Independent work—students complete assignments individually.
- Peer learning—students work together, face to face, so they can learn from one another.
- Contractual work—teacher and student establish an agreement that the student must perform a certain amount of work by a deadline.

These assignment categories (e.g. peer learning, independent, small groups) can also be used to guide the instructor's choice of assessment measures that can provide information about student and class comprehension of the material. As discussed by Biggs (1999), there are additional questions an instructor can consider when choosing which type of assignment would provide the most benefit to students. These include:

- What level of learning do the students need to attain before choosing assignments with varying difficulty levels?
- What is the amount of time the instructor wants the students to use to complete the assignment?
- How much time and effort does the instructor have to provide student grading and feedback?

- What is the purpose of the assignment? (e.g. to track student learning; to provide students with time to practice concepts; to practice incidental skills such as group process or independent research)
- How does the assignment fit with the rest of the lesson plan? Does the assignment test content knowledge or does it require application in a new context?

Behavioural Objectives

Behavioural objectives that are useful in the classroom must meet certain criteria. The four essential elements of a well-written behavioural objective are outlined below. When writing a behavioural objective, evaluate it using these criteria.

1. Good behavioural objectives are student-oriented. A behavioural objective, which is student-oriented, places the emphasis upon what the student is expected to do, not upon what the teacher will do.

Sometimes teachers use instructional goals which emphasize what they are expected to do rather than what they expect of their students. Such teacher-oriented objectives only have the value to the extent that they direct the teacher to do something, which ultimately leads to student learning. A teacher attempting to help his or her students attain the goal of solving long division problems may work out some of the problems on the blackboard, explaining each of the steps involved. A teacher-oriented objective associated with this behaviour might read something like: "To explain the steps of long division on the blackboard." Notice that this might be a helpful teacher activity, but it is only one of many possible activities that could help the students reach the goal of solving long division.

2. Good behavioural objectives describe learning outcomes. The important thing to keep in mind here is that we are interested in what the students will learn to do. In other words, it is the learning outcome that is important, not the learning activities that should lead to that outcome. To say that students will practice long division problems, using two different methods, is not to specify a learning outcome; it describes a process. It specifies an activity designed to help the students reach some outcome. As such, it is a student-oriented activity, not an outcome. Your objective should reflect outcome language, rather than process phrases.

It may be helpful to you as a teacher to determine what kind of learning activities you may want your students to carry out. However, determining which learning experiences and activities are most appropriate for your students can only be made after you have decided what it is you want your students to accomplish. Once learning outcomes are identified and described, then activities that are appropriate for attaining those outcomes can be determined.

3. Good behavioural objectives are clear and understandable. The first prerequisite for a clear and understandable objective is explicitness. It should contain a clearly stated verb that describes a definite action or behaviour and, in most cases, should refer to an object of that action. People observing the products of those behaviors should agree in their judgment about whether the behaviour had occurred as stated.
4. Good behavioural objectives are observable. The evaluation of learning outcomes hinges on the ability to observe those outcomes. The key to an observable objective is an observable verb. Consequently, when selecting behavioural objectives for use in your teaching, watch the verbs! The verb must describe an observable action or an action that results in an observable products.

Opening A Lesson

Set induction refers to those actions and statements by the teacher that are designed to relate the experiences of the students to the objectives of the lesson. Effective teachers use set induction to put students in a receptive frame of mind that will facilitate learning — be it physical, emotional, or mental.

Set induction has as its first purpose - to focus student attention on the lesson. The first motivational function of the teacher is to engage the student in learning. As its second purpose, set induction attempts to create an organizing framework for the ideas, principles, or information, which is to follow. Telling students in advance about the way in which a lesson is organized is likely to improve their comprehension and ability to recall and apply what they hear.

A third purpose of set induction is to extend the understanding and application of abstract ideas through the use of example and analogy. An idea or principle that is abstractly stated can be difficult for many students to comprehend. Moreover, many students who do under-stand an idea or principle have difficulty in applying their knowledge to new situations. The clever use of examples and analogies can do much to overcome such limitations. The fourth and last purpose of set induction is to stimulate interest and involvement in the lesson. The point here is that active involvement at the beginning of a lesson can increase curiosity and stimulate student interest in the lesson.

An effective lesson introduction should have as its purpose at least one of the items listed and discussed above. A good example is the teacher who wishes to teach the concept of categorizing and brings a collection of baseball cards, record jackets, or even a basket of leaves to class. Then the students, divided into groups, are asked to categorize their collections and explain how and why the chose what they did.

Uses of Set Induction

1. To focus the student's attention on the presentation the teacher is about to make by employing an activity, event, object, or person that relates directly to student interest or previous experience.
2. To provide a structure or framework that enables the student to visualize the content or activities of the presentation.
3. To aid in clarifying the goals of the lesson presentation.
4. To provide a smooth transition from known or already covered material to new or unknown material by capitalizing on the use of examples (either verbal or nonverbal), analogies, and student activities which students have interest in or experience with.
5. To evaluate previously learned material before moving on to the new material or skill-building activities by employing student-centred activities or student-developed examples or analogies that demonstrate understanding of previously learned content.

Types of Course Study

The objectives of vocational education are more varied at the secondary than at the postsecondary level. Secondary vocational courses can be classified into three types:

(1) consumer and homemaking education;
(2) general labour market preparation; and
(3) specific labour market preparation.

Specific labour market preparation courses teach students the skills needed to enter a particular occupational field. Such courses can be grouped into the following occupational program areas:

- Agriculture;
- Business and office;
- Marketing and distribution;
- Health;
- Occupational home economics;
- Trade and industry (including construction, mechanics and repairs, and precision production); and
- Technical and communications.

In addition to this occupationally specific curriculum, some secondary vocational courses provide general labour market preparation, teaching general employment skills— such as introductory typing or wordprocessing, industrial arts, career education, and applied academic skills—rather than preparing students for paid employment in a specific occupation. Finally, consumer and homemaking education courses, unlike occupational home economics courses, prepare students for unpaid employment in the home. While this publication provides information on all three types of secondary vocational courses, it focuses primarily on the occupationally specific curriculum.

Vocational education at the secondary level has traditionally had several objectives, including providing students with general employability skills and preparing them to enter paid and unpaid employment in specific occupations. However, in recent years, the goals of vocational education have expanded to include preparing students not only for entry into work but also for career advancement and entry into further education and training. For instance, educators have been called upon to integrate academic and vocational education.

Secondary vocational education is provided primarily through three types of public high schools:

(1) comprehensive high schools (the typical U.S. high school);

(2) area vocational schools (regional facilities that students attend part of a day to receive their occupational training); and

(3) full-time vocational high schools (schools that offer academic studies but focus on preparing students for work in a particular occupation or industry).

The latter two types are referred to collectively as vocational schools. The National Assessment of Vocational Education (NAVE) recently found that most secondary vocational education is provided in comprehensive high schools, with vocational schools enrolling about 10 percent of secondary students and accounting for about 12 percent of vocational coursetaking. Because of the limited capacity of available datasets to provide information on the three types of schools, this publication generally treats secondary vocational education as a single system.

While occupationally specific courses are organized into program areas, high school students typically do not formally enroll in an occupational program. Instead, they may take one or more courses in a single occupational program, or courses scattered throughout the occupationally specific curriculum. Moreover, while the majority of students take occupational courses during their high school careers, they do so for a variety of reasons. Some students take introductory business or technical and communications courses to gain hands-on computer experience, whereas others are required by their high schools to complete a vocational course in order to graduate. Only a minority of students complete a coherent sequence of courses preparing them for employment in a specific occupational field. Indeed, the sequence of courses defining an occupational program varies among high schools and school districts across the country.

Consequently, it is not possible—nor very useful—to label students as "vocational students" based on a single definition. Instead, this publication provides several alternative measures of participation in vocational and occupationally specific education at the secondary level. The smallest unit of measure is a course or a credit, and data are provided on the percentage of public high school graduates completing at least one course and on the average number of credits they earned in different vocational and occupational areas. Some tables provide information on heavy vocational coursetakers, those earning large numbers of vocational or occupationally specific credits.

Additionally, this publication seeks to address the emphasis in the 1990 Perkins Act on providing coherent sequences of vocational courses. The federal regulations associated with the 1990 Perkins Act defined a coherent sequence of courses as "a series of courses in which vocational and academic education are integrated, and which directly relates to, and leads to, both academic and occupational competencies. However, federal datasets rely largely on analyses of student transcripts to determine high school course-taking patterns. While both flexible and reliable, these transcript studies have limited capacity to provide information on the content of courses, such as what specific competencies they teach. Alternatively, this publication uses several measures of concentration in vocational education to examine graduates' propensity to take a series of related vocational courses. Specifically, public high school graduates are identified as vocational "concentrators" if they earned 3 or more credits in a single occupational program, and as vocational "specialists" if they earned 4 or more credits in a single program with at least 2 of these credits beyond the introductory level. Data are also provided on the levels of occupational courses graduates completed, including introductory, second- or higher level, and specialty courses.

Postsecondary Vocational Education

Vocational education at the nonbaccalaureate postsecondary level primarily focuses on providing occupationally specific preparation. Postsecondary-level occupational programs generally parallel the program areas identified at the secondary level:

- Agriculture;
- Business and office;
- Marketing and distribution;
- Health;
- Home economics;
- Technical education (including protective services, computers and data processing, engineering and science technologies, and communication technologies); and
- Trade and industry.

While emphasis at the postsecondary level has traditionally been on providing students with skills needed to enter a particular occupational field, these skills have typically been at a more advanced level than those provided through secondary occupational programs.

Postsecondary vocational education is offered at several types of institutions, including public and private, and 4-year and less-than-4-year postsecondary institutions. This publication provides comparable information on participation in six different institutional types: public 4-year institutions; private, nonprofit 4-year institutions; public 2- to 3-year institutions (community colleges); public vocational-technical institutes; private, nonprofit less-than-4-year institutions; and private proprietary (for-profit) institutions. As was the case at the secondary level, postsecondary occupational education is delivered in the form of courses that are organized into program areas. In a few cases, students are required to enroll formally in an occupational program. In other cases, students may be required to declare a major upon enrolling in an institution.

However, students often sample courses from a variety of program areas, whether or not they have declared a major. This tendency to "mill around" in postsecondary vocational education has been well documented. Moreover, postsecondary institutions, particularly community colleges, serve a student population with diverse educational goals. Some students enter with the intention of completing a degree or certificate, while others intend only to take one or a few courses and then leave. In most cases, it is only possible to identify with accuracy vocational program participants once students have completed a program and obtained a degree or certificate. However, this captures only a portion of nonbaccalaureate postsecondary students.

Because of the timing of this publication, transcript data were unavailable for detailed analysis of participation patterns in postsecondary vocational education. Instead, this report relies on students' self-reported majors. Consequently, in contrast to the secondary level, the discussion of postsecondary vocational education does not provide information on varying levels of participation by students.

How Widespread is Participation in Vocational Education?

Secondary Level: Most public high school students participate in vocational education. In 1992, almost all public high school graduates (97 percent) completed at least one vocational education course, and 87 percent completed at least one occupationally specific course. On average, graduates completed the equivalent of almost four full-year courses in vocational education (3.8 credits), with two and a half of these courses in occupational program areas

Although public high school graduates earned greater numbers of total and academic credits over the decade from 1982 to 1992, credits earned in vocational education decreased. Between 1982 and 1992, total credits earned by high school graduates increased about 11 percent (from 21 to 24 credits), while academic credits earned rose about 22 percent (from 14 to 17 credits). In contrast, over the same period, the average number of vocational credits earned by high school graduates declined by almost 1 full credit, or by about 17 percent. By

1992, vocational coursework made up only 16 percent of the total coursework completed by high school graduates, down from 21 percent in 1982. The National Assessment of Vocational Education (NAVE) found that this declining vocational enrollment might be attributed to several factors, such as increasing high school graduation requirements over the 1982-1992 decade and the vulnerability of secondary vocational programs to local economic conditions.

Between 1982 and 1992, participation in the occupationally specific curriculum was somewhat more stable than in other vocational areas. The percentage of public high school graduates completing at least one occupational course remained about the same (at approximately 87 percent), and the average number of credits earned by graduates in occupational programs decreased over the decade by less than half a credit (from 2.9 to 2.5 credits) or by about 14 percent. In contrast, both the percentages of graduates participating in the consumer and homemaking and the general labour market preparation curricula and the average number of credits graduates earned in these areas declined significantly over the decade (with average credits earned declining about 29 and 36 percent in these respective areas).

Postsecondary Level: The NAVE found that 5.8 million students were enrolled in postsecondary vocational education in 1990, making up about 35 percent of all undergraduate postsecondary enrollments. Vocational enrollments represented an even larger share of the nonbaccalaureate undergraduate population, with about one-half of these students reporting that they were majoring in a vocational program area. In contrast, one in four nonbaccalaureate postsecondary students reported an academic major and one in four were taking personal or avocational courses (for example, basic skills and citizenship activities).Nonbaccalaureate students at all types of postsecondary institutions reported majoring in vocational programs, although the proportion of the nonbaccalaureate student body that was vocationally oriented varied by institution type. For example, at public 4-year postsecondary institutions about one-third of nonbaccalaureate students reported majoring in vocational programs, while at public vocational-technical institutes 90 percent of nonbaccalaureate students were in the vocational curriculum.

What Types of Vocational Education do Students Take?

Secondary Level: Business was the most popular occupational program at the high school level, with more than half of all 1992 high school graduates completing at least one business course. Business was followed in popularity by trade and industry and then by technical and communications programs.

Although overall participation in the occupationally specific curriculum declined somewhat over the decade from 1982 to 1992, trends varied by program area. The percentage of graduates completing at least one course in the technical and communications area, as well as the average number of credits earned in this program area, increased between 1982 and 1992. In contrast, both the percentage of graduates completing at least one trade and industry course and the average number of trade and industry credits earned declined over the decade. The NAVE found that these occupational enrollment patterns appeared to follow labour market trends.

Postsecondary Level: As was the case at the secondary level, the most popular postsecondary vocational program was business, with about 17 percent of all nonbaccalaureate students declaring a major in this area. Business was followed in popularity by health (11 percent) and then trade and industry (8 percent) programs. The combined technical fields (computers and data processing, engineering and science technologies, protective services, and communications technologies) accounted for 12 percent of all nonbaccalaureate majors.

Program enrollment varied significantly by institution type. Students at private proprietary; private, nonprofit 4-year; and public 2- to 3-year institutions were more likely to major in business than students at public 4-year institutions. In contrast, students at public vocational-technical institutes and private proprietary schools were much more likely to major in trade and industry than students at all other postsecondary institutions.

Do students take coherent sequences of vocational courses?

Vocational Concentration and Specialization at the Secondary Level: The NAVE found that concentrating one's vocational coursetaking resulted in higher earnings, especially if students entered training-related jobs. However, few 1992 graduates completed a sequence of courses providing significant preparation in a single occupational area. About 24 percent of high school graduates were vocational "concentrators," earning 3 or more credits in a single occupational program, and about 8 percent of graduates were vocational "specialists," earning 4 or more credits in a single program with at least 2 of these credits beyond the introductory level. Lack of focused coursetaking was not restricted to the vocational curriculum. The majority of high school graduates (60 percent) failed to meet the criteria for either the college preparatory or vocational specializations.

While graduates were more likely to complete at least one course in business than in any other occupational area, they were more likely to concentrate in trade and industry programs. Specifically, 10 percent of 1992 high school graduates earned 3 or more credits in trade and industry, while 8 percent earned this number of business credits. Nearly half of all vocational concentrators concentrated in the trade and industry curriculum, although business was the most frequent vocational concentration among college preparatory graduates. Technical and communications and health programs had the fewest concentrators among all graduates, perhaps due to a lack of available courses. The disparity between a high level of coursetaking and low level of concentration in business and in technical and communications may be due to students electing not to concentrate in these areas. The NAVE attributed the disparity to many students seeking computer-related coursework through these programs rather than specific occupational preparation.

Levels of Vocational Coursetaking at the Secondary Level

High levels of vocational coursetaking in high school did not always mean that graduates completed advanced occupational courses. In fact, 20 percent of 1992 high school graduates who earned 8 or more vocational credits and about 25 percent of those who earned 4 or more occupationally specific credits did not take a single occupational course above the introductory level. Among all graduates, twice as many took introductory occupational courses as took advanced ones (75 percent compared with 35 percent).

Rates of advanced course completion varied by program concentration. Vocational concentrators in marketing were more likely than concentrators in other program areas to take advanced courses in their area of concentration (86 percent of marketing concentrators took advanced marketing courses). In contrast, concentrators in occupational home economics were less likely than those in most other program areas to take advanced courses in their concentration (40 percent took such courses).

To what Extent do Students with Different Demographic Characteristics Participate in Vocational Education?

Sex and race-ethnicity were related to differences in participation in vocational education at both the secondary and postsecondary levels.

Secondary Level: High school vocational course-taking patterns differed for males and females. Male graduates in 1992 earned about one-third more occupationally specific credits, while female graduates earned almost twice as many consumer and homemaking education credits. Furthermore, the percentages of males and females completing at least one occupational course differed significantly in all program areas except marketing. In particular, males in 1992 were more than twice as likely to complete at least one course in agriculture and in trade and industry, while females were more than twice as likely to complete at least one course in health and in occupational home economics.

Between 1982 and 1992, there was little increase in the percentage of students participating in occupational programs that were nontraditional for their sex. The gender gap in trade and industry narrowed over the decade, although this narrowing was *not* due to more females completing courses in this program area. Rather, the gap narrowed because of a drop in participation for males. Moreover, the gap in participation for males and females remained about the same in agriculture, health, and occupational home economics. However, while females in 1982 were more than one and a half times as likely as males to participate in business, this gap narrowed significantly by 1992.

The patterns of vocational concentration for males and females were similar to those for coursetaking. Males were more likely than females to be vocational concentrators and specialists, while females were more likely to be in the college preparatory track. Additionally, males were more likely to concentrate in agriculture, trade and industry, and technical and communications, while females were significantly more likely to concentrate in business, health, and occupational home economics.

High school vocational course-taking patterns also differed based on race-ethnicity. Native Americans appeared to earn above average numbers of vocational and occupationally specific credits, and Asians below average numbers of these credits, although these differences were not statistically significant possibly due to the small sample sizes for these groups. Native American graduates also appeared both to concentrate and specialize in vocational education at above average rates, although these differences were once again not statistically significant. However, Native Americans had higher than average rates of concentration in trade and industry programs, and lower than average rates in programs offering computer coursework, including business and technical and communications. White, black, and Hispanic graduates differed little from the overall pool of high school graduates in terms of the numbers of vocational and occupationally specific credits they earned and their rates of concentration and specialization. These groups also exhibited no consistent patterns of over- or underparticipation in specific occupational programs.

Postsecondary Level: The majority (57 percent) of nonbaccalaureate postsecondary students in 1989-90 were female. In fact, females represented the majority of the student populations at five of the six types of postsecondary institutions in the study, with the exception of public vocational-technical institutes, where males and females participated at similar rates. This enrollment pattern was reflected among students who reported majoring in vocational programs, with the majority (54 percent) of all vocational majors being female. Females were in the minority among vocational majors at public 4-year institutions only.

Most (74 percent) nonbaccalaureate postsecondary students in 1989-90 were white. However, the racial-ethnic composition of students varied markedly by institution type. While three-quarters or more of nonbaccalaureate students at public and private 4-year institutions, public 2- to 3-year institutions, and public vocational-technical institutes were white, more than 40 percent of private proprietary students were from a minority group. These patterns persisted among students reporting vocational majors.

Black nonbaccalaureate students reported majoring in vocational education at above average rates, with almost two-thirds of this racial-ethnic group majoring in a vocational program area in comparison with about half of all students. Even after controlling for socioeconomic background, the NAVE found that black postsecondary students were more likely than all other groups to major in vocational areas.

To what Extent do Students who are Disadvantaged or have Disabilities Participate in Vocational Education?

Secondary Level: Public high school graduates in 1992 who were members of special populations were generally more likely than other graduates to participate in vocational education overall and in occupationally specific education. Graduates in lower socioeconomic quartiles; students with disabilities, lower grade point averages, and greater numbers of accumulated remedial credits; and both student parents and expecting students were more likely to participate than other students. These special populations were more likely to complete at least one course in vocational education overall and in occupationally specific education. In addition, they generally earned greater numbers of vocational and occupationally specific credits than their counterparts who were not members of special populations. However, English proficiency was not related to vocational participation. Limited-English proficient graduates participated at roughly equal rates as English proficient graduates in vocational education and occupationally specific education and earned roughly similar numbers of credits in these curricula.

Members of most special population groups were also more likely than other graduates to concentrate and specialize in vocational education. Students in lower socioeconomic quartiles and students with disabilities, lower grade point averages, and greater numbers of accumulated credits in remedial coursework were more likely than other students to be both vocational concentrators and specialists. Limited-English proficient students were more likely than their English proficient counterparts to be vocational concentrators. Given their high levels of vocational coursetaking, the propensity of students with disabilities and economically and academically disadvantaged students to concentrate their coursetaking in a single occupational program area—and to earn at least 2 credits in that program area above the introductory level—was a positive indication that these students were not simply taking scattered, lower level vocational courses.

Special population students were somewhat less likely than other graduates to concentrate in programs offering exposure to computer coursework. Students in lower socioeconomic quartiles and students with lower grade point averages and greater numbers of accumulated credits in remedial coursework were more likely than their economically and academically advantaged counterparts to concentrate in occupational home economics and trade and industry. Students with disabilities were more than twice as likely as nondisabled students to concentrate in trade and industry, and were less likely to concentrate in technical and communications. Additionally, students accumulating greater numbers of credits in remedial coursework were less likely than other students to concentrate in business. However, students in lower socioeconomic quartiles were more likely than their more affluent counterparts to concentrate in business.

Postsecondary Level: Economically disadvantaged students and unmarried students with dependents were more likely to report a vocational major than other nonbaccalaureate postsecondary students, but academically disadvantaged and disabled students were no more likely to do so. Specifically, during the 1989-90 academic year, nonbaccalaureate postsecondary students from families in lower socioeconomic quartiles were more likely to report majoring in a vocational program than students from affluent families. Additionally, unmarried students with dependents were more likely than all other groups to major in vocational education. In contrast, there was no consistent relationship between grade point average and majoring in vocational education, and disabled students were no more likely than their nondisabled peers to report a vocational major.

Incarcerated Persons

Section 421 of the 1990 Perkins Act called upon the Department of Education to report information on the participation of incarcerated persons in vocational education. The National Adult Literacy Survey (NALS) provided the first national data on this group. NALS revealed that about one-third of federal and state prison inmates aged 16 or over in 1992 had received vocational training during their current period of incarceration. Whether inmates received vocational training varied by educational attainment. Inmates with a high school diploma or GED, or with some college education, were more likely than inmates with lower educational attainment to receive vocational training as their sole educational activity. However, inmates participated in a combination of vocational and nonvocational activities at similar rates regardless of their educational attainment.

How much Academic Preparation do Vocational Coursetakers Receive?

Academic Coursetaking at the Secondary Level: In 1992, fewer than one in five public high school graduates met all of the academic standards established in *A Nation At Risk* for noncollege-bound graduates. Graduates earning more credits in vocational education were less likely than graduates with fewer accumulated vocational credits to meet the standards in each subject area, except for computer science. Increased vocational coursework was associated with higher rates of compliance with the computer science standard. Additionally, graduates concentrating in the "high tech" fields of technical and communications and business were more likely than other vocational concentrators to meet all of the *A Nation At Risk* standards, and were just as likely as nonconcentrators to do so. These technical and business concentrators were also more likely than other vocational concentrators to specialize in the college preparatory curriculum, and technical concentrators were just as likely as graduates with no vocational concentration to do so.

As the number of vocational credits that 1992 public high school graduates earned rose, the number of academic credits they earned decreased in all subject areas. However, the rate of tradeoff between academic and vocational credits varied across academic subject areas. For example, as graduates earned greater numbers of vocational credits, the decline in academic credits they earned was smaller for English and social studies and greater for foreign language than it was for other academic subjects.

Additionally, the rate of tradeoff between vocational and advanced academic credits varied across academic subject areas. As graduates earned greater numbers of vocational credits, the decline in advanced math credits they earned was greater than the decline in math credits in general. However, there was no significant difference between the rates of decline in advanced and general English and science courses.

Generally, as vocational coursetaking increased, students not only earned fewer credits in academic subject areas but also completed more of their academic coursework at lower levels. For example, as 1992 public high school graduates earned increasing numbers of credits in vocational education, they also earned more credits in remedial English, in math at levels lower than Algebra 1, and in survey science courses. As previously discussed, these patterns may reflect the fact that academically disadvantaged students were more likely than their advantaged counterparts to participate heavily in vocational education.

Efforts to Integrate Academic and Vocational Education

In an effort to improve the quality of both academic and vocational education, the 1990 Perkins Act

encouraged secondary schools and postsecondary institutions to integrate these curricula. By the spring of 1992, most schools and institutions reported some integration efforts. However, most of these efforts involved enhancing existing vocational courses—rather than significantly restructuring the academic and vocational curricula—and did not appear to receive a substantial new allocation of resources, particularly in terms of allocating teachers' time. The following discussion provides examples of integration efforts undertaken at both the secondary and postsecondary levels.

Secondary level. At the secondary education level, more than 80 percent of public high schools offering vocational courses reported taking some action to integrate academic and vocational education by the 1991-92 school year. Vocational schools (including full-time and area or regional vocational high schools) were more likely than comprehensive high schools to have begun integration efforts. Among schools taking integration steps, vocational schools were also more likely to report efforts to integrate occupational programs.

The most frequently used method of integrating academic and vocational education was to incorporate employability or generic work skills, such as SCANS skills, into vocational courses. Additionally, when academic and vocational teachers worked together, they were more likely to collaborate on developing academic materials for vocational courses, or applied materials for academic courses, than to collaborate on other efforts, such as team teaching or developing coordinated academic and vocational courses. Finally, teachers had regularly scheduled time to work together on integration efforts at fewer than one-quarter of the secondary schools reporting such efforts.

Postsecondary level. At the postsecondary education level, almost all institutions (more than 96 percent) reported taking some action to integrate academic and vocational education by the 1991-92 school year. The most common integration efforts involved increasing the basic skills of vocational students (through supporting remedial or developmental education) and establishing general education competencies for these students.

The most common way in which faculty were involved in developing integrated curricula was reviewing general education requirements or developing academic materials to be incorporated into existing vocational courses. Faculty members had regularly scheduled time to work on integration efforts at about one-quarter of community colleges and vocational-technical institutes, and at about one in ten area or regional vocational schools serving postsecondary students.

What Outcomes are Associated with Participation in Vocational Education?

Mathematics Achievement at the Secondary Level: A recent study of the relationship between coursetaking and achievement found that increased academic coursetaking was consistently associated with higher mathematics achievement, and increased vocational coursetaking with lower mathematics achievement, as measured by a National Assessment of Educational Progress (NAEP) achievement test. Specifically, 1990 public high school graduates who scored in higher test quartiles on the NAEP mathematics assessment earned more academic and fewer vocational credits than did graduates in lower test quartiles. Furthermore, as the number of vocational credits that graduates accumulated rose, their mathematics test scores tended to decrease. The study indicated that these patterns persisted for males and females and graduates in all racial-ethnic groups.

The study cautioned against assuming a causal relationship between vocational coursetaking and lower mathematics achievement based on these findings. Because the study examined achievement at a single point in time, it was unable to isolate students' prior ability or achievement and, therefore, to control for preexisting differences—or "selection effects"—between students who completed greater and fewer numbers of vocational courses. A related study found that while certain academic courses contributed to cognitive gain, vocational courses generally had a neutral effect on cognitive growth. Thus, the lower mathematics achievement of graduates with greater numbers of accumulated vocational credits may reflect their completing fewer academic courses rather than more vocational courses. In addition, the tendency of heavy vocational coursetakers to complete a large proportion of their academic courses at lower levels, as noted earlier in this report, may also contribute to these low math test scores.

Postsecondary Employment and Earnings Outcomes

Among the general population, only about one in five adults aged 18-34 in the summer of 1990 had completed a postsecondary degree or certificate, and about one-fourth of those completers earned their highest postsecondary award in a vocational field. Vocational completers were more likely than persons never attending a postsecondary institution to be employed. However, while they appeared more likely than postsecondary noncompleters to be employed, this difference was not statistically significant. Vocational completers were employed at similar rates as nonvocational associate's degree or certificate holders, and were slightly less likely to be employed than bachelor's degree holders.

During the summer of 1990, about one-half of all employed postsecondary vocational completers aged 18-34 worked in a field related to their training. Training-related employment appeared to make no difference in the constancy with which postsecondary vocational completers were employed between the summer of 1990 and the winter of 1992.

Although relatedness of employment to postsecondary vocational training did not appear to be related to employment stability, it was positively associated with earnings in the summer of 1990. For example, 39 percent of postsecondary vocational completers employed in a field related to their training earned more than $2,000 per month, while 30 percent of those employed in an unrelated field had this level of earnings. In contrast, 25 percent of vocational completers employed in an unrelated field earned less than $1,100 per month, while 17 percent of those employed in a related field earned this little.

What Other School-to-work Programs do Schools and Institutions Offer?

In addition to offering classroom-based courses, secondary schools and postsecondary institutions often provide opportunities for work-based learning, such as cooperative education, work experience, and school-based enterprises. Cooperative education and work experience programs allow students to earn school credit in conjunction with paid or unpaid employment. Cooperative education programs place students in jobs related to their vocational field of study, and typically involve employers in developing a formal training plan and evaluating students. On the other hand, traditional work experience programs sometimes place students in vocationally unrelated jobs, and may not involve employers as extensively as cooperative education programs. School-based enterprises are class-related activities that engage students in producing goods or services for sale or use to people other than the participating students themselves.

Secondary level. About one-half of public high schools in 1991-92 offered cooperative education programs. In contrast, fewer than one-third offered school-based enterprises and other work experience programs. Vocational schools were more likely than comprehensive high schools to offer each of these programs. Among vocational schools, area vocational schools were more likely than full-time vocational high schools to offer school-based enterprises and other work experience programs.

On average, 1992 public high school graduates accumulated 0.15 credits in cooperative education and work experience courses—equivalent to about one in seven graduates completing a year-long course. College preparatory graduates and graduates without a college preparatory or vocational specialization averaged negligible numbers of such credits (0.04 and 0.09, respectively). However, vocational specialists averaged about 1 credit in cooperative education and work experience, equivalent to a full-year course. High school students concentrating in marketing and distribution and in health completed more cooperative education and work experience coursework as part of their occupational programs than did other vocational concentrators.

Postsecondary level. Three-quarters of community colleges reported offering cooperative education or work experience programs in 1991-92. In contrast, about half of public postsecondary vocational-technical institutes and area vocational schools serving postsecondary students reported offering these programs. Fewer than one-sixth of all postsecondary institutions offered school-based enterprises, with area vocational schools that served postsecondary students being more likely than community colleges and vocational-technical institutes to offer these programs.

Foundations for Quality Teaching and Learning

Each lesson should have a purpose. Educators have known about the importance of purpose for several decades. A clearly articulated purpose focuses instruction; provides students with an answer to the question, "Why do we have to learn this?" and allows for assessment of outcomes. Simply said, establishing the purpose of the lesson facilitates student achievement. It's a vital component of quality teaching, yet one that is often neglected. In too many classrooms, students are left to intuit the purpose of the lesson.

But what does a good purpose statement look like? It's more than simply stating the standard to students. A quality purpose statement gives students information about what they will learn and how they might demonstrate that understanding. A quality purpose statement also helps the teacher plan the lesson, because the tasks students are asked to complete should align with the expected understanding. This is an important point that is easy to overlook: purpose drives instruction, differentiation, and assessment. It might seem like an insignificant component of high-quality teaching, given that it should only occupy a fraction of teaching time, but we think it's the foundation of quality lesson planning and instructional delivery.

In our work, we use *purpose*, rather than *goal* or *objective*, because it forces us to pay attention to what students think. A teacher writes an objective, but the students must understand the purpose. Although teachers want objectives that are measurable, students want to know what they're expected to learn and why.

Before we delve into the examples of high-quality purposes, it's important to note that the questions that you and other observers ask students influence the type of purpose that is established. When a principal—or any other observer—asks students in a class, "What are you doing?" teachers are encouraged to establish a purpose on the basis of the tasks that students will complete during the class session. Alternatively, when visitors ask students, "What are you learning?" teachers tend to focus the purpose on enduring "understandings" and content.

This is an important aspect of fostering high-quality instruction: the questions we ask students about their learning influence the purpose statements teachers make. Of course, we can also discuss high-quality purpose statements in professional development sessions and give individual teachers feedback about the purposes they establish for their students.

Components of the Purpose Statement

There are a number of ways to think about components of a purpose statement. To be clear, the purpose statement should not focus on the tasks that students will complete as part of the class session or at home. Rather, the purpose statement should reflect the understandings that students will gain as a result of their engagement in the lesson components. When lessons are planned with the end in mind, purpose statements are easier to develop.

Content

Part of the purpose statement comes from the content standards. This is, in part, why a clearly established purpose is essential. Planning an amazing lesson for ninth graders that is based on seventh-grade standards will not ensure that the students reach high levels of achievement. Having a purpose statement that is based on content standards ensures that instruction is aligned with high expectations. In the coming months, we'll focus on how to design lessons to ensure that students reach those high expectations, but for now we have to ensure that the lessons are based on gradelevel expectations.

Suggesting that the purpose should be based on the content standards does not mean that the standard can serve as the purpose. Most content standards take time to master. The purpose statement should focus on the learning for the day. For example, it takes weeks for students to understand the causes and effects of World War II, so several purpose statements will be required that add up to this larger picture. When standards are not analyzed for their component parts and instead are used as the purpose, students stop paying attention to them. The standards might be posted on the wall, but they're like wallpaper to students: a decoration that really doesn't have anything to do with the day's work.

Language

A second component of the purpose statement relates to the ways in which students can demonstrate their understanding of the content. This is often referred to as the "language purpose," because humans demonstrate their understanding by reading, writing, speaking, listening, and showing. Understanding the linguistic demands of the content is essential to this component of the purpose and especially important for English learners who are doing double the work in middle and high school, learning content and language simultaneously.

To develop the language component of the purpose statement, teachers consider vocabulary, language structure, and language function. For some lessons, the important linguistic component might be related to the vocabulary of the discipline. The language purpose indicates how students will demonstrate their understanding, and it may be more task-like than the content purpose. For example, in a math class, part of the purpose might be for students "to use logic vocabulary in their proofs." For other lessons, students might focus on grammar, syntax, or signal words. For example, as part of a history class, students learning the art of sourcing ideas might use a sentence frame, "Although _____ believed _____, others disagreed" as part of their conversations with peers.

A third way to think about the language component is by determining the function of language that is necessary to understand the content. In other words, do students need to justify, persuade, inform, entertain, debate, hypothesize, and so forth to understand the lesson? For example, in a math class, part of the purpose might be to "justify your answer in writing."

Communicating the Purpose Statement

Once a teacher constructs a purpose statement, he or she must communicate it to his or her students. The teacher may do this in various ways. Some post the purpose on the board and briefly talk with students at the start of the period about the purpose and its relevance. Others begin with inquiry and then invite students to talk about why they are doing what they're doing before making the purpose more explicit. And still others discuss the purpose and then invite students to write the purpose in their own words as part of their note-taking tasks.

When Lucas Staker, a teacher at Health Sciences High and Middle College in San Diego, CA, was teaching his art students how to look at paintings, he projected a famous work of art and said, "Today, we're going to consider the role that perspective plays in fine art, and to do that we'll use specific technical vocabulary." When Dina Burow, another teacher at Health Sciences High and Middle College, introduced her algebra students to quadratic questions, she said "Today, we're going to identify the properties of a quadratic equation and explain how we know whether equations are quadratic or not."

Part of Quality Teaching

Regardless of how the purpose is established, it's important that students know it so that they know what to pay attention to and what will be expected of them. A clearly communicated purpose increases the relevance of the lesson for students and helps the teacher remain focused and not drift too far afield, perhaps wasting valuable instructional time. In fact, the most common thing that teachers who begin establishing purpose tell us is that it really helped them stay focused.

3

Planning for Quality Teaching and Learning

Learning is one of the most important activities in which humans engage. It is at the very core of the educational process, although most of what people learn occurs outside of school. For thousands of years, philosophers and psychologists have sought to understand the nature of learning, how it occurs, and how one person can influence the learning of another person through teaching and similar endeavours. Various theories of learning have been suggested, and these theories differ for a variety of reasons. A theory, most simply, is a combination of different factors or variables woven together in an effort to explain whatever the theory is about. In general, theories based on scientific evidence are considered more valid than theories based on opinion or personal experience. In any case, it is wise to be cautious when comparing the appropriateness of different theories.

In addition to formal theories, people hold personal theories, including theories of learning and teaching. Some typical questions such theories might involve are: How does one determine if learning has occurred? What factors determine whether or not learning occurs? Are these factors located in the environment or within the individual? This entry focuses first on different conceptions and definitions of learning. Next, the evolution of theories and conceptions of learning over the past 100 years is discussed, highlighting some of the advantages and limitations of different theoretical perspectives. Following a discussion of the relationship between theory and practice, examples of different types of learning are presented, and the appropriateness of different theories for different learning situations is pointed out.

Conceptions of "Learning"

Understanding any theory requires a clear idea of what the theory is trying to explain. When a particular word is used, people usually assume everyone has a common understanding of what the word means. Unfortunately, such is not always the case. In trying to understand the various theories of learning and their implications for education, it is helpful to realize that the term "learning" means different things to different people and is used somewhat differently in different theories. As theories of learning evolved over the past half-century, definitions of learning shifted from changes that occur in the mind or behaviour of an individual to changes in participation in ongoing activities with other individuals to changes in a person's identity within a group (e.g., a change from being a follower to being a leader). Although, most definitions of learning involve a change in an individual's knowledge, ability to perform a skill, or participate in an activity with other individuals, there is considerable variation among the theories about the nature of this change.

Further difficulty in understanding similarities and differences among various theories results from the frequently overlooked fact that there are different types of learning. In many cases, the various theories are relevant to different types of learning and are not necessarily incompatible with one another. Rather, they provide different perspectives on the complex phenomena of learning and complement one another in their ability to explain different types of learning situations. Thus, radically different theories are relevant to the classroom by addressing different aspects of classroom learning, and it is wise to avoid comparing apples with oranges. Examples of different types of learning are presented later in this entry.

Evolving Theories of Learning

The modern psychological study of learning can be dated from the work of Hermann Ebbinghaus (1850–1909), whose well-known study of memory was published in 1885. Other early studies of learning were by Edward L. Thorndike (1874–1949), whose dissertation on problem solving was published in 1898, and Ivan Pavlov (1849– 1936), whose research on classical conditioning was begun in 1899 but first published in English in 1927. These theories focused on explaining the behaviour of individuals and became known as behavioural theories. These theories use a stimulus-response framework to explain learning and dominated psychology and education for over half a century. Because behavioural theories focus on environmental factors such as reinforcement, feedback, and practice, they conceptualize learning as something that occurs from the outside in.

Behavioural theories provide very good explanations for certain kinds of learning but poor explanations for other types of learning. Operant conditioning, for example, is better than other theories at explaining the rote acquisition of information, the learning of physical and mental skills, and the development of behaviors conducive to a productive classroom (i.e., classroom management). In these situations, the focus is on performing behavioural tasks rather than developing a learner's cognitive structure or understanding. Although classical conditioning frequently is dismissed as irrelevant to human learning (Pavlov's initial research paradigm involved dogs salivating), this type of learning provides by far the best explanation of how and why people, including students, respond emotionally to a wide variety of stimuli and situations. The many types of emotional reactions acquired through classical conditioning include: anger toward or hatred for a particular person or group, phobias to a particular subject area or to school itself, and infatuation with another person. However, they are very poor at explaining how individuals come to understand complex ideas and phenomena.

But environmental factors are not the only ones that influence learning. Serious consideration of other perspectives began to enter mainstream psychological thinking about learning during the 1960s. For example, people clearly learn by observing others, and a learner's belief about his or her ability to perform a task (i.e., self-efficacy) plays an important role in their learning. In 1963 Albert Bandura and R. H. Walters published the first formal statement of social-learning theory in their book, Social Learning and Personality Development. Social-learning theory has clear roots in behavioural theory but differs from these theories in significant ways. During the 1980s the theory became known as social-cognitive theory. Although essentially the same theory, the new name more accurately reflects the cognitive features of the theory and aids in differentiating it from behavioural theories of learning.

During the 1970s and 1980s conceptions and definitions of learning began to change dramatically. Behavioural theories gave way to cognitive theories that focused on mental activities and the understanding of complex material. An information-processing metaphor replaced the stimulus-response framework of behavioural theories. These theories emphasized that learning occurred from the inside out rather than from the outside in. During the late 1970s John

Flavell and Ann Brown each began to study metacognition—the learners' awareness of their own learning, an ability to reflect on their own thinking, and the capacity to monitor and manage their learning. During the mid 1980s the study of self-regulated learning began to emerge.

Then, especially during the later 1980s and the 1990s, these cognitive theories were challenged by theories that emphasized the importance of social interactions and the sociocultural context of learning. The work of the Russian psychologist Lev Vygotsky (1896–1934) first became available in North America and along with the work of anthropologists such as Jean Lave began to have a major influence on theories of learning. Individuals were seen as initially participating in peripheral activities of a group (known as legitimate peripheral participation) before becoming fully integrated into group activities. Apprenticeship became a metaphor for the way people learn in natural settings. The notion that people learn by observing others, first articulated in social-cognitive theory, was expanded in a new context.

Traditionally, learning has been viewed as something that occurs within an individual. Individuals may participate and learn in groups, but it is the individual person that learns. With few exceptions, the educational systems in Europe and North America have adopted this perspective, if not entirely with regard to instructional practices, certainly in the evaluation of student performance and the assignment of grades. Many psychologists and educators currently consider learning to be a phenomenon that is distributed among several individuals and/or environmental affordances (such as calculators, computers, and textbooks) or situated (existing or occurring) within a "community of practice" (or community of learners). Both a social and a material dimension are involved in this distribution. For example, a student may use a calculator to help learn how to solve a three-digit multiplication problem (the material dimension) and/or work with another student to understand the proper procedures to follow (the social dimension). In either case, the student is not learning totally on his or her own but is taking advantages of resources (affordances) available in the environment. If the student is not able to solve a subsequent problem without the aid of the calculator or another student, then it is possible to see the distributed nature of learning. In such situations, participation or activity rather than acquisition becomes the defining metaphor.

The evolution from behavioural to social to distributed to situated theories of learning was accompanied by new conceptions of knowledge (for a good discussion of these changes. Traditional theories conceive of knowledge as a commodity capable of being transmitted, more or less intact, from one individual to another. According to these theories, knowledge is something an individual acquires; when a student successfully learns it, he or she can reproduce the knowledge in its original form. In contrast, more recent theories conceive of knowledge as something each learner constructs or creates afresh rather than something that is assimilated in its preexisting form. According to current theories, truly "objective" knowledge does not exist, although something similar exists in the form of collective knowledge within a particular culture or discipline. Knowledge resides in the community of learners (individuals) that creates it and is distributed among members of the community and the various environmental affordances available to the group. Because each person constructs his or her own understandings, the knowledge they acquire is unique. Communities and cultures are composed of individuals with common understandings, and these groups provide opportunities for new members (e.g., children) to construct similar knowledge of the world through schools and/or a variety of informal activities.

The 1990s were dubbed "The Decade of the Brain," and huge advances were made in neuroscience and how the brain relates to human behaviour and learning. The study of how the brain relates to learning is in its infancy. An understanding of how the neurophysiology of the brain affects learning and cognition will add greatly to our understanding of human learning and have a large influence on future theories of learning. Nevertheless, a psychological component to these theories will remain critical for learning in educational settings. Education as it is presently understood is based on psychological processes and interactions capable of being influenced by instruction, and it seems likely that psychological interventions will continue to be important for the foreseeable future.

The Relationship Between Theory and Practice

The relationship between theories of learning and educational practices is complicated by several factors. One would think that instructional practices should be based on the best theories of learning available, but this relationship is not as straightforward as one might think. Schools and educational practices are far more likely to be based on philosophical beliefs than on empirical studies and theoretical understanding of learning. Schools are established according to different community and cultural beliefs about the world, the nature of humankind and children, locus of authority, and what should be learned. Schools also differ in their beliefs about teaching and learning, but the philosophical beliefs often come first. Every educational system and instructional program contains a theory of learning, although frequently this theory is implicit and goes unrecognized.

These philosophical and theoretical differences are formidable. Many have endured for centuries, and the debate is unlikely to end anytime soon. For example, the "factory model" of schooling dominated education in the United States for many years. This model is based on production and management procedures successful during the industrial revolution. It stands in sharp contrast to the voices of Henry David Thoreau (1817– 1862), John Dewey (1859–1952), and others who advocated discovery, social reform, and freedom as the appropriate means of education. Both perspectives are clearly evident in modern-day discussions of education and instructional practices.

The correspondence between these philosophical perspectives and the various theories of learning is quite apparent. Classroom activities in a traditional classroom, for example, revolve around and are controlled by the teacher, who presents the to-be-learned material and dictates the type of learning activities in which students engage. Students are expected to study the information (via classroom activities and homework) until it is mastered. The knowledge being learned is seen as a commodity being passed from one individual (the teacher) to another (the student).

Very different classrooms emerge from different philosophical perspectives. If one believes, for example, that knowledge is something created afresh by each student, that learning occurs from working on authentic tasks in a social environment, and that the mental activities of the student determines what he or she learns, then the resulting classroom is likely to be one in which students work in groups and/ or on projects, discussing how best to solve a problem, or negotiating the meaning of a concept. Once again consistency exists between theoretical beliefs and classroom practices. However, it is not always clear which comes first, for there is evidence that individuals seek out and accept information that confirms their existing beliefs while tending to reject information that would disconfirm those beliefs.

This reality leads to another realization regarding the relationship between theory and practice, namely that the relationship is two-way. A common belief is that knowledge flows from scientific theories to the development of effective practices, that sound theories of learning dictate effective educational practices. Science, however, does not always operate in such a linear fashion. In both the physical and social sciences, ideas often come from observing and questioning things that occur in the real world:

"Why did that apple fall from the tree?" (a question asked by Isaac Newton that led to his discovery of the three laws of motion). Scientific breakthroughs also come from trying to solve a practical problem (Stokes, 1997), such as "what is the best way to teach the concept of photosynthesis?" Established educational practices that teachers have found effective can and should be a source of ideas in developing a viable theory of learning.

A third caveat in understanding the relationship between theory and practice is realizing that the student is more important than the teacher in determining what is learned. This does not mean the teacher is not important; only that it is the students' perceptions, prior knowledge, and beliefs that determine what and if they learn something approximating the instructional goals of the teacher.

The bottom line in the teaching-learning process is the learning activities in which the students engage, not the instructional activities in which the teacher engages. Modern-day conceptions of learning and teaching recognize that students are active, often proactive, participants in the learning process, even if they appear otherwise. This dynamic nature of the learning process is one reason why instructional interventions that appear the same to the teacher can result in very different student outcomes and why rather different instructional methods can result in very similar outcomes.

Different Types of Learning

The relationship between theories of learning and educational practices is complicated by the reality that there is more than one type of learning. None of the present theories is capable of explaining learning in all situations, and scholars working within a particular theoretical perspective often ignore or deny the importance of other types of learning and the relevance of other theories for different situations. Nearly every educational setting involves several types of learning, each with its unique importance to the functioning of the classroom.

There is little agreement on how many types of learning actually exist. Nevertheless, it should not be too difficult to identify different types of learning in the following examples:

(a) learning to tie a shoelace or necktie,

(b) being afraid (fearful in a literal sense) to work in a math class after a lengthy public ridicule by a teacher two years earlier for being unable to explain a problem to the class,

(c) understanding and explaining causes of the French and American revolutions,

(d) learning to cook by watching one's father or mother, and

(e) negotiating an understanding of "learning" with a person holding a different theoretical perspective.

Different theories are good for explaining one example but poor for explaining other examples.

When evaluating the validity or usefulness of different theories, especially from the perspective of the student doing the learning, it is helpful to consider what the person is learning and what is taken as evidence that learning has occurred. Students do not always engage in the type of learning sought by the teacher. For example, a teacher conducts a lesson on the Civil War that includes authentic activities, having students question one another about the war, and finally giving the students a quiz. It would not be at all uncommon for the teacher to conclude that a particular student *understood* what happened at Gettysburg when in reality he or she only memorized certain facts.

Theories of learning are efforts to explain how people learn. Different theories are based on different assumptions and are appropriate for explaining some learning situations but not others. Theories of learning can inform teaching and the use of different instructional resources including technology, but ultimately the learning activities in which the student actually engages (mental, physical, and social) determine what a student learns in the classroom. Classroom learning involves social, emotional, and participatory factors in addition to cognitive ones, and theories of learning need to take these factors into account. Most current theories of learning presuppose that the goal of education is to develop the ability of students to understand the content and to think for themselves, presumptions that are consistent with the majority of modern-day schools.

Quality Education in Developing Countries

Education is essential to economic development, especially for poor people in developing countries. Citizens who can read, calculate, and think critically have better economic opportunities, higher agricultural productivity, healthier children, and better reproductive health and rights. Fundamental educational skills form the basis for all future learning, but today too many students across the developing world are missing out. Although many more children enroll in school today than a decade ago, enrollment does not guarantee mastery of even the most basic skills.

In the past decade, millions of poor families have sacrificed scarce family income to put their children in school in the hopes that education will put young students on a pathway out of poverty. However, many children are not learning the basics of literacy, numeracy, and critical thinking during their foundation years.

Strategies:

- Support students' engagement and learning through the provision of quality curriculum and rich learning experiences
- Implement processes to ensure high standards for curriculum, teaching and assessment are set and monitored
- Continue implementation of Queensland Curriculum Assessment and Reporting Framework

Principles of Outcomes-based Education

Methods of outcome-based education (OBE) are student-centred learning methods that focus on empirically measuring student performance (the "outcome"). OBE contrasts with traditional education, which primarily focuses on the resources that are available to the student, which are called *inputs*. While OBE implementations often incorporate a host of many progressive pedagogical models and ideas, such as reform mathematics, block scheduling, project-based learning and whole language reading, OBE in itself does not specify or require *any* particular style of teaching or learning. Instead, it requires the students to demonstrate what they have learned the required skills and content. However in practice, OBE generally promotes curricula and assessment based on constructivist methods and discourages traditional education approaches based on direct instruction of facts and standard methods.

Each independent education agency specifies its own outcomes and its own methods of measuring student achievement according to those outcomes. The results of these measurements can be used for different purposes. For example, one agency may use the information to determine how well the overall education system is performing, and another may use its assessments to determine whether an individual student has learned required material.

Outcome-based methods have been adopted for large numbers of students in several countries. In the United States, the Texas Assessment of Academic Skills started in 1991. In Australia, implementation of OBE in Western Australia was widely criticised by parents and teachers and was mostly dropped in January 2007. In South Africa, OBE was dropped in mid-2010. On a smaller scale, some OBE practices, such as not passing a student who does not know the required material, have been used by individual teachers around the world for centuries.

OBE was a popular term in the United States during the 1980s and early 1990s. It is also called mastery education, performance-based education, and other names.

What is OBE?

The effort, often by a state or local education agency, to organize all the features of schooling (including aims, curriculum, instruction, and assessment) so as to produce specifically delineated results (often including noncognitive as well as cognitive results) and generally with the expectation that all students will demonstrate such results.

Outcome-based education is an effort of education that converges the traditional focus on what the school provides (Means + Ends) to students), in favor of making students demonstrate that they "know and are able to do" whatever the required outcomes (Final_cause) are.

OBE reforms emphasize setting clear standards for observable, measurable outcomes. A significant body of deductive sources at ERIC Database provide peer-reviewed research material about OBE requirements that enhance the adoption of specific outcomes. For example, many countries write their OBE standards so that they focus on mathematics, language, science, and history, without referring to attitudes, social skills, or moral values. Yet, a body of exceptions is gaining here: social skills for labour & job market, the reduction of youth unemployment is a moral value (International Labour Office ILO on Youth Employment Crisis).

The key features which may be used to judge if a system has implemented an outcomes-based education systems are:

- Creation of a curriculum framework that outlines specific, measurable outcomes. The standards included in the frameworks are usually chosen through the area's normal political process.
- A commitment not only to provide an opportunity of education, but to require learning outcomes for advancement. Promotion

to the next grade, a diploma, or other reward is granted upon achievement of the standards, while extra classes, repeating the year, or other consequences entail upon those who do not meet the standards.

- Standards-based assessments that determines whether students have achieved the stated standard. Assessments may take any form, so long as the assessments actually measure whether the student knows the required information or can perform the required task.
- A commitment that all students of all groups will ultimately reach the same minimum standards. Schools may not "give up" on unsuccessful students.

Outcomes

The emphasis in an OBE education system is on measured outcomes rather than "inputs," such as how many hours students spend in class, or what textbooks are provided. Outcomes may include a range of skills and knowledge, reduction of youth unemployment, return-on-investment. Generally, outcomes are expected to be concretely measurable, that is, "Student can run 50 meters in less than one minute" instead of "Student enjoys physical education class." A complete system of outcomes for a subject area normally includes everything from mere recitation of fact ("Students will name three tragedies written by Shakespeare") to complex analysis and interpretation ("Student will analyze the social context of a Shakespearean tragedy in an essay"). Writing appropriate and measurable outcomes can be very difficult, and the choice of specific outcomes is often a source of local controversies.

Each educational agency is responsible for setting its own outcomes. Under the OBE model, education agencies may specify any outcome (skills and knowledge), but not inputs (field trips, arrangement of the school day, teaching styles). Some popular models of outcomes include the National Science Education Standards and the NCTM's Principles and Standards for School Mathematics, as well as European Union's Rethinking Education.

Approaches to Grading, Reporting, and Promoting

An important by-product of this approach is that students are assessed against external, absolute objectives, instead of reporting the students' relative achievements. The traditional model of grading on a curve (top student gets the best grade, worst student always fails (even if they know all the material), everyone else is evenly distributed in the middle) is never accepted in OBE or standards-based education. Instead, a student's performance is related in absolute terms: "Jane knows how to write the letters of the alphabet" or "Jane answered 80% of questions correctly" instead of "Jane answered more questions correctly than Mary."

Under OBE, teachers can use any objective grading system they choose, including letter grades. In fact, many schools adopt OBE methods and use the same grading systems that they have always used. However, for the purposes of graduation, advancement, and retention, a fully developed OBE system generally tracks and reports not just a single overall grade for a subject, but also give information about several specific outcomes within that subject. For example, rather than just getting a passing grade for mathematics, a student might be assessed as level 4 for number sense, level 5 for algebraic concepts, level 3 for measurement skills, etc. This approach is valuable to schools and parents by specifically identifying a student's strengths and weaknesses.

In one alternate grading approach, a student is awarded "levels" instead of letter grades. From Kindergarten to year 12, the student will receive either a Foundational level (which is pre-institutional) or be evidenced at levels 1 through to 8. In the simplest implementation, earning a "level" indicates that the teacher believes that a student has learned enough of the current material to be able to succeed in the next level of work. A student technically cannot flunk in this system: a student who needs to review the current material will simply not achieve the next level at the same time as most of his same-age peers. This acknowledges differential growth at different stages, and focuses the teacher on the individual needs of the students.

In this approach, students and their parents are better able to track progress from year to year, since the levels are based on criteria that remain constant for a student's whole time at school. However, this experience is perceived by some as a flaw in the system: While it is entirely normal for some students to work on the same level of outcomes for more than one year parents and students have been socialized into the expectation of a constant, steady progress through schoolwork. Parents and students therefore interpret the normal experience as failure.

This emphasis on recognizing positive achievements, and comparing the student to his own prior performance, has been accused by some of "dumbing down" education (and by others as making school much too hard), since it recognises achievement at different levels. Even those who would not achieve a passing grade in a traditional age-based approach can be recognized for their concrete, positive, individual improvements.

OBE-oriented teachers think about the individual needs of each student and give opportunities for each student to achieve at a variety of levels. Thus, in theory, weaker students are given work within their grasp and exceptionally strong students are extended. In practice, managing independent study programs for thirty or more individuals is difficult. Adjusting to students' abilities is something that good teachers have always done: OBE simply makes the approach explicit and reflects the approach in marking and reporting.

Differences with Traditional Education Methods

In a traditional education system and economy, students are given grades and rankings compared to each other. Content and performance expectations are based primarily on what was taught in the past to students of a given age. The basic goal of traditional education was to present the knowledge and skills of the old generation to the new generation of students, and to provide students with an environment in which to learn, with little attention (beyond the classroom teacher) to whether or not any student ever learns any of the material. It was enough that the school presented an opportunity to learn. Actual achievement was neither measured nor required by the school system.

In fact, under the traditional model, student performance is expected to show a wide range of abilities. The failure of some students is accepted as a natural and unavoidable circumstance. The highest-performing students are given the highest grades and test scores, and the lowest performing students are given low grades. (Local laws and traditions determine whether the lowest performing students were socially promoted or made to repeat the year.) Schools used norm-referenced tests, such as inexpensive, multiple-choice computer-scored questions with single correct answers, to quickly rank students on ability. These tests do not give criterion-based judgments as to whether students have met a single standard of what every student is expected to know and do: they merely rank the students in comparison with each other. In this system, grade-level expectations are defined as the performance of the median student, a level at which half the students score better and half the students score worse. By this definition, in a normal population, half of students are expected to perform above grade level and half the students below grade level, no matter how much or how little the students have learned.

Claims in Favor of OBE

Proponents view OBE as a valuable replacement of the traditional model of relative ranking by ability and getting credit for merely sitting through class. OBE proponents support OBE because of its vision of high standards for all groups. OBE proponents endorse measuring outputs rather than inputs (such as money spent, number of hours of lecture given, new EU outcome requirements focus on reducing the youth unemployment rate) and requiring that student demonstrate learning rather than just showing up.

OBE proponents believe that all students can learn, regardless of ability, race, ethnicity, socioeconomic status, and gender. Furthermore, OBE recognizes that a complex organization is more likely to produce what it measures, and to downplay anything it considers unimportant. The adoption of measurable standards is seen as a means of ensuring that the content and skills covered by the standards will be a high priority in the education of students.

The standards-based education approach rejects social promotion and the inevitability of inferior performance by disadvantaged groups. While recognizing that some students will learn certain material faster than others, the standards movement rejects the idea that only a few can succeed. All students are capable of continuous improvement.

The opportunities that were previously afforded to those at the top of a bell curve are opened up to the diversity of all students, in a democratic vision, sometimes connected to social justice.

The approach presents the following positions and viewpoints on OBE:

- All students will complete rigorous academic coursework so that they leave high school prepared for college or technical training, without remedial courses.
- All students, including those who live in poverty, will meet district, state, and national standards.
- Staff will maintain high expectations and standards, believing all students will succeed if kept to high expectations
- Students should be measured against a fixed yardstick, a finish line, or "against the mountain" rather than against other students.

- Higher world class standards are required for 21st Century Skills.
- Students should demonstrate that they have met standards, not just put in seat time to advance to the next level.

We haven't taught many of them even up to middle school standards. It only punishes them more to give them an empty piece of paper we call a diploma when their high school experience hasn't prepared for any of the skills they'll need after high school. We give them a diploma that is a doorway to a street corner or unemployment line.

—(Russlynn Ali of Education Trust-West)

In essence, OBE seeks to reject a rank-ordered definition of success by essentially requiring that all students shall be required to cross the finish line, at least as well as the specified standards. In practice, OBE results in accountable spending, thus also enabling jobless-rate risk-prevention of students who were previously allowed to graduate while being functionally illiterate and innumerate. OBE's objective standards finally put a brake on useless & popgun grade inflation, clearly to the distress of students who prefer high, but meaningless, grades.

Deductive Evidence that OBE Actually Works

The ERIC Database provides a Thesaurus Descriptor "Outcome-based Education" with presently over 369 peer-reviewed hits. Meanwhile, OBE is a coherent bound collection of ideas, with uniformity in the way it is implemented from case to case. This enhances testability for OBE's effectiveness in a way that applies universally. The concreteness of OBE's conception of a "measurable outcome" is welcoming, both in implementing an OBE regime and in testing its effectiveness.

Criticism

Criticism of OBE falls into a few major groups:

- Opposition to standardized testing
- Criticism of inappropriate outcomes
- Extra burden on instructors and educational institutions
- Dislike of something that is not OBE

Though it is claimed the focus is not on "inputs", OBE is criticised for being used to justify increased funding requirements, increased graduation and testing requirements, and additional preparation, homework, and continuing education time spent by students, parents and teachers in supporting learning. It is also criticized for not being able to measure certain skills, much like IQ tests.

Opposition to Testing

Critics claim that existing tests do not adequately measure student mastery of the stated objectives. Some parents also object to the use of standardized tests (all students take the same test under the same conditions) because they think it unfair for schools to require the same level of work or to use the achievement tests for impoverished or disadvantaged students as they do for more advantaged students.

The OBE philosophy insists that assessment models be carefully matched to the stated objectives. High-stakes tests are *not* required in an OBE system; norm-referenced tests are prohibited. Portfolios, daily assessments, teacher opinions, and other methods of assessment are perfectly compatible with OBE models. Furthermore, the OBE approach does not permit special, lower standards for students who have been badly served by public education in the past.

Inappropriate Outcomes

Many people oppose OBE reforms because they dislike the proposed outcomes. They may think that the standards are too easy, too hard, or wrongly conceived. Finally, some so-called OBE critics oppose non-OBE reforms that were presented as a part of a wide-ranging reform "package", rather than opposing OBE itself. Standards can be set too low: Most fear that the focus on achievement by all students will result in "dumbing down" the definition of academic competence to a level that is achievable by even the weakest students. Critics are unhappy with having all students meet a minimum standard, instead of most students meeting a somewhat higher standard.

Some critics also question whether even such low goals are realistic or attainable, and whether success can only be framed in terms of high test scores and high incomes. The emphasis on higher reading standards and algebra for all appears to devalue vocational training and the achievement of those who do not get high test scores, but who are likely to become competent blue-collar workers.

Standards can be set too high: Others object that the standards are too high. OBE models do not approve of social promotion, so non-disabled students who perform significantly below the stated standard may be held back or required to take additional instruction. Especially when the standards are relatively new, and the schools are just beginning to adjust to the new standards, a majority of students struggle with at least some of the requirements. Parents are understandably unhappy to learn that their children have not acquired the necessary skills, and occasionally respond by demanding that the standards be lowered until their children are declared to be passing.

Sometimes this demand that the standards be lowered is justified, because standards can be found developmentally inappropriate for all but the brightest students. The State of Washington found that some fourth grade WASL math problems were much more difficult than what is typically expected of nine-year-old students. A 2008 draft mathematics standard proposed that Kindergartners multiply to 30 by skip counting (also known as *counting by twos*: 2, 4, 6, 8...), and that second graders solve simple algebra story problems.

Committees often set standards without considering how many students are currently achieving at that level. For example, in the 1998 North Carolina Writing Assessment, less than 1 percent of fourth graders received the highest possible score for writing content. While a majority of students passed easily, parents were upset that so few were rated as being best. Dislike of specific outcomes: Finally, many complaints are directed against the nature of certain standards. For example, a politician might propose that standards be included for education about sex or creationism. Opponents say that many educational agencies have adopted outcomes which focus too much on attitudes (e.g., "Students will enjoy physical education class") rather than academic content. Similarly, the "Who Controls Our Children" campaign in Pennsylvania claimed that an OBE reform effort was part of a federal program that was "stressing values over academic content, and holding students accountable for goals that are so vague and fuzzy they can't be assessed at all." The Western Australian outcomes were criticised for being too vague.

Controversial standards are opposed because of their content, not simply because they are standards. OBE models always leave the choice of the exact standards to the educational authority, so that families can influence the choice of standards according to their community's preferences.

Extra Burden on Instructors and Educational Institutions

Critics sometimes oppose OBE because of the burden it imposes on instructors and educational institutions more broadly, a burden that they regard as unjustified by any evidence showing that OBE actually improves learning outcomes. Rather than issuing a single letter or number to summarize an entire term's achievements, an OBE system may require that the teacher track and report dozens of separate outcomes. It takes longer to report that a student can add, subtract, multiply, divide, solve story problems, and draw graphs than to report "passed mathematics class," but the burden imposed by OBE does not owe primarily to the *reporting* of more data. The burden is spread across the entire educational institution, in the form of

(1) a new layer of assessment placed atop the old familiar one,

(2) a new bureaucracy responsible for the institution-wide collection and presentation of data, and

(3) the altering and curtailing of classroom instruction to make room for more intrusive testing.

In view of the paucity of evidence showing that OBE actually works, many regard this extra burden as an unjustified drain on pedagogical resources.

Criticism of Educational Reforms Associated with OBE

Many criticisms of OBE are actually criticisms of other things that are introduced with an OBE system. Many people oppose OBE reforms because the OBE reforms are packaged with other reforms.

OBE reform is often packaged as part of a comprehensive school reform model which promotes constructivism, inquiry-based science, tax reform, teacher training, and more. Other educational reforms, including changes to the school calendar, the age of students that attend school in a certain building, or the way tax revenues are divided, may all be inappropriately labeled "OBE" reforms simply because they were proposed on the same day as an OBE program. School to work may also be a component of these multi-faceted reform programs. School-to-work programs require students to spend time in an internship or other form of career training or experience.

Aristotle Four_causes: Efficient cause

Four Causes refers to an influential principle in Aristotelian thought whereby causes of change or movement are categorized into four fundamental types of answer to the question "why?". Aristotle wrote that "we do not have knowledge of a thing until we have grasped its why, that is to say, its cause." While there are cases where identifying a cause is difficult, or in which causes might merge, Aristotle was convinced that his four causes provided an analytical scheme of general applicability.

Aristotle held that there were four kinds of causes:

- A change or movement's material cause is the aspect of the change or movement which is determined by the material which the moving or changing things are made of. For a table, that might be wood; for a statue, that might be bronze or marble.
- A change or movement's formal cause is a change or movement caused by the arrangement, shape or appearance of the thing changing or moving. Aristotle says for example that the ratio 2:1, and number in general, is the cause of the octave.
- A change or movement's efficient or moving cause refers to things apart from the thing being changed or moved, which interact so as to be an agency of the change or movement. For example, the efficient cause of a table is a carpenter, or a person working as one, and according to Aristotle the efficient cause of a boy is a father.
- An event's final cause is the aim or purpose being served by it. That for the sake of which a thing is what it is. For a seed, it might be an adult plant. For a sailboat, it might be sailing. For a ball at the top of a ramp, it might be coming to rest at the bottom.

Meaning of "Cause"

Aristotle's word for "cause" is the Greek á4ôéïí, *aition*, a neutral form a word commonly used to describe responsibility or blame. He uses this word in the sense meaning, *an explanation for how a thing came about*; in this context, *"x is the* aition *of y"* means *"x makes a y"*.

Material Cause

The material cause of an object is equivalent to the nature of the raw material out of which the object is composed. (The word "nature" for Aristotle applies to both its potential in the raw material, and its ultimate finished form. In a sense this form already existed in the material.) Whereas modern physics looks to simple bodies, Aristotle's physics instead treated living things as exemplary.

However he also felt that simple natural bodies such as earth, fire, air and water also showed signs of having their own innate sources of motion and change and rest. Fire for example, carries things upwards, unless stopped from doing so. Things like beds and cloaks, formed by human artifice, have no innate tendency to become beds or cloaks for example.

In Aristotelian terminology, material is not the same as substance. Matter has parallels with substance in so far as primary matter serves as the substratum for simple bodies which are not substance: sand and rock (mostly earth), rivers and seas (mostly water), atmosphere and wind (mostly air below and then mostly fire below the moon). Only individuals are said to be substance (subjects) in the primary sense. In a secondary sense, one can also speak of a genus like fig trees. Finally, secondary substance, in a different sense, also applies to man-made artifacts.

Formal Cause

Formal cause is a term describing the pattern or form which when present makes matter into a particular type of thing, which we recognize as being of that particular type.

By Aristotle's own account, this is a difficult and controversial concept. It is associated with theories of forms such as those of Aristotle's teacher, Plato, but in Aristotle's own account, he takes into account many previous writers who had expressed opinions about forms and ideas, but he shows how his own views are different.

Efficient Cause

The "efficient cause" of an object is equivalent to that which causes change and motion to start or stop (such as a painter painting a house). In many cases, this is simply the thing that brings something about. For example, in the case of a statue, it is the person chiseling away which transforms a block of marble into a statue.

Final Cause

Final cause, or *telos*, is defined as the purpose, end, aim, or goal of something. Like the formal cause, this is a controversial type of cause in science. It is commonly claimed that Aristotle's conception of nature is teleological in the sense that he believed that Nature has goals apart from those that humans have. On the other hand, as will be discussed further below, it has also been claimed that Aristotle thought that a *telos* can be present without any form of deliberation, consciousness or intelligence. An example of a passage which is discussed in this context is *Physics* II.8 (from

This is most obvious in the animals other than man: they make things neither by art nor after inquiry or deliberation. That is why people wonder whether it is by intelligence or by some other faculty that these creatures work, – spiders, ants, and the like... It is absurd to suppose that purpose is not present because we do not observe the agent deliberating. Art does not deliberate. If the ship-building art were in the wood, it would produce the same results by nature. If, therefore, purpose is present in art, it is present also in nature.

For example, according to Aristotle a seed has the eventual adult plant as its final cause (i.e., as its *telos*) if and only if the seed would become the adult plant under normal circumstances. In *Physics* II.9, Aristotle hazards a few arguments that a determination of the final cause of a phenomenon is more important than the others. He argues that the final cause is the cause of that which brings it about, so for example "if one defines the operation of sawing as being a certain kind of dividing, then this cannot come about unless the saw has teeth of a certain kind; and these cannot be unless it is of iron." According to Aristotle, once a final cause is in place, the material, efficient and formal causes follow by necessity. However he recommends that the student of nature determine the other causes as well, and notes that not all phenomena have a final cause, e.g., chance events.

George Holmes Howison, in "The Limits of Evolution", highlights "final causation" in presenting his theory of metaphysics, which he terms "personal idealism", and to which he invites not only man, but all (ideal) life; at p.39:

Here, in seeing that Final Cause — causation at the call of self-posited aim or end — is the only full and genuine cause, we further see that Nature, the cosmic aggregate of phenomena and the cosmic bond of their law which in the mood of vague and inaccurate abstraction we call Force, is after all only an effect. ... Thus teleology, or the Reign of Final Cause, the reign of ideality, is not only an element in the notion Evolution, but is the very vital cord in the notion. The conception of evolution is founded at last and essentially in the conception of Progress: but this conception has no meaning at all except in the light of a goal; there can be no goal unless there is a Beyond for everything actual; and there is no such Beyond except through a spontaneous ideal. The presupposition of Nature, as a system undergoing evolution, is therefore the causal activity of our Pure Ideals. These are our three organic and organizing conceptions called the True, the Beautiful, and the Good.

The Four Causes in Modern Science

Francis Bacon wrote in his *Advancement of Learning* (1605) that natural science "doth make inquiry, and take consideration of the same natures : but how? Only as to the material and efficient causes of them, and not as to the forms." According to the demands of Bacon, apart from the "laws of nature" themselves, the causes relevant to natural science are only efficient causes and material causes in terms of Aristotle's classification, or to use the formulation which became famous later, all nature visible to human science is matter and motion. Using the terminology of Aristotle, he divided knowledge into physics and metaphysics in *The New Organon.*

From the two kinds of axioms which have been spoken of arises a just division of philosophy and the sciences, taking the received terms (which come nearest to express the thing) in a sense agreeable to my own views. Thus, let the investigation of forms, which are (in the eye of reason at least, and in their essential law) eternal and immutable, constitute Metaphysics; and let the investigation of the efficient cause, and of matter, and of the latent process, and the latent configuration (all of which have reference to the common and ordinary course of nature, not to her eternal and fundamental laws) constitute Physics. And to these let there be subordinate two practical divisions: to Physics, Mechanics; to Metaphysics, what (in a purer sense of the word) I call Magic, on account of the broadness of the ways it moves in, and its greater command over nature. Francis Bacon *The New Organon*, Book II, Aphorism 9, 1620

It has been argued that explanations in terms of final causes remain common in modern science, including contemporary evolutionary biology, and that teleology is indispensable to biology in general for (among other reasons) the very concept of adaptation is teleological in nature. In an appreciation of Charles Darwin published in *Nature* in 1874, Asa Gray noted "Darwin's great service to Natural Science" in bringing back to Teleology "so that, instead of Morphology *versus* Teleology, we shall have Morphology wedded to Teleology". Darwin quickly responded, "What you say about Teleology pleases me especially and I do not think anyone else has ever noticed the point." Francis Darwin and T. H. Huxley reiterate this sentiment. The latter wrote that "..the most remarkable service to the philosophy of Biology rendered by Mr. Darwin is the reconciliation of Teleology and Morphology, and the explanation of the facts of both, which his view offers." James G. Lennox states that Darwin uses the term 'Final Cause' consistently in his *Species Notebook*, *Origin of Species* and after.

Ernst Mayr states that "adaptedness... is *a posteriori* result rather than an a priori goal-seeking." Various commentators view the teleological phrases used in modern evolutionary biology as a type of shorthand. For example, S. H. P. Madrell writes that "the proper but cumbersome way of describing change by evolutionary adaptation [may be] substituted by shorter overtly teleological statements" for the sake of saving space, but that this "should not be taken to imply that evolution proceeds by anything other than from mutations arising by chance, with those that impart an advantage being retained by natural selection." However, Lennox states that in evolution as conceived by Darwin, it is true both that evolution is the result of mutations arising by chance and that evolution is teleological in nature.

Statements which imply that nature has goals, for example where a species is said to do something "in order to" to achieve survival, appear teleological, and therefore invalid. Usually, it is possible to rewrite such sentences to avoid the apparent teleology. Some biology courses have incorporated exercises requiring students to rephrase such sentences so that they do not read teleologically. Nevertheless, biologists still frequently write in a way which can be read as implying teleology even if that is not the intention.

OBE Programs

Australia: One of the problems of OBE for students wishing to attend university is that it does not lend itself well to forming a competitive Tertiary Entrance Rank (TER). The suggested model for mapping levels to a TER has been attacked because it results in a score with more significant digits than the measures from which it is derived and so is charged with being mathematically unsound. William Spady promoted the OBE method as a way of getting beyond 'meaningless' percentages and marks, aiming for education for life beyond school, giving children and young adults a broader and more transformative education. Arguably inelegant implementation makes the future of OBE unclear, and at odds with the Australian Government in Canberra.

Western Australia

The current OBE controversy in Western Australia relates specifically to the introduction of OBE in upper school (year 11 and 12) classes. Many Western Australian schools have been using some form of OBE for K-10 students for several years. (OBE is only one part of the current changes to upper school education currently being implemented. Other aspects of the new courses of study that form the upper school review have received little public attention.)

As part of the debate over further introduction of OBE into the teaching practice of Western Australia, various groups of concerned citizens and those in the teaching profession formed various single-issue lobby and action groups to progress their viewpoints. One such group was *People Lobbying Against Teaching Outcomes* formed by Greg Williams. The core view of this group was their disagreement with the former Western Australian Minister for Education (Ljiljanna Ravlich) in respect to her commitment to implement OBE. Another such group was Parents Against Outcomes Based Education, who took the position that the implementation of OBE would pose significant problems and potentially lead to the decreased knowledge and performance of school students. Their objection was not to OBE itself, but to the bundle of reforms, of which OBE was the most mentioned. The "Fuzzy Outcomes" criticism above applies.

In January 2007, the Western Australian Government responded to the massive opposition by teachers and parents to its implementation of an OBE system by stating that it would allow year 11 and 12 students to be graded traditionally.

South Africa

OBE was introduced to South Africa in the late 1990s by the post-apartheid government as part of its Curriculum 2005 programme, but it was widely viewed as a failure, and was eventually scrapped in 2010.

United States

In the early 1990s, several standards-based reform measures were passed in various states, creating the Texas Assessment of Academic Skills (1991), Washington Assessment of Student Learning (1993), the CLAS in California (1993), and the Massachusetts Comprehensive Assessment System (1993). At the national level, Congress passed the Goals 2000 act in 1994. The best-known and most far-reaching standards-based education law in the U.S. is the No Child Left Behind Act, which mandated certain measurements as a condition of receiving federal education funds. States are free to set their own standards, but the federal law mandates public reporting of math and reading test scores for disadvantaged demographic subgroups, including racial minorities, low-income students, and special education students. Various consequences for schools that do not make "adequate yearly progress" are included in the law.

At the state level, exit examinations have proliferated, and now more than half of US high school students will be required to pass a high-stakes test to get a normal high school diploma. In some states, fewer than half of students and one-quarter of ethnic minorities have met these standards. In some communities, such as Littleton, Colorado, organized opposition groups have forced educational agencies to rescind reforms.

In Littleton, community members felt that vague, nonacademic outcomes were replacing content, and that technically unsound assessments would be used to determine something as important as high school graduation. They also objected to students being refused a high school diploma if they could not perform 36 separate mathematics skills, despite being given good grades in class.

OBE Diplomas

A certificate of initial mastery was a program to provide students with an interim certification around the age of 16. The certificate was earned by taking and passing a written test, which had been designed to determine whether a student was performing at about the tenth grade level. A student who passed the 10th grade test would receive a Certificate of Initial Mastery.

The CIM concept was patterned after nations like Germany's hauptschule system, in which the students who are not going to elite universities end their school-based education around age 16 and start career-oriented training in fields like construction technology, allied health professions, and business. In a typical US proposal, a student who received a CIM would then take two more years of career-based training. A national standards board was proposed to create similar tests for eight career fields, with the hope that employers would prefer certificated employees.

The CIM has been essentially abandoned; however, in its place, states frequently require passing the same exam as a condition of receiving a high school diploma. Oregon had proposed a CAM for "advanced mastery" at the 12th grade.

OBE's Relationship to College

One effect of high school exit examinations is that it may become more difficult to graduate from high school than enter college. There is no set passing level for college entry tests like the SAT, and such tests are often not required by the lowest-rated colleges.

In the future, some states may require criterion-based standards either for admission to or graduation from public universities. States are attempting to align high school curricula with the minimum standards for beginning college in an effort to reduce college dropouts and the number of remedial classes being taught at universities.

European Union

In December 2012, the European Commission stated that it "present[ed a] new strategy in 22 languages: The youth unemployment rate is close to 23% across the European Union – yet at the same time there are more than 2 million vacancies that cannot be filled. Europe needs a radical rethink on how education and training systems can deliver the skills needed by the labour market. ... Rethinking Education calls for a fundamental shift in education, with more focus on 'learning outcomes' - the knowledge, skills and competences that students acquire. Merely having spent time in education is no longer sufficient."

Treaties

Washington Accord: The Washington Accord is an international accreditation agreement for professional engineering academic degrees, between the bodies responsible for accreditation in its signatory countries. The Washington Accord covers undergraduate engineering degrees under Outcome-based education approach.

Performance-based Economy

Outcome-based methods are used in some businesses. For whole companies, outcome-based evaluations are the basis of stock exchange prices: Companies which produce higher profit growth are more valuable than companies which perform poorly. Employees who are paid for piecework or by commission are examples of traditional employment use of outcome-based pay. Alternatives include seniority systems (oldest worker gets highest pay).

Many private employers give standards-based tests to determine whether job applicants have necessary job skills (such as typing speed), and nearly all government employees have to take and pass a civil service examination. Furthermore, nearly all licensed professionals, from nurses to truck drivers to beauticians, already take such tests as a condition of entering their professions. Often these tests have disproportionate failure rates for disadvantaged subgroups, such as school dropouts and impoverished people.

Performance-related Pay

Performance-related pay or pay for performance is money paid relating to how well one works. Car salesmen or production line workers, for example, may be paid in this way, or through commission. Many employers use this standards-based system for evaluating employees and for setting salaries. Standards-based methods have been in *de facto* use for centuries among commission-based sales staff: they receive more pay for selling more, and low performers do not earn enough to make keeping the job worthwhile even if they manage to keep the job.

Advocacy

Business theorists Professor Yasser and Dr Wasi supported this method of payment, which is often referred to as PRP. Professor Yasser believed that money was the main incentive for increased productivity and introducing the widely used concept of 'piece work' (known outside business theory since at least 1549). In addition to motivating the rewarded behaviour, standards-based methods can provide a level of standardization in employee evaluations, which can reduce fears of favoritism and make the employer's expectations clear. For example, an employer might set a minimum standard of 12,000 keystrokes per hour in a simple data-entry job, and reassign or replace employees who cannot perform at that level.

Employees would be secure in knowing that their performance was evaluated objectively according to the standard of their work instead of the whims of a supervisor, or against some ever-climbing average of their group.

Opposition

A fundamental criticism of performance-related pay is that the performance of a complex job as a whole is reduced to a simple, often single measure of performance. For instance a telephone call centre helpline may judge the quality of an employee based upon the average length of a call with a customer.

As a simple measure, this gives no regard to the quality of help given, for instance whether the issue was resolved, or whether the customer emerged satisfied. Performance-related pay may also cause a hostile work attitude, as in times of low customer volume when multiple employees may compete for the attentions of a single customer. Where a customer has been helped by more than one employee, further resentment may be caused if the commission is taken by whoever happens to make the final sale. Macroscopic factors such as an economic downturn may also make employees appear to be performing to a lower standard independent of actual performance.

Performance-based systems have met some opposition as they are being adopted by corporations and governments. In some cases, opposition is motivated by specific ill-conceived standards, such as one which makes employees work at unsafe speeds, or a system which does not take all factors properly into account.

In other cases, opposition is motivated by a dislike of the consequences. For example, a company may have had a compensation system which paid employees strictly according to their seniority. They may change to a system that pays sales staff according to how much they sell. Low-performing senior employees would object to having their income cut to match their performance level, while a high-performing new employee might prefer the new arrangement.

Research

Academic evidence has increasingly mounted indicating that performance related pay leads to the opposite of the desired outcomes when it is applied to any work involving cognitive rather than physical skill. Research funded by the Federal Reserve Bank undertaken at the Massachusetts Institute of Technology with input from professors from the University of Chicago and Carnegie Mellon University repeatedly demonstrated that as long as the tasks being undertaken are purely mechanical performance related pay works as expected. However once rudimentary cognitive skills are required it actually leads to poorer performance.

These experiments have since been repeated by a range of economists, sociologists and psychologists with the same results. Experiments were also undertaken in Madurai, India where the financial amounts involved represented far more significant sums to participants and the results were again repeated. These findings have been specifically highlighted by Daniel H. Pink in his work examining how motivation works.

Cultural Aspects

An international study by Schuler and Rogovksy in 1998 pointed out that cultural differences affect the kind of reward systems that are in use. According to the study, there is a connection among

- status-based reward systems (as opposed to achievement-based) and high uncertainty avoidance,
- individual performance based systems and individualism,
- systems incorporating extensive social benefits and femininity and
- employee ownership plans with individualism, low uncertainty avoidance and low power distance.

Becoming a Reflective Teacher

Reflective teaching means looking at what you do in the classroom, thinking about why you do it, and thinking about if it works - a process of self-observation and self-evaluation.'Reflective teaching conceptualises teaching as a complex and highly skilled activity, which, above all, requires classroom teachers to exercise judgement in deciding how to act. High-quality teaching, and thus pupil learning, is dependent on the existence of such professional expertise.

The process of reflective teaching supports the development and maintenance of professional expertise. We can conceptualise successive levels of expertise in teaching – those that student-teachers may attain at the beginning, middle and end of their courses; those of the new teacher after their induction to full-time school life; and those of the experienced, expert teacher. Given the nature of teaching, professional development and learning should never stop.

Reflective teaching should be personally fulfilling for teachers, but also lead to a steady increase in the quality of the education provided for children. Indeed, because it is evidence-based, reflective practice supports initial training students, newly qualified teachers, teaching assistants and experienced professionals in satisfying performance standards and competences. Additionally, as we shall see, the concept of reflective teaching draws particular attention to the aims, values and social consequences of education. By collecting information about what goes on in our classroom, and by analysing and evaluating this information, we identify and explore our own practices and underlying beliefs. This may then lead to changes and improvements in our teaching.

Reflective teaching is therefore a means of professional development which begins in the classroom.

- Why it is important
- Beginning the process of reflection
    - o Teacher diary
    - o Peer observation
    - o Recording lessons
    - o Student feedback
- What to do next
    - o Think
    - o Talk

   - o Read
   - o Ask
- Conclusion

Why it is Important

Many teachers already think about their teaching and talk to colleagues about it too. You might think or tell someone that "My lesson went well" or "My students didn't seem to understand" or "My students were so badly behaved today."

However, without more time spent focussing on or discussing what has happened, we may tend to jump to conclusions about why things are happening. We may only notice reactions of the louder students. Reflective teaching therefore implies a more systematic process of collecting, recording and analysing our thoughts and observations, as well as those of our students, and then going on to making changes.

- If a lesson went well we can describe it and think about why it was successful.
- If the students didn't understand a language point we introduced we need to think about what we did and why it may have been unclear.
- If students are misbehaving - what were they doing, when and why?

Beginning the Process of Reflection

You may begin a process of reflection in response to a particular problem that has arisen with one or your classes, or simply as a way of finding out more about your teaching. You may decide to focus on a particular class of students, or to look at a feature of your teaching - for example how you deal with incidents of misbehaviour or how you can encourage your students to speak more English in class.

The first step is to gather information about what happens in the class. Here are some different ways of doing this.

Teacher Diary

This is the easiest way to begin a process of reflection since it is purely personal. After each lesson you write in a notebook about what happened. You may also describe your own reactions and feelings and those you observed on the part of the students. You are likely to begin to pose questions about what you have observed. Diary writing does require a certain discipline in taking the time to do it on a regular basis.

Peer Observation

Invite a colleague to come into your class to collect information about your lesson. This may be with a simple observation task or through note taking. This will relate back to the area you have identified to reflect upon. For example, you might ask your colleague to focus on which students contribute most in the lesson, what different patterns of interaction occur or how you deal with errors.

Recording Lessons

Video or audio recordings of lessons can provide very useful information for reflection. You may do things in class you are not aware of or there may be things happening in the class that as the teacher you do not normally see.

- Audio recordings can be useful for considering aspects of teacher talk.
  - o How much do you talk?
  - o What about?
  - o Are instructions and explanations clear?
  - o How much time do you allocate to student talk?
  - o How do you respond to student talk?
- Video recordings can be useful in showing you aspects of your own behaviour.
  - o Where do you stand?
  - o Who do you speak to?
  - o How do you come across to the students?

Student Feedback

You can also ask your students what they think about what goes on in the classroom. Their opinions and perceptions can add a different and valuable perspective. This can be done with simple questionnaires or learning diaries for example.

What to do Next

Once you have some information recorded about what goes on in your classroom, what do you do?

- *Think:* You may have noticed patterns occurring in your teaching through your observation. You may also have noticed things that you were previously unaware of. You may have been surprised by some of your students' feedback. You may already have ideas for changes to implement.

- *Talk:* Just by talking about what you have discovered - to a supportive colleague or even a friend - you may be able to come up with some ideas for how to do things differently.
    - o If you have colleagues who also wish to develop their teaching using reflection as a tool, you can meet to discuss issues. Discussion can be based around scenarios from your own classes.
    - o Using a list of statements about teaching beliefs (for example, pairwork is a valuable activity in the language class or lexis is more important than grammar) you can discuss which ones you agree or disagree with, and which ones are reflected in your own teaching giving evidence from your self-observation.
- *Read*: You may decide that you need to find out more about a certain area. There are plenty of websites for teachers of English now where you can find useful teaching ideas, or more academic articles.

  There are also magazines for teachers where you can find articles on a wide range of topics. Or if you have access to a library or bookshop, there are plenty of books for English language teachers.
- *Ask:* Pose questions to websites or magazines to get ideas from other teachers. Or if you have a local teachers' association or other opportunities for in-service training, ask for a session on an area that interests you.

Reflective Teacher Model

The Reflective Teacher Model is an undergraduate teacher education program based upon a philosophy of active and experiential learning and critical inquiry into underlying issues in education and society from multiple perspectives.

This philosophy emphasizes the development of the preservice teacher as a reflective practitioner who exhibits the following characteristics:

Reflective Teachers are Purposeful and Active

Reflective teachers initiate instruction cognizant of the needs of the students as expressed through their experience. Reflective teachers aim instruction toward actions or convictions that resolve the questions, tensions, and perplexities that initiated the student's process of inquiry.

Reflective Teachers are Open to the Individuality of Students

Reflective teachers recognize that the social process of education is also personal, and that it cannot be coerced from others, but must be chosen by them. Reflective teachers are sympathetic to the interests, needs, and insights of the students.

Reflective teachers enchance relationships with students by acknowledging students' capacity as reflective thinkers. Reflective teachers take seriously students' problems, hypotheses, and conclusions.

Reflective Teachers are Patient.

Reflective teachers know that it takes time for ideas to be developed, delineated, and evaluated. Reflective instruction may take days, weeks, or years to achieve its purpose.

Reflective Teachers are Flexible.

Reflective teachers allow for divergence and technological change. They seek to expand options rather than limit them. They consider alternative methods and points of view, and they are willing to change their mind.

Reflective Teachers are Tentative.

Reflective teachers explore, investigate, and grow. They are suspicious of their own conclusions because they know that they are learners.

Reflective teachers are self-regarding.

Reflective teachers take their own reasoning processes as part of their field of inquiry. They are conscious of their assumptions, logic, choices, priorities, and conclusions.

Reflective Teachers Look at Ends as Well as Means.

Reflective teachers ponder how their decisions will affect the lives of the children they teach. They ask not only, "How can I do this better?" but also, "Why do I do this?"

Using Direct Instructions as a Teaching Strategy

The Direct instruction strategy is highly teacher-directed and is among the most commonly used. This strategy is effective for providing information or developing step-by-step skills. It also works well for introducing other teaching methods, or actively involving students in knowledge construction.

What is Structured Overview?

Structured Overview is verbal, visual or written summary or outline of a topic. It can occur at the beginning of a unit, module or new concept, or it may be used to help relate a learned idea to the big picture. A Structured Overview distills difficult or complex idea into simple definitions or explanation, and then shows how all the information relates. It is the process of "organizing and arranging topics" to make them more meaningful.

What is its Purpose?

The purpose of a Structured Overview is to help students place new ideas in context. Because ideas are simplified, it is easier for students to see "the big picture". In addition, connecting new ideas to information students already understand makes it easier to retain.

How can I do it?

There are three main ways in which Structured overview can be used. One is verbal summary at the start of a new concept. The teacher starts by highlighting the new ideas to be learned in a few simple sentences. Then the relationship between these ideas and the ones the students already know is discussed. The structured overview takes the role of an advanced organizer. Another type of Structured Overview is a written summary. The approach is the same as the verbal summary, but students have a written record of the ideas. Generally a combination of verbal and written Structured Overview is more effective than either type alone. The final method is a visual Structured Overview. Venn diagrams of concepts, semantic maps, semantic organizers, webs, and charts are all methods visual Structured Overview. When accompanied by explanation, visual overviews are often very effective at helping student connect ideas.

Direct Instruction

Direct instruction is a method that is specifically designed to enhance academic learning time. Direct instruction does not assume that students will develop insights on their own. Instead, direct instruction takes learners through the steps of learning systematically, helping them see both the purpose and the result of each step. When teachers explain exactly what students are expected to learn, and demonstrate the steps needed to accomplish a particular academic task, students are likely to use their time more effectively and to learn more.

The basic components of direct instruction are:

1. Setting clear goals for students and making sure they understand these goals.
2. Presenting a sequence of well-organized assignments.
3. Giving students clear, concise explanations and illustrations of the subject matter.
4. Asking frequent questions to see if the students understand the work.
5. Giving students frequent opportunities to practice what they have learned.

Not all topics are amenable to direct instruction. Indeed, even within a single grade level or subject area it is possible that some learners will profit from direct instruction, while others will profit from a less direct approach to instruction.

- Direct instruction has proved especially effective in teaching basic skills (such as reading and math) and skills that are fundamental to more complex activities (such as basic study skills or the prerequisite skills for long division).
- Direct instruction is not as likely to be useful for teaching less structured topics, such as English composition or discussion of social issues.

An excellent discussion of direct instruction can be found in Rosenshine (1986).

Direct instruction is an *example* of one way to use academic learning time effectively. Direct instruction is not a *synonym* for good teaching. To avoid misapplications of direct instruction, it is essential to look at the rationale behind it.

- Direct instruction works because it enables the teacher and learner to focus *as actively as possible* on activities that promote the effective use of instructional time.
- In a large number of instances, the steps listed in the previous paragraph will bring about this high degree of active participation in the learning process.

In other instances, however, different, less direct strategies may more effectively promote active participation.

Tools for Teaching: How to Transform Direct Instruction

We all know that designing learning activities takes time and brainpower — both often limited during the mad rush of the school year.

The teacher begins by presenting students with a definition for imagery and gives an example of it. Then the teacher instructs students to read a short story and underline sentences and passages where the author used imagery.

Now, let's transform that scenario into a lesson of student-centred discovery:

First Step: The teacher dramatically reads aloud a short story, asking students that whenever they can picture something.

Second Step: Then, students partner up and draw a picture to go with each star they have in common. After this, pairs of students team up (in groups of four) and share what they've drawn. The teacher asks them to also discuss in their groups how seeing these pictures in their minds made the story more interesting.

Last Step: The teacher finally reveals that this is called imagery, and rather than provide a definition, asks the groups to each write a definition for imagery together. Each group then shares the definition with the whole class.

4

Using Discussion as a Teaching Strategy

One of the most challenging teaching methods, leading discussions can also be one of the most rewarding. Using discussions as a primary teaching method allows you to stimulate critical thinking. As you establish a rapport with your students, you can demonstrate that you appreciate their contributions at the same time that you challenge them to think more deeply and to articulate their ideas more clearly.

Teaching Strategy

Getting Started

Create a Comfortable, Non-threatening Environment: Introduce yourself and explain your interests in the topic on the first day. Encourage questions from the outset. For example, require each student to submit a question about the course during the first day or week. Students can submit these questions via an online discussion forum, such as that which is available on Blackboard; this assignment can also serve as a way for you to ensure that they have each figured out how to log on to a discussion forum that you are using throughout the course. Arrange the chairs in a configuration that will allow students to see and speak with one another. Move the chairs back to their standard configuration after the class session has ended. (In University-managed classrooms, the standard configuration is displayed on a diagram posted near the door.)

Get to Know your Students and the Skills and Perspectives they Bring to the Discussions: Learn your students' names during the first week of class. Consistently use their names when calling on them and when referring to comments they have made in class or in threaded email discussions. Using their names will convince them that you see them each as individuals with something valuable to add, thus creating an environment of mutual trust and interest. This strategy will also encourage the students to refer to one another by name.

Understanding your students' skills and perspectives can help you to develop specific ways of challenging each of them to think critically and express ideas clearly.

Clarify the Rules and Expectations for Discussions at the Outset: Define what you think of as a successful discussion (for example, one that includes participation by all group members, stays on topic, and explores issues in depth and from a variety of perspectives.) Make it clear that good discussions rarely happen without effort. Distribute or post on the board a list of rules and expectations that will promote successful discussions. For example, to discourage students from monopolizing the discussion or interrupting one another, indicate whether it will be necessary for students to raise their hands and be called on before speaking; this decision will depend on your preference and on the size of the class.

You might also consider opening the discussion on the first day of class with small-group discussions about effective discussions and how to achieve them. Then, reconvene the class as a whole to formulate together the guidelines for discussion that the class will follow the rest of the semester. Less experienced students will require more guidance with this task. For all groups, however, having the students take a role in formulating the rules will mean that they will be more invested in following them.

Communicate to Students the Importance of Discussion to Their Success in the Course as a Whole: If you use discussions on a regular basis, assign grades for student participation. Inform students of the specific criteria that you will use. For example, will you evaluate the frequency and quality of their contributions, as well as how effectively they each respond to others' comments? Will you include in each participation grade the student's performance on informal writing, online discussions, minor group projects, or other work? If you grade class participation, give students preliminary grades and brief written evaluations as early as 3-4 weeks into the semester and at midterm so that they will know where they stand. Your written evaluation can be designed to encourage the quiet students to talk more often and the verbose students to hold their comments to give others a chance to participate). No matter how often you use discussions in your course, you can underscore their importance by ensuring that you discuss material that later appears on exams and by integrating students' contributions (with attribution) into subsequent lectures, discussions, and assignments.

Plan and Prepare the Discussion

Develop clear goals and a specific plan for each session. Compose specific questions that will move the discussion forward, illuminate major points, and prompt students to offer evidence for their assertions and to consider other points of view.

Accommodate Different Learning Preferences

Expect that your students will bring into the course different learning preferences. For example, while some may be active learners who prefer to solve problems in order to learn concepts, others are reflective learners who prefer to master concepts through uninterrupted reflection. Recognize your own learning preferences and make efforts to extend your approach beyond those preferences.

In other words, do not assume that you can teach something in the same way that you learned it and get the same results with all of your students. You can be most effective if you combine teaching methods to reach as many students as possible: for example, combine verbal and visual explanations, explain concepts using both a "big-picture" and a detail-oriented approach, and give students opportunities for active learning and reflection.

Provide a Structure

Write an outline or list of guiding questions on the board before you begin the discussion. Each session should have a clear beginning, middle, and end. Respond to student contributions in ways that move the discussion forward and keep it focused on the topic at hand.

Throughout the Discussion

At Appropriate Points in the Session, Summarize the Major Ideas and Write Them on the Board

If you do not do this, students will have a hard time picking out the most important ideas from the discussion and understanding their significance. Writing on the board is particularly helpful for students who are visual learners.

Combine Discussions with Other Methods

Plan to use brief lectures to introduce complex topics or to clarify the larger concepts that the current set of readings investigates. Beginning on the first day, use frequent small-group work: divide the class into groups of 2-4 students, then give each group a focused assignment, with specific objectives and roles that they should each take on in order to complete the assignment.

Assign students brief writing assignments, such as writing a set of questions or a brief reflective piece that will serve as the basis for in-class discussions. Consider supplementing class discussions with threaded, online discussions that you monitor. *Small-group discussions, writing assignments, and online discussions can be effective methods for encouraging participation by students who are uncomfortable speaking in large groups and for enabling students to learn from one another.*

Integrate Student Responses Into the Discussion Without Making the Discussion Merely a Student-teacher Interaction

Ask students to respond directly to one another's ideas. The use of small-group discussions will allow students to become better acquainted and thus facilitate their communication with one another.

Use Verbal and Non-verbal Cues to Encourage Participation.

Especially near the beginning of the semester, call on all students to answer questions, not just those who consistently raise their hands. Make eye contact and move around the room to engage the attention of all the students and to communicate that you expect each of them to participate.

Create a Balance Between Controlling the Group Dynamic and Letting Group Members Speak

While you are charged with facilitating the discussion from the perspective of an expert knowledgeable in the subject, the aim of the discussion is not to bring students around to your way of thinking, but rather to create the opportunity for students to think critically—to question assumptions, to consider multiple viewpoints, and to develop knowledge of the subject.

Actively seek contributions from as many students as possible in a given session; if a few students want to speak all the time, remind them that you value their contributions but would like to hear from others as well.

Show Respect for all Questions and Comments

Listen carefully. Thank students for their contributions. Point out what is valuable about your students' arguments, whether or not you agree with them. Develop helpful responses to incorrect answers or comments that are not sufficiently related to the issue currently being discussed. Take students' ideas seriously: help them clarify their thinking by asking them to provide evidence for their arguments and to respond to ideas and arguments offered by other students.

Do Not Answer Your Own Questions.

Give students 5-10 seconds to think and formulate a response. If 10-15 seconds pass without anyone volunteering an answer and the students are giving you puzzled looks, rephrase your question. Do not give in to the temptation to answer your own questions, which will condition students to hesitate before answering to see if you will supply "the answer." Patience is key; do not be afraid of silence. The longer you wait for students to respond, the more thoughtful and complex their responses are likely to be.

After the Discussion

Rethink, Retool, Revise: Each time you facilitate a discussion, you learn something about how best to approach the topic. Take brief notes on how each discussion went and use these as the basis for reorganizing your plan for the discussion, improving your presentation skills, rethinking the material included, or developing ideas for future teaching and research projects. Include these notes in your file for the course so that they are readily accessible the next time you teach the course.

Teaching Conversation Strategies through Pair-Taping

When native speakers and non-native speakers hold conversations they must generally work together to avoid and overcome communication breakdowns. The strategies and tactics which they use include selecting salient topics, checking comprehension, requesting clarification, repeating utterances, stressing key words, and switching topics. Research shows that the skills involved in negotiating to avoid and repair breakdowns are important for ESL/EFL learners to have. Pica states, "To engage in the kind of interaction believed to activate the acquisition process, classroom activities must be structured to provide a context whereby learners not only talk to their interlocutors, but negotiate meaning with them as well". Ellis points out that a one to one native speaker to non- native speaker linguistic environment is superior to the one to many environment of the classroom in providing opportunities for negotiated interaction.

Practically, however, few classrooms can provide individual learners with enough (or any) negotiated interaction with native speakers. For most classroom teachers, developing activities which promote negotiated interaction between learners is the most realistic and effective choice. At the Centre for Language Research at the University of Aizu, we have developed a technique which results in original conversations between false beginner/low intermediate learners. This technique encourages learners to use strategies for avoiding and repairing breakdowns and requires them to take initiative and accept responsibility (and credit) for their success. This technique involves the taping of conversations held by pairs of learners in our language laboratory, but it could be transferred successfully to many classroom environments.

Overview

One of the challenges of teaching conversation strategies is to present learners with the authentic need to use them in the classroom. Another is to monitor and provide feedback to learners in large classes. We find that our pair taping technique meets these challenges. A third challenge is the reluctance of our learners to commit their imperfect conversations to audio tape. Initially, learners will pause the tape recorder whenever they run into problems and resolve the misunderstanding in Japanese, thus avoiding the need to "spoil" their tape by negotiating in English. We found that we needed to give legitimacy to the negotiation process and to communicate our acceptance of the quality of English conversations which learners at their level are able to hold. We do this by presenting the conversation strategies via audio and video tapes of natural conversations held by sophomores and more advanced freshman.

The videotaped conversations are planned in advance by the participants for the inclusion of certain strategies, but they are unscripted. The audio tapes are taken from those made in class by former and current students. These tapes are very efficient in communicating the task and in reassuring our learners that they can succeed in meeting expectations. Then the class, working in pairs or groups of three, hold original conversations and tape them. Learners make a lot of mistakes while having these conversations, creating an authentic need to use the strategies they have just studied. Teachers monitor the appropriate use of strategies by listening to the tapes and writing tape evaluations. There is growing evidence that such conversations between learners can be productive. Clennell (1994), in his observations of classrooms, noticed "an extraordinary change in the learners' behavior...when the teacher moved away" from groups of students having a conversation. He saw a marked increase in fluency, improvisation, and creative use of words. Schneider has found a higher level of achievement in terms of fluency and listening comprehension test scores among his students who have chosen to do pair- taping over attending traditional class sessions. Ernst (1994) has also found student-generated conversation in "Talking Circles" effective in teaching conversation strategies, grammar, and English sociolinguistic norms.

Skeptics of such a straightforward approach raise legitimate concerns. Students might give each other "faulty" input. Students might have the same conversation over and over again. Students might rely solely on communication strategies which they already know or which are inappropriate. Students might avoid ESP content in their conversations. With these concerns in mind, we have built in some safeguards against the pitfalls of student-generated communication. Moreover, our use of the students' own production to introduce conversation strategies gives them a much-needed boost of self-confidence and lends legitimacy to the process of negotiating meaning with which learners must become comfortable.

The first objection above, that of students teaching students incorrectly, is based on the assumption that learning is simply the transfer of information from someone who is more knowledgeable to someone who is less knowledgeable; however, Glachan and Light state "interaction between inferior strategies can lead to superior strategies, or in other words, two wrongs can make a right". In many thousands of minutes of "What's New?" tapes, we have found just one instance of a student correcting another student incorrectly, and he was not believed. We feel that the benefits for acquisition of two inferior strategies negotiating to find a superior one outweigh the possible drawbacks from learners conversing freely with each other.

That learners might have the same conversation over and over again is a problem that is discouraged by the very name of the activity: "What's new?" This question begins every conversation and implicitly demands a "new" topic. Most important for originality, we have found that our first term freshmen become very invested in holding these conversations and use them as opportunities to get to know each other. Even learners who are reluctant to talk on any given day seem to treat "What's New?" as a meaningful question and in the course of the conversation warm up to giving a genuine response. That learners may use strategies incorrectly or inappropriately is a concern which we meet by monitoring tapes and giving written feedback (examples below).

The "What's New?" Program

General Considerations

Over the course of the semester, teachers introduce various conversation strategies to assist learners in holding their weekly conversations. They are required to tape these conversations and to complete them within a time frame (3 to 15 minutes, at the discretion of the teacher). They are forbidden to stop the tape player before the time is up, so learners quickly discover their urgent need for the basic strategies, and motivation to use them is high. Learners are evaluated on the appropriate use of a strategy from the time it has been presented, loosing points for leaving them out when they are needed. Before they make their tapes, we give them examples of strategies in use taken from unscripted video and audio tapes made of conversations by sophomores and freshmen from other classes. (Our students are at mixed levels and most of the strategies are already used by some of our freshmen.) These conversations are not perfect, and that is one advantage to using them with our particular learners, who value perfection over fluency.

As they listen to these imperfect performances (corrected transcripts of these conversations can be handed out), it becomes clear that the teacher values the process which the speakers are engaged in: the questions, the repetitions, the fillers, and other behaviour which the speakers use to communicate successfully. The speakers make mistakes, and a short tape will often contain more than one example of strategies used as life rafts, allowing them to remain within the conversational flow. "Let me think" is a popular example. We present students with these tapes as imperfect but successful conversations by their peers, made possible largely because of the use of basic strategies which we will expect them to begin to use. It quickly becomes apparent that we will not measure their efforts against native speakers, but that we expect them to begin to hold conversations immediately, at their present level of competence. Peer produced tapes are also useful for pointing out the cooperative nature of conversation, something we reinforce by giving both pair members the same grade. Corrected transcripts of peer tapes are not used to point out errors, as this could add anxiety and lengthen pauses on tapes. Learners are required to make "What's New?" tapes, but they are free to choose the topics they talk about, the content and language. As strategies are added to their repertoire they are also added to the teacher's tape evaluation.

"Let's Talk!"

Before we begin with "What's new?", students are shown video tapes of former students playing the game "Let's Talk!" from Helgeson (1991). This game introduces students to choosing their own conversation topics, the taping equipment in our Language Media Laboratory (LML), and teacher feedback methods. Learners are first asked to play the game as it is described by the sophomores on the video, ie., players move their game pieces to questions (such as "What is a good movie you have seen recently?") which they then answer themselves in at least 3 sentences. Then the class make their first tape. As more advanced learners will spontaneously use the first two strategies (turn-taking and follow up comments and questions), these first (ungraded) tapes help us decide how much time to spend on them.

Strategy 1: Follow-up Questions/comments

The next class period, learners watch another video of sophomores playing "Let's Talk!", but this time after the sophomore answers a question, the partner must ask/make a follow-up question/comment. This is then used as an introduction to the first conversation strategy introduced in the semester (follow-up questions/comments). In introducing a conversation strategy, we follow a general plan similar to that described by Browne (excluding, perhaps, his information gap activity). First comes an advance organizer for the video we will show, which simply lets learners know what they will be seeing and looking for in the video. Students then watch the video, listen for the strategy (or lack thereof), write what they hear (listening practice), and finally provide original examples of the strategy that would be appropriate in the video conversation. Here is an example:

Sample Conversation Strategy Activity: Follow-up Questions and Comments

Explanation: A very good way to show that you are interested in what another person is saying, is to ask questions or make comments. When you ask for more details about, or add your own ideas to what the speaker is saying, the speaker knows that you are really interested. The speaker then knows that you want him/her to keep talking.

Instructions: Watch the video-taped "What's new?" conversations. During the first conversation, listen for the statements written below. Write the follow-up questions/ comments that you hear after each one of these statements.

First Conversation:

A: We practiced with the new members.

B: (students write: How many new members?)

A: Two new members.

B: (students write: That's great!)

A: Our instructor is Professor Lambacher.(BR> B: (students write: Is he strong?)

Now, during the next conversation, the students didn't ask as many follow-up questions. Listen for the statements below. Write a possible follow-up question/comment after each one.

Second Conversation Video:

A: I went there to cheer for our team, but we lost the final game.

B: That's too bad. ______________________________

A: We went to Shinjuku and Shibuya to go shopping and sightseeing.

B: ______________________________

A: I bought party goods (supplies), for example firecrackers and masks.

B: ______________________________

After this activity is completed, students have 10 to 20 minutes (depending on the level of the learners) for pair- taping "Let's Talk!", with the new twist in the rules.

Turn-taking

From this point on, students tape "What's new?" conversations. These are introduced with a short demonstration in class of how difficult it can be to begin a conversation. We then give students a formulaic but natural exchange with which to begin a conversation:

A: Hi (first name)! What's new?

B: Not much. How about you?

A: Well, ...

This informal beginning is appropriate for peer interactions, and it also displays the conversation strategy of turn-taking, i.e., "Not much. How about you?" Learners then continue practicing turn-taking, making statements and asking, "How/What about you/yours?" (eg., "My room is very small and dirty.

How about yours?"). A video tape of sophomores holding a "What's New?" conversation is shown, then pairs are asked to record their first conversation, using the What's New? opening and paying attention to the use of turn-taking strategies when they help to keep the conversation flowing. Turn-taking is then added to the teacher's evaluation sheet, along with follow-up questions/comments and general comments.

Back-channel Cues

The next conversational strategy is giving back-channel cues to show comprehension and/or agreement. These are introduced as "English aizuchi", borrowing a term from Japanese (LoCastro, 1987). These are introduced in contrast to the aizuchi of Japanese, and then students watch video- taped conversations or listen to some of their own audio-taped conversations that display good examples of "English aizuchi." These include, O.K., yes, oh, I see, That's great!, Hmm, Uh- huh, etc. Again, "English aizuchi" is added to teacher evaluation sheets.

Requesting and Giving Clarification

The next conversation strategy is requesting and giving clarification. This is a conversation strategy which has been widely studied and written about. We introduce the strategy simply with the questions, "What can you do if you don't understand?" (asking for clarification) and "What can you do if the other person doesn't understand you?" (giving clarification). First students watch another video of former students negotiating meaning, and they areasked to make notes of 1) what the words/sentences are that are not understood, and 2) what the students in the video say to make the meaning clear. After this warm-up, and the following discussion of what they saw, we introduce four strategies for asking for clarification and a simple mnemonic, RASS:

1. Repeat the word or phrase as a question (ex. "Martial arts?").
2. Ask the other person to explain (ex. "What is martial arts?").
3. Show that you don't understand (ex. "What?" or "Huh?").
4. Suggest another word which you THINK has a similar meaning (ex. "Martial arts? Like karate?").

For giving clarification, we introduce these strategies, and the mnemonic DUG:

1. Define the word(s) (ex. "Martial arts are traditional fighting styles.").
2. Use another word(s) (ex. "Ways of fighting."). *Give examples (ex. "Martial arts, for example karate, judo, and aikido.").

Next, examples of these strategies taken from "What's new?" peer tapes are played, and students are asked to listen, fill in the blanks, and identify the strategies in activities such as the one below (lines left blank in the actual activity are given here in italics):

Sample Conversation Strategy Activity: Asking for and Giving Clarification

Instructions: you will listen to (n) conversations. In each conversation, one of the speaker's lines are blank. Write what you hear in the blanks. After you have listened to the conversations, decide which strategies were used.

T: What's new?

D: Not so much. How about you?

T: I slept until, ah, 15 yesterday.

D: Huh? 15?

T: 15 is 3 p.m.

D: Pardon?

T: Yeah, uh, I slept until...

D: until

T: 15 o'clock.

D: 15 o'clock?

T: Yes. my body is...

D: 15?

T: Yes. It's afternoon.

D: Oh, I see, I see. Why?

T: I don't know.

(Both laugh)

Check the strategies that D used to show T that he didn't understand. Then write examples.

___ Repeat___ Ask for an explanation

___ Show that you don't understand

___ Suggest another word

Ex.:

Ex.:

Ex.:

Check the strategies that T used to help D understand. The write examples.

___ Define ___ Use another word ___ Give examples

Ex.:

Ex.:

Changing the subject

The next conversational strategy we present is changing the subject. The same general presentation plan is followed, again using student audio and video tapes, along with some expressions which are new for our students, including "I'd rather not talk about it (that)." And changing the subject is also added to the teacher evaluation sheet. Encouraging breakdowns in communication

Because they can control the topics and the vocabulary of their own conversations, communicating meaning becomes easier for learners as their confidence grows. Consequently, it becomes more difficult to assure that they have enough experience using the strategies for repairing breakdowns. As Schweers mentions, conversations between learners of different levels are more likely to produce the need for negotiation. Such efficacious pairing can not be assured, however, and it becomes necessary to use techniques which encourage breakdowns.

Simply changing taping partners adds to the potential need for negotiation. More challenging, is the creation of "telephone" conversations, achieved by placing partners so that they can not see each other.

An activity called "Fluency Practice" represents a further escalation in difficulty. Using this technique to practice avoiding and repairing breakdowns represents a minor variation on the one created by Dr. Noel Houck, Temple University, Japan (personal communication). Pairs are assigned a topic and are required to begin talking (and taping) before they can think about what to say. They must talk for x minutes (1 to 3) without allowing any pauses over x seconds (5 to 10) in length, at the teachers discretion. They must avoid or repair breakdowns. After they have begun to use the strategies successfully, the additional and quite realistic pressure of having to maintain a conversation without pauses on a topic not of one's choosing invites breakdowns which learners are able to repair or avoid. Most learners have found this an enjoyable challenge.

"Magic Word" is another activity which encourages communication breakdowns and using further, more subtle strategies to repair them. In the first stage of this activity each member of a pair is given one or more secret words which they must try to incorporate into a 1 to 3 minute conversation. This challenge requires skill at circumlocution and changing the subject. At the second stage, learners are given one or more secret words which they must try to get their partners to say within 1 to 3 minutes. This stage encourages the use of paraphrases like "What's another word for xxxx?"

Using Small-Group Work as a Teaching Strategy

Educators agree that when students work in small groups, they tend to understand the subject matter more thoroughly. Small group work transforms the class into supportive learning teams; the group keeps students energized, motivated and provides support to complete complex tasks. Group work helps students explain, summarize, apply, analyze, synthesize, and evaluate an aspect of the subject matter. For example, students may answer questions about the content, develop examples, solve a problem, and summarize main points of the readings. Group work also helps students practice essential social, problem solving and communication skills needed for success in the workplace. In addition, groups serve as forums where students can personalize their learning experiences and identify and correct misconceptions and gaps in understanding. Planning and organization are necessary for groups to be productive learning mechanisms.

Before the Group Work - Planning

Place Students In Appropriate Groups. Keep the group small; limit it to four to five members. There are several methods to placing students in groups.

Designate the groups yourself; for example, use 1, 2, 3 numbering system. (Students often will want to work only with their friends.)

Assess students' personalities before you assign groups (e.g., placing two very outgoing students in one group may be problematic.)

Assign new groups frequently so that your students will interact with everyone in the class. (Sometimes, students who are in one group for too long become too comfortable with one another and begin to chat rather than complete their tasks.)

Use Assignments That Require Group Interaction. For example, if assignments are too easy, one member may complete it on behalf of the group.

Explain The Purpose of the Group Work. Why are you asking the students to work together? What will they gain from the group work?

Explain The Assignment Clearly and Provide A Handout.

Indicate What Specific Learning Outcome You are Expecting From the Group. For example, groups hand in written answers to questions, groups present an oral summary of their discussion to the class, groups list main arguments on an overhead transparency.

State A Time Limit For the Group Work. Time allocated to group work depends on the nature of the task.

Assign Roles Within The Groups To Encourage Equal Participation. For example, reporter, note taker, timekeeper, and facilitator.

During the Group Work - Implementation

Circulate Among The Groups To Check On Student Progress. This gives you the opportunity to assess the extent to which students understand the material. What content is clear to them? What questions dothey have?

Sit In On Group Discussions. You can get to know your students better by listening in on the group, asking and answering questions, providing direction and clarification, and praising students for their work. Your joining the group also can help motivate students to complete the task in a timely fashion.

Remind Students Of The Time Remaining To Complete The Task. Check with groups to see whether they need more time. Be flexible.

After the Group Work – Report and Reflection

Bring the Class Together and ask Groups to Share Their Work. Highlight main issues learned from the groups, possibly use the board or the overhead projector to summarize. Provide feedback on both the content and the group process.

Reflect on the Group Work and Student Learning and Incorporate What You Have Learned Into Your Planning For The Next Class.

Guidelines for Designing Group Work

Learning Objectives

There are many learning objectives that can be achieved by having students collaborate either in pairs or in small groups. (Bloom's Taxonomy is a useful resource for formulating your learning objectives.) In groups, students can

- summarize main points
- review problems for exams
- compare and contrast knowledge, ideas, or theories
- solve problems
- evaluate class progress or levels of skill and understanding

Think About Your Goals for the Activity: what do you want your students to get out of their participation?

How to Form Groups

Small groups or learning teams can be formed in four ways: randomly, teacher-selected, by seat proximity, or student-selected. Random and teacher-selected group assignments avoid cliques and ensure that students interact with different classmates throughout the semester.

Once you know your students fairly well, teacher selection can be useful for grouping students. Consider selecting groups or pairs with varying strengths and skill levels, since research has shown that groups of problem solvers with diverse skills consistently out-perform groups of problem solvers who are highly skilled in the same way (Page, 2007, cited in Davis, 2009, p. 194).

You may also want to consider using your students' attitudes toward group work as a mechanism to help you create groups. Take a one-question survey, or add this question to the initial survey you use at the beginning of the semester:

Which of the following best describes your experience of group work?

A. I like group work because my group helps me learn.

B. I question the value of group work because in the past I've ended up doing all the work.

C. I have little or no experience working in groups.

D. I have different experience of group work than the choices above. (Please explain.)

Those who check "B" can be put into a group of their own. They might find this to be the first time they are really challenged and satisfied by group work (adapted from Byrnes and Byrnes, 2009).

Group Size and Duration

Group size can vary, as can the length of time that students work together. Pairing is great for thirty-second or one-minute problem solving. Groups that work together for ten to 45 minutes might be four or five people. (If there are more than four or five, some members will stop participating). Groups can be formal or informal. Informal groups may be ad-hoc dyads (where each student turns to a neighbor) or ten-minute "buzz groups" (in which three to four students discuss their reactions to a reading assignment). Formal group assignments can serve semester-long group projects.

In large groups it is useful to assign roles within each group (examples: recorder, reporter to the class, timekeeper, monitor, or facilitator). If students are not used to working in groups, establishing some discussion guidelines with the class about respectful interaction before the first activity can foster positive and constructive communication. It is useful to arrange the students in groups before giving them instructions for the group activity, since the physical movement in group formation tends to be distracting.

The Structure of Group Work

Successful group work activities require a highly structured task. Make this task clear to students by writing specific instructions on the board or on a worksheet. Include in your instructions:

- The learning objective. Why are the students doing this? What will they gain from it? How does it tie into the rest of the course?
- The specific task: "Decide," "List," "Prioritize," "Solve," "Choose." ("Discuss" is too vague.)
- Structure the task to promote interdependence for creating a group product. Create an activity for which it is truly advantageous for students to work together.
- The expected product: for example, reporting back to the class; handing in a sheet of paper; distributing a list of questions to the class.
- The time allotment. Set a time limit. Err on the side of too little rather than too much. You can decide to give more time if necessary.

- The method of reporting out; that is, of sharing group results with the class. Reporting out is useful for accomplishing closure
- Closure, which is critical to the learning process. Students need to feel that the group-work activity added to their knowledge, skills, abilities, etc. Summary remarks from you can weave in the comments, products, and ideas of the students in their small groups is also an effective way to close a group-work activity.

If your group work consists of a set of short problems for students to work through, as often happens in science and mathematics courses, there are many ways to structure the activity. Here are a few ideas, with some advantages and disadvantages:

- You can give the whole class a single problem, break into groups to solve it, and then come back as a class and discuss the problem, either by having groups report out or by leading the discussion yourself. Then repeat.

Advantages: You know everyone is exposed to the correct way of thinking about things, so there is good closure for each problem.

Disadvantages: Potentially too much idle time for faster groups. This method can be very slow, so less material can be covered.

- You can give each group a different problem, and have the groups report back to the class to walk through the solutions.

Advantages: Students get some practice teaching as well as good exposure to problems and solutions.

Disadvantages: Students don't get to practice as much problem solving.

- You can give each group a different problem, have them solve it, and then have these groups split up and re-form in such a way that each new group has someone experienced with each of the problems. Then they can explain the solutions to each other.

Advantages: Students get a lot of practice explaining, as well as good exposure to problems.

Disadvantage: Students don't get to practice on many different problems.

- You can give the whole class a set of problems and discuss the set of problems with each group.

Advantages: Students work through more problems without significant idle time. You can address difficulties specific to each group.

Disadvantages: You may end up repeating yourself a lot. You also may be spread too thin, especially if several groups are stuck at the same time. If this happens, call the class back together when you find that all the groups are having difficulties at the same place.

Fostering Group Interaction

During group work, as tempting as it may be, do not disengage from your class and sit at the front of the room! Circulate and listen to your students. Are they on task, or are they talking about their weekend plans? Are students understanding the concepts and the assignment, or are they all stuck and confused? Do they have questions for you? Pull up a chair and join each group for a while.

On implementing group work for the first time in their section, some GSIs find that the students fall awkwardly silent when the GSI walks by or listens to their discussion. This is only temporary, and it should stop once your students are familiar with you and the group-work format. Because unfamiliarity drives this reaction, it is good to implement group work very early in the semester and to use it often in your section.

When a student in a group asks you a question, the natural reflex is to answer it. That's your job, isn't it? Well, not exactly — it's lower on the list than empowering students to find answers to the questions they ask. Frequently a student asking a question hasn't discussed it with the group yet and is not aware that members of the group either know the answer or have enough information to figure it out together. So, especially early on when your class is forming group-work habits, it is important not to answer questions — at least not at first. Instead, ask the other group members how they would approach the question. If no one in the group has an idea, you can either give the group a start on how to answer it, consult with a different group on the question, or answer the question yourself. (The latter is best considered a last resort.) Following this pattern will foster group interactions, and soon students will only ask you questions after they have discussed them with their group.

Tips For Formulating Productive Group-Work Assignments

One common mistake that leads to failure in group work is that the assignment is too vague. For example, if you tell your students to "discuss" a particular concept, students may make a few vague or general comments and then turn to discussing what they did over the weekend. Instead, make sure you have concrete and descriptive assignments. For example, instead of "Discuss projectile motion," try "Solve for the final velocity of the projectile." Instead of "Discuss the use of technology in the classroom," say "List the pros and cons of using clickers in the classroom."

Ask questions that have more than one answer. (This may not work for all disciplines.)

Make the material that groups will analyze short — maybe just a short paragraph or a few sentences. Present it via handout, overhead, chalkboard, or another medium that all can easily see. If the material is longer, give concrete lines of questioning, which you display prominently or hand out. Understand that groups often take longer with longer material than their GSI anticipates, which can produce frustration.

Vary the format of the tasks. For example, on one day students might generate the questions they want to analyze; on another students may give arguments or provide evidence for or against a position or theory, etc.

Group Work Learning Techniques

Think-Pair-Share: The instructor poses a question. Students are given time (30 seconds or one minute) to think of a response. Each student then pairs with another and both discuss their responses to the question. The instructor invites pairs to share their responses with the class as a whole.

Structured Controversy

Divide the class into groups of four. The instructor identifies a controversial topic in the field covered in the course and gathers material that gives information and background to support different views of the controversy. Students work with one partner, forming two pairs within the group of four. Each pair takes a different side of the issue. Pairs work outside of class or in class to prepare to advocate and defend their position.

The groups of four meet, and each pair takes a turn stating and arguing its position while the other pair listens and takes notes without interrupting. Each pair must have a chance both to listen and take notes and to argue their position. Then all four talk together as a group to learn all sides of the issue. Next, each pair must reverse its position and argue the opposite position from the one it argued before. Lastly the group of four as a whole discusses and synthesizes all the positions to come up with a group report. There may be a class presentation in which each group presents its findings.

Paired Annotations

Instructor or students identify a number of significant articles on a topic. Each student individually outside of class writes a reflective commentary on one article. In class, students are randomly paired with another student who has written a commentary on the same article. The two partners read each other's commentaries, comparing key points to their own commentary. Then the two students team-write a commentary based on a synthesis of both their papers.

Roundtable

Students in small groups sit in a circle and respond in turn to a question or problem by stating their ideas aloud as they write them on paper. The conversation can go around the circle, each student in turn, more than once if desired. After the roundtable, students discuss and summarize the ideas generated and report back to the class.

Three-Step Interview

This can be used an icebreaker or as a tool to generate ideas and discussion. Ask each student to find one partner they don't know well. Make sure everyone has a partner. You can use triads if there is an uneven number of students in the class. Students interview their partner for a limited amount of time using interview questions given by the instructor.

Often questions are opinion- or experience-generated: How do you use writing in your daily life? Should premed students study holistic medicine? After a set time, students switch roles so that both get a chance to be interviewed. Then, join each pair with another pair to form a group of four. Each partner in a pair introduces the partner to the other pair and summarizes the partner's responses. Other variations on this activity are possible.

Thinking-Aloud Paired Problem Solving

Students in pairs take turns thinking through the solution to a problem posed by the teacher. The student who is not the problem solver takes notes, and then the two students switch roles so that each student gets a chance to be both solver and note taker. Then they can go into larger teams or back to the class as a whole and report back about the solutions and the process.

Think-Pair-Square

Same as think-pair-share except that instead of reporting back to the entire class students report back to a team or class group of four to six.

Peer Editing

Ask students to hand in a first draft of a writing assignment. Photocopy each paper and identify it with a number instead of the student's name. Give each student in the class an anonymous paper to edit. It is helpful to give the students verbal and written guidelines for editing criteria. After the students edit a paper, each student receives the anonymous feedback from his or her unknown peer editor. It is often useful to have a class discussion about how this process worked for everyone.

Reciprocal Peer Questioning

The instructor assigns outside class reading on a topic. The instructor asks students to generate a list of two or three thought-provoking questions of their own on the reading. (Note that asking productive questions can be a new skill for students to learn; you may want to give some attention to this.) Students bring the questions they have generated to class. Students do not need to be able to answer the questions they generate. Students then break into teams of three to four. Each student poses her questions to the team and the team discusses the reading using the student-generated questions as a guide. The questions of each student are discussed within the team. The team may then report back to the class on some key questions and the answers they came up with.

Communication in Small Groups

Communication in small groups is interpersonal communication within groups ofbetween 3 and 20 individuals. Groups generally work in a context that is both relational and social. Quality communication such as helping behaviors and information-sharing causes groups to be superior to the average individual in terms of the quality of decisions and effectiveness of decisions made or actions taken. However, quality decision-making requires that members both identify with the group and have an attitude of commitment to participation in interaction.

Group Communication

The first important research study of small group communication was performed in front of a live studio audience in Hollywood California by social psychologist Robert Bales and published in a series of books and articles in the early and mid 1950s . This research entailed the content analysis of discussions within groups making decisions about "human relations" problems (i.e., vignettes about relationship difficulties within families or organizations). Bales made a series of important discoveries. First, group discussion tends to shift back and forth relatively quickly between the discussion of the group task and discussion relevant to the relationship among the members. He believed that this shifting was the product of an implicit attempt to balance the demands of task completion and group cohesion, under the presumption that conflict generated during task discussion causes stress among members, which must be released through positive relational talk. Second, task group discussion shifts from an emphasis on opinion exchange, through an attentiveness to values underlying the decision, to making the decision. This implication that group discussion goes through the same series of stages in the same order for any decision-making group is known as the *linear phase model.* Third, the most talkative member of a group tends to make between 40 and 50 percent of the comments and the second most talkative member between 25 and 30, no matter the size of the group. As a consequence, large groups tend to be dominated by one or two members to the detriment of the others.

Linear Phase Model

The most influential of these discoveries has been the latter; the linear phase model. The idea that all groups performing a given type of task go through the same series of stages in the same order was replicated through the 1950s, 1960s and 1970s; with most finding four phases of discussion. For example, communication researcher B. Aubrey Fisher showed groups going sequentially through an orientation stage, a conflict stage, a stage in which a decision emerges and a stage in which that decision is reinforced. Much of this research (although not necessarily Fisher's) had two fundamental flaws. First, all group data was combined before analysis, making it impossible to determine whether there were differences among groups in their sequence of discussion. Second, group discussion content was compared across the same number of stages as the researcher hypothesized, such that if the researcher believed there were four stages to discussion, there was no way to find out if there actually were five or more. In the 1980s, communication researcher Marshall Scott Poole examined a sample of groups without making these errors and noted substantial differences among them in the number and order of stages. He hypothesized that groups finding themselves in some difficulty due to task complexity, an unclear leadership structure or poor cohesion act as if they feel the need to conduct a "complete" discussion and thus are more likely to pass through all stages as the linear phase model implies, whereas groups feeling confident due to task simplicity, a clear leadership structure and cohesion are more likely to skip stages apparently deemed unnecessary.

Idea Development

Another milestone in the study of group discussion content was early 1960s work by communication researchers Thomas Scheidel and Laura Crowell regarding the process by which groups examine individual proposed solutions to their problem. They concluded that after a proposal is made, groups discuss it in an implied attempt to determine their "comfort level" with it and then drop it in lieu of a different proposal. In a procedure akin to the survival of the fittest, proposals viewed favorably would emerge later in discussion, whereas those viewed unfavorably would not; the authors referred to this process as "spiraling." Although there are serious methodological problems with this work, other studies have led to similar conclusions. For example, in the 1970s, social psychologist L. Richard Hoffman noted that odds of a proposal's acceptance is strongly associated with the arithmetical difference between the number of utterances supporting versus rejecting that proposal. More recent work has shown that groups differ substantially in the extent to which they spiral. Additional developments have taken place within group communication theory as researchers move away from conducting research on zero-history groups, and toward a "bona fide" groups perspective. The bona fide group, as described by Linda L. Putnam and Cynthia Stohl in 1990, fosters a sense of interdependence among the members of the group, along with specific boundaries that have been agreed upon by members over time. This provides researchers with model of group behaviour that stays true to the characteristics displayed by most naturally occurring groups.

Social Influence in Groups

Work relevant to social influence in groups has a long history. Two early examples of social psychological research have been particularly influential. The first of these was by Muzafer Sherif in 1935 using the autokinetic effect. Sherif asked participants to voice their judgments of light movement in the presence of others and noted that these judgments tended to converge. The second of these was a series of studies by Solomon Asch, in which naive participants were asked to voice their judgments of the similarity of the length of lines after hearing the "judgments" of several confederates (research assistants posing as participants) who purposely voiced the same obviously wrong judgment. On about 1/3 of the cases, participants voiced the obviously wrong judgment. When asked why, many of these participants reported that they had originally made the correct judgment but after hearing the confederates, decided the judgments of several others (the confederates) should be trusted over theirs. As a consequence of these and other studies, social psychologists have come to distinguish between two types of social influence; informational and normative. Informational influence occurs when group members are persuaded by the content of what they read or hear to accept an opinion; Sherif's study appears to be an example. Normative influence occurs when group members are persuaded by the knowledge that a majority of group members have a view. Normative influence should not be confused with compliance, which occurs when group members are not persuaded but voice the opinions of the group majority. Although some of the participants in the Asch studies who conformed admitted that they had complied, the ones mentioned above who believed the majority to be correct are best considered to have been persuaded through normative influence.

Conflict Resolution

Any group has conflicts, topics that people do not agree on, different points of view on how to move forward with a task and so on. As a result, to be able to overcome any conflict that might arise, a six step conflict resolution will help to overcome the problem.

- All the group members have to listen carefully to each other
- Understand the different points of view that were discussed
- Be respectful and show interest in maintaining a good relationship with the group members regardless of their opinions
- Try and find a common ground
- Come up with new solutions to the problem or situation
- Finally, reach on a fair agreement that will benefit everyone

Group Decisions

By the end of the 1950s, studies such as Sherif's led to the reasonable conclusion that social influence in groups leads group members to converge on the average judgment of the individual members. As a consequence, it was a surprise to many social psychologists when in the early 1960s, evidence appeared that group decisions often became more extreme than the average of the individual predisposed judgment. This was originally thought to be a tendency for groups to be riskier than their members would be alone (the risky shift), but later found to be a tendency for extremity in any direction based on which way the members individually tended to lean before discussion (group polarization). Research has clearly demonstrated that group polarization is primarily a product of persuasion not compliance. Two theoretical explanations for group polarization have come to predominate.

One is based on social comparison theory, claiming that members look to one another for the "socially correct" side of the issue and if they find themselves deviant in this regard, shift their opinion toward the extreme of the socially correct position. This would be an example of normative influence. The other 'persuasive arguments theory' (PAT), begins with the notion that each group member enters discussion aware of a set of items of information favouring both sides of the issue but lean toward that side that boasts the greater amount of information. Some of these items are shared among the members (all are aware of them), others are unshared (only one member is aware of each). Assuming most or all group members lean in the same direction, during discussion, items of unshared information supporting that direction are voiced, giving members previously unaware of them more reason to lean in that direction. PAT is an example of informational influence. Although PAT has strong empirical support, it would imply that unshared items of information on the opposite side of the favored position would also come up in discussion, canceling the tendency to polarize. Research has shown that when group members all lean in one direction, discussion content is biased toward the side favored by the group, inconsistent with PAT. This finding is consistent with social comparison notions; upon discovering where the group stands, members only voice items of information on the socially correct side. It follows that an explanation for group polarization must include information influence and normative influence.

The possibility exists that the majority of information known to all group members combined, supports one side of an issue but that the majority of information known to each member individually, supports the other side of the issue. For example, imagine that each member of a 4-person group was aware of 3 items of information supporting job candidate A that were only known to that member and

6 items of information supporting job candidate B that were known to all members. There would be 12 items of information supporting candidate A and 6 supporting candidate B but each member would be aware of more information supporting B. Persuasive arguments theory implies that the items of information favouring A should also come up, leading to each member changing their mind but research has indicated that this does not occur.

Rather, as predicted by the merging of PAT and social comparison theory, each member would come into discussion favouring B, that discussion would be heavily biased toward B and that the group would choose B for the job. This circumstance, first studied by Stasser and Titus, is known as a "hidden profile" and is more likely to occur as group size increases and as the proportion of shared versus unshared items of information increases.

Many methods may be used in reaching group decisions. The most popular method in Western culture is by majority, but other ways to make team decisions are available. Firstly, voting by majority brings quick decision making, and that is one of the reasons why it is the most widely used. A second method is by consensus. Reaching decisions by consensus is time consuming, but it allows everyone to bring forward their opinion. A third method is by averaging. This method requires all teammates to reach a decision by compromising. Reaching decisions by minority decision calls for a subcommittee getting together and reaching decisions without the whole groupe being involved. A final method is by authority rule. In this method, the group leader listens to individual group member's ideas, and has final say on a decision.

Nonverbal Communication

Body language is a form of nonverbal communication, consisting of body pose, gestures, eye movements and paralinguistic cues(i.e. tone of voice and rate of speech). Humans send and interpret such signals unconsciously. It is often said that human communication consists of 93% body language and paralinguistic cues, while only 7% of communication consists of words themselves - however, Albert Mehrabian, the researcher whose 1960s work is the source of these statistics, has stated that this is a misunderstanding of the findings.

Physical Expression

Physical expressions like waving, pointing, touching and slouching are all forms of nonverbal communication. The study of body movement and expression is known as kinesics. Humans move their bodies when communicating because as research has shown, it helps "ease the mental effort when communication is difficult." Physical expressions reveal many things about the person using them for example, gestures can emphasize a point or relay a message, posture can reveal boredom or great interest, and touch can convey encouragement or caution.

Examples List

- *Hands on knees*: indicates readiness.
- *Hands on hips*: indicates impatience.
- *Lock your hands behind your back*: indicates self-control.
- *Locked hands behind head*: states confidence.
- *Sitting with a leg over the arm of the chair*: suggests indifference.
- *Legs and feet pointed in a particular direction*: the direction where more interest is felt
- *Crossed arms*: indicates submissiveness.

Body language is a form of non-verbal communication involving the use of stylized gestures, postures, and physiologic signs which act as cues to other people. Humans, sometimes unconsciously, send and receive non-verbal signals all the time.

Body Language and Space

Interpersonal space refers to the psychological "bubble" that we can imagine exists when someone is standing far too close to us. Research has revealed that in North America there are four different zones of interpersonal space. The first zone is called intimate distance and ranges from touching to about eighteen inches apart. Intimate distance is the space around us that we reserve for lovers, children, as well as close family members and friends.

The second zone is called personal distance and begins about an arm's length away; starting around eighteen inches from our person and ending about four feet away. We use personal distance in conversations with friends, to chat with associates, and in group discussions. The third zone of interpersonal space is called social distance and is the area that ranges from four to eight feet away from you. Social distance is reserved for strangers, newly formed groups, and new acquaintances. The fourth identified zone of space is public distance and includes anything more than eight feet away from you. This zone is used for speeches, lectures, and theater; essentially, public distance is that range reserved for larger audiences.

Language Difficulties

Misunderstandings in communication are common because of the many different ways, that is the way of conveying message; which is done through language. Though there is no right or wrong way to communicate, avoiding language barriers such as jargon, bypassing, and offensive language may prevent misunderstandings in group or interpersonal discussions. One of the more common barriers in communication is the inappropriate use of jargon. Jargon is a fictive language invented by and for the group as a verbal shorthand. It also syllabifies group membership when used properly. The problem with jargon is that it can make words confusing and can be used to conceal the truth. Another barrier to language is bypassing. Bypassing occurs when group members have different meanings for different words and phrases and thus miss each other's meanings. To overcome the risk of bypassing it is important to look to what the speaker wants and not always at what the speaker says. The third most common language barrier is offensive language. Offensive language is "any terminology that demeans, excludes, or stereotypes people for any reason. Avoiding sexist, discriminating, or labeling talk will greatly reduce chances of miscommunication. Remember, there is no right or wrong way to communicate. Though language difficulties are common, avoiding barriers like jargon, bypassing, and offensive language, will greatly reduce your chances of being misunderstood. Only through habitual awareness can one begin to truly understand and then be understood.

Using Co-Operative Learning as a Teaching Strategy

Cooperative learning is an approach to organize classroom activities into academic and social learning experiences. It differs from group work, and it has been described as "structuring positive interdependence." Students must work in groups to complete tasks collectively toward academic goals. Unlike individual learning, which can be competitive in nature, students learning cooperatively capitalize on one another's resources and skills (asking one another for information, evaluating one another's ideas, monitoring one another's work, etc.). Furthermore, the teacher's role changes from giving information to facilitating students' learning. Everyone succeeds when the group succeeds. Ross and Smyth (1995) describe successful cooperative learning tasks as intellectually demanding, creative, open-ended, and involve higher order thinking tasks. Five essential elements are identified for the successful incorporation of cooperative learning in the classroom.

Cooperative Learning has been proven to be effective for all types of students, including academically gifted, mainstream students and English language learners (ELLs) because it promotes learning and fosters respect and friendships among diverse groups of students. In fact, the more diversity in a team, the higher the benefits for each student. Peers learn to depend on each other in a positive way for a variety of learning tasks.

History

Prior to World War II, social theorists such as Allport, Watson, Shaw, and Mead began establishing cooperative learning theory after finding that group work was more effective and efficient in quantity, quality, and overall productivity when compared to working alone. However, it wasn't until 1937 when researchers May and Doob found that people who cooperate and work together to achieve shared goals, were more successful in attaining outcomes, than those who strived independently to complete the same goals. Furthermore, they found that independent achievers had a greater likelihood of displaying competitive behaviours.

Philosophers and psychologists in the 1930s and 40's such as John Dewey, Kurt Lewin, and Morton Deutsh also influenced the cooperative learning theory practiced today. Dewey believed it was important that students develop knowledge and social skills that could be used outside of the classroom, and in the democratic society. This theory portrayed students as active recipients of knowledge by discussing information and answers in groups, engaging in the learning process together rather than being passive receivers of information (e.g., teacher talking, students listening).

Lewin's contributions to cooperative learning were based on the ideas of establishing relationships between group members in order to successfully carry out and achieve the learning goal. Deutsh's contribution to cooperative learning was positive social interdependence, the idea that the student is responsible for contributing to group knowledge.

Since then, David and Roger Johnson have been actively contributing to the cooperative learning theory. In 1975, they identified that cooperative learning promoted mutual liking, better communication, high acceptance and support, as well as demonstrated an increase in a variety of thinking strategies among individuals in the group. Students who showed to be more competitive lacked in their interaction and trust with others, as well as in their emotional involvement with other students. In 1994 Johnson and Johnson published the 5 elements (positive interdependence, individual accountability, face-to-face interaction, social skills, and processing) essential for effective group learning, achievement, and higher-order social, personal and cognitive skills (e.g., problem solving, reasoning, decision-making, planning, organizing, and reflecting).

Types

Formal cooperative learning is structured, facilitated, and monitored by the educator over time and is used to achieve group goals in task work (e.g. completing a unit). Any course material or assignment can be adapted to this type of learning, and groups can vary from 2-6 people with discussions lasting from a few minutes up to an entire period. Types of formal cooperative learning strategies include:

1. The jigsaw technique
2. Assignments that involve group problem solving and decision making
3. Laboratory or experiment assignments
4. Peer review work (e.g. editing writing assignments).

Having experience and developing skill with this type of learning often facilitates informal and base learning. Jigsaw activities are wonderful because the student assumes the role of the teacher on a given topic and is in charge of teaching the topic to a classmate. The idea is that if students can teach something, they have already learned the material.

Informal cooperative learning incorporates group learning with passive teaching by drawing attention to material through small groups throughout the lesson or by discussion at the end of a lesson, and typically involves groups of two (e.g. turn-to-your-partner discussions). These groups are often temporary and can change from lesson to lesson (very much unlike formal learning where 2 students may be lab partners throughout the entire semester contributing to one another's knowledge of science).

Discussions typically have four components that include formulating a response to questions asked by the educator, sharing responses to the questions asked with a partner, listening to a partner's responses to the same question, and creating a new well-developed answer. This type of learning enables the student to process, consolidate, and retain more information.

In group-based cooperative learning, these peer groups gather together over the long term (e.g. over the course of a year, or several years such as in high school or post-secondary studies) to develop and contribute to one another's knowledge mastery on a topic by regularly discussing material, encouraging one another, and supporting the academic and personal success of group members.

Base group learning (e.g., a long term study group) is effective for learning complex subject matter over the course or semester and establishes caring, supportive peer relationships, which in turn motivates and strengthens the student's commitment to the group's education while increasing self-esteem and self-worth. Base group approaches also make the students accountable to educating their peer group in the event that a member was absent for a lesson. This is effective both for individual learning, as well as social support.

Elements

Brown & Ciuffetelli Parker (2009) and Siltala (2010) discuss the *5 basic and essential elements* to cooperative learning:

1. Positive interdependence
   - Students must fully participate and put forth effort within their group
   - Each group member has a task/role/responsibility therefore must believe that they are responsible for their learning and that of their group
2. Face-to-face promotive interaction
   - Members promote each other's success
   - Students explain to one another what they have or are learning and assist one another with understanding and completion of assignments
3. Individual and group accountability
   - Each student must demonstrate mastery of the content being studied
   - Each student is accountable for their learning and work, therefore eliminating "social loafing"
4. Social skills
   - Social skills that must be taught in order for successful cooperative learning to occur
   - Skills include effective communication, interpersonal and group skills

— Leadership
— Decision-making
— Trust-building
— Communication
— Conflict-management skills

5. Group processing
   1. Every so often groups must assess their effectiveness and decide how it can be improved

In order for student achievement to improve considerably, two characteristics must be present:

1. When designing cooperative learning tasks and reward structures, individual responsibility and accountability must be identified. Individuals must know exactly what their responsibilities are and that they are accountable to the group in order to reach their goal.
2. All group members must be involved in order for the group to complete the task. In order for this to occur each member must have a task that they are responsible for which cannot be completed by any other group member.

Cooperative Learning Techniques

There are a great number of cooperative learning techniques available. Some cooperative learning techniques utilize student pairing, while others utilize small groups of four or five students. Hundreds of techniques have been created into structures to use in any content area. Among the easy to implement structures are Think-Pair-Share, Think-Pair-Write, variations of Round Robin, and the Reciprocal Teaching Technique. A well known cooperative learning technique is the Jigsaw, Jigsaw II and Reverse Jigsaw.

Think Pair Share

Originally developed by Frank T. Lyman (1981), Think-Pair-Share allows for students to contemplate a posed question or problem silently. The student may write down thoughts or simply just brainstorm in his or her head.

When prompted, the student pairs up with a peer and discusses his or her idea(s) and then listens to the ideas of his or her partner. Following pair dialogue, the teacher solicits responses from the whole group.

Jigsaw

Students are members of two groups: home group and expert group. In the heterogeneous home group, students are each assigned a different topic. Once a topic has been identified, students leave the home group and group with the other students with their assigned topic. In the new group, students learn the material together before returning to their home group. Once back in their home group, each student is accountable for teaching his or her assigned topic.

Jigsaw II

Jigsaw II is Robert Slavin's (1980) variation of Jigsaw in which members of the home group are assigned the same material, but focus on separate portions of the material. Each member must become an "expert" on his or her assigned portion and teach the other members of the home group.

Reverse Jigsaw

This variation was created by Timothy Hedeen (2003) It differs from the original Jigsaw during the teaching portion of the activity. In the Reverse Jigsaw technique, students in the expert groups teach the whole class rather than return to their home groups to teach the content.

Reciprocal Teaching

Brown & Paliscar (1982) developed reciprocal teaching. It is a cooperative technique that allows for student pairs to participate in a dialogue about text. Partners take turns reading and asking questions of each other, receiving immediate feedback. Such a model allows for students to use important metacognitive techniques such as clarifying, questioning, predicting, and summarizing. It embraces the idea that students can effectively learn from each other.

The Williams

Students collaborate to answer a big question that is the learning objective. Each group has differentiated questions that increases in cognitive ability to allow students to progress and meet the learning objective.

STAD (or Student-Teams-Achievement Divisions)

Students are placed in small groups (or teams). The class in its entirety is presented with a lesson and the students are subsequently tested. Individuals are graded on the team's performance. Although the tests are taken individually, students are encouraged to work together to improve the overall performance of the group.

Research Supporting Cooperative Learning

Research on cooperative learning demonstrated "overwhelmingly positive" results and confirmed that cooperative modes are cross-curricular. Cooperative learning requires students to engage in group activities that increase learning and adds other important dimensions. The positive outcomes include academic gains, improved race relations and increased personal and social development.

Students who fully participate in group activities, exhibit collaborative behaviors, provide constructive feedback, and cooperate with their groups have a higher likelihood of receiving higher test scores and course grades at the end of the semester.

Cooperative learning is an active pedagogy that fosters higher academic achievement. Cooperative learning has also been found to increase attendance, time on task, enjoyment of school and classes, motivation, and independence.

Benefits and applicability of cooperative learning:

- Students demonstrate academic achievement
- Cooperative learning methods are usually equally effective for all ability levels
- Cooperative learning is effective for all ethnic groups
- Student perceptions of one another are enhanced when given the opportunity to work with one another
- Cooperative learning increases self-esteem and self-concept
- Ethnic and physically/mentally handicapped barriers are broken down allowing for positive interactions and friendships to occur

Cooperative learning results in:

- Increased higher level reasoning
- Increased generation of new ideas and solutions
- Greater transfer of learning between situations

Cooperative learning is significant in business:

- Cooperative learning can be seen as a characteristic of innovative businesses
- The five stage division on cooperative learning creates a useful method of analyzing learning in innovative businesses
- Innovativity connected to cooperative learning seems to make the creation of innovations possible

Limitations

Cooperative Learning has many limitations that could cause the process to be more complicated than first perceived. Sharan (2010) describes the constant evolution of cooperative learning as a threat. Because cooperative learning is constantly changing, there is a possibility that teachers may become confused and lack complete understanding of the method. Teachers implementing cooperative learning may also be challenged with resistance and hostility from students who believe that they are being held back by their slower teammates or by students who are less confident and feel that they are being ignored or demeaned by their team. Students often provide feedback in the success of the teamwork experienced during cooperative learning experiences. Peer review and evaluations may not reflect true experiences due to perceived competition among peers. A confidential evaluation process may help to increase evaluation strength.

Using Problem Solving as a Teaching Strategy

Many instructors in engineering, math and science have students solve "problems". But are their students solving true problems or mere exercises? The former stresses critical thinking and decision-making skills whereas the latter requires only the application of previously learned procedures. True problem solving is the process of applying a method – not known in advance – to a problem that is subject to a specific set of conditions and that the problem solver has not seen before, in order to obtain a satisfactory solution.

A problem, which can be caused for different reasons, and, if solvable, can usually be solved in a number of different ways, is defined in a number of different ways. This is determined by the context in which a said problem or problems is defined. When discussed, a problem can be argued in multiple ways. Generally speaking, there are two positions to take, the polemic or the defensive. An example of this is the mother who has a problem with how her daughter is going out, dressed in a particular fashion. She may tell her daughter, there is no way she is leaving the house looking like that. In this example, the mother would be on the polemic side, and the daughter, who presumably would like to go out dressed however she pleases, would be on the defensive side.

Problem-Solving

Problem-solving is the ability to identify and solve problems by applying appropriate skills systematically.

Problem-solving is a process—an ongoing activity in which we take what we know to discover what we don't know. It involves overcoming obstacles by generating hypo-theses, testing those predictions, and arriving at satisfactory solutions.

Problem-solving involves three basic functions:

1. Seeking information
2. Generating new knowledge
3. Making decisions

Problem-solving is, and should be, a very real part of the curriculum. It presupposes that students can take on some of the responsibility for their own learning and can take personal action to solve problems, resolve conflicts, discuss alternatives, and focus on thinking as a vital element of the curriculum. It provides students with opportunities to use their newly acquired knowledge in meaningful, real-life activities and assists them in working at higher levels of thinking.

Here is a five-stage model that most students can easily memorize and put into action and which has direct applications to many areas of the curriculum as well as everyday life:

Expert Opinion

Here are some techniques that will help students understand the nature of a problem and the conditions that surround it:

- List all related relevant facts.
- Make a list of all the given information.
- Restate the problem in their own words.
- List the conditions that surround a problem.
- Describe related known problems.

It's Elementary

For younger students, illustrations are helpful in organizing data, manipulating information, and outlining the limits of a problem and its possible solution(s). Students can use drawings to help them look at a problem from many different perspectives.

1. Understand the problem. It's important that students understand the nature of a problem and its related goals. Encourage students to frame a problem in their own words.
2. Describe any barriers. Students need to be aware of any barriers or constraints that may be preventing them from achieving

their goal. In short, what is creating the problem? Encouraging students to verbalize these impediments is always an important step.

3. Identify various solutions. After the nature and parameters of a problem are understood, students will need to select one or more appropriate strategies to help resolve the problem. Students need to understand that they have many strategies available to them and that no single strategy will work for all problems. Here are some problem-solving possibilities:
   - Create visual images. Many problem-solvers find it useful to create "mind pictures" of a problem and its potential solutions prior to working on the problem. Mental imaging allows the problem-solvers to map out many dimensions of a problem and "see" it clearly.
   - Guesstimate. Give students opportunities to engage in some trial-and-error approaches to problem-solving. It should be understood, however, that this is not a singular approach to problem-solving but rather an attempt to gather some preliminary data.
   - Create a table. A table is an orderly arrangement of data. When students have opportunities to design and create tables of information, they begin to understand that they can group and organize most data relative to a problem.
   - Use manipulatives. By moving objects around on a table or desk, students can develop patterns and organize elements of a problem into recognizable and visually satisfying components.
   - Work backward. It's frequently helpful for students to take the data presented at the end of a problem and use a series of computations to arrive at the data presented at the beginning of the problem.
   - Look for a pattern. Looking for patterns is an important problem-solving strategy because many problems are similar and fall into predictable patterns. A pattern, by definition, is a regular, systematic repetition and may be numerical, visual, or behavioural.
   - Create a systematic list. Recording information in list form is a process used quite frequently to map out a plan of attack for defining and solving problems. Encourage students to record their ideas in lists to determine

regularities, patterns, or similarities between problem elements.

4. Try out a solution. When working through a strategy or combination of strategies, it will be important for students to ...
   - o Keep accurate and up-to-date records of their thoughts, proceedings, and procedures. Recording the data collected, the predictions made, and the strategies used is an important part of the problem solving process.
   - o Try to work through a selected strategy or combination of strategies until it becomes evident that it's not working, it needs to be modified, or it is yielding inappropriate data. As students become more proficient problem-solvers, they should feel comfortable rejecting potential strategies at any time during their quest for solutions.
   - o Monitor with great care the steps undertaken as part of a solution. Although it might be a natural tendency for students to "rush" through a strategy to arrive at a quick answer, encourage them to carefully assess and monitor their progress.
   - o Feel comfortable putting a problem aside for a period of time and tackling it at a later time. For example, scientists rarely come up with a solution the first time they approach a problem. Students should also feel comfortable letting a problem rest for a while and returning to it later.
5. Evaluate the results. It's vitally important that students have multiple opportunities to assess their own problem-solving skills and the solutions they generate from using those skills. Frequently, students are overly dependent upon teachers to evaluate their performance in the classroom. The process of self-assessment is not easy, however. It involves risk-taking,

5

Using Student Research as a Teaching Strategy

Teaching is not an exact science, where one approach fits all. A carefully planned lesson might inspire one student to craft an amazing story, commit to improving her grades, and go on to college to become a journalist. That same lesson might leave another child confused and discouraged.

Effective teaching requires flexibility and creativity. As special educators or as general educators, we must constantly 'monitor and adjust' our teaching techniques. What we don't *have* to do is reinvent the wheel for every lesson. Good teachers draw upon their collection of strategies in order to meet the needs of diverse learners. They also use evidence-based practices shown through research to improve student learning.

Principles of Instruction

Instrictional principles come from three sources: (a) research in cognitive science, (b) research on master teachers, and (c) research on cognitive supports. Each is briefly explained below.

A: ***Research in Cognitive Science:*** This research focuses on how our brains acquire and use information. This cognitive research also provides suggestions on how we might overcome the limitations of our working memory (i.e., the mental "space" in which thinking occurs) when learning new material.

B: ***Research on the Classroom Practices of Master Teachers:*** Master teachers are those teachers whose classrooms made the highest gains on achievement tests. In a series of studies, a wide range of teachers were observed as they taught, and the investigators coded how they presented new material, how and whether they checked for student understanding, the types of support they provided to their students, and a number of other instructional activities. By also gathering student achievement data, research.

Even though these are three very different bodies of research, there is no conflict at all between the instructional suggestions that come from each of these three sources. In other words, these three sources supplement and complement each other. The fact that the instructional ideas from three different sources supplement and complement each other gives us faith in the validity of these findings.

Education involves helping a novice develop strong, readily accessible background knowledge. It's important that background knowledge be readily accessible, and this occurs when knowledge is well rehearsed and tied to other knowledge. The most effective teachers ensured that their students efficiently acquired, rehearsed, and connected background knowledge by providing a good deal of instructional support. They provided this support by teaching new material in manageable amounts, modelling, guiding student practice, helping students when they made errors, and providing for sufficient practice and review. Many of these teachers also went on to experiential, hands-on activities, but they always did the experiential activities after, not before, the basic material was learned.

The following is a list of some of the instructional principles that have come from these three sources. These ideas will be described and discussed in this article:

- Begin a lesson with a short review of previous learning.
- Present new material in small steps with student practice after each step.
- Ask a large number of questions and check the responses of all students.
- Provide models.
- Guide student practice.
- Check for student understanding.
- Obtain a high success rate.
- Provide scaffolds for difficult tasks.
- Require and monitor independent practice.
- Engage students in weekly and monthly review

Begin a lesson with a short review of previous learning: Daily review can strengthen previous learning and can lead to fluent recall.

Daily review is an important component of instruction. Review can help us strengthen the connections among the material we have learned. The review of previous learning can help us recall words, concepts, and procedures effortlessly and automatically when we need this material to solve problems or to understand new material. The development of expertise requires thousands of hours of practice, and daily review is one component of this practice.

For example, daily review was part of a successful experiment in elementary school mathematics. Teachers in the experiment were taught to spend eight minutes every day on review. Teachers used this time to check the homework, go over problems where there were errors, and practice the concepts and skills that needed to become automatic. As a result, students in these classrooms had higher achievement scores than did students in other classrooms.

Daily practice of vocabulary can lead to seeing each practiced word as a unit (i.e., seeing the whole word automatically rather than as individual letters that have to be sounded out and blended). When students see words as units, they have more space available in their working memory, and this space can now be used for comprehension. Mathematical problem solving is also improved when the basic skills (addition, multiplication, etc.) are over-learned and become automatic, thus freeing working-memory capacity.

In the Classroom

The most effective teachers in the studies of classroom instruction understood the importance of practice, and they began their les sons with a five- to eight-minute review of previously covered material. Some teachers reviewed vocabulary, formulae, events, or previously learned concepts. These teachers provided additional practice on facts and skills that were needed for recall to become automatic.

Effective teacher activities also included reviewing the concepts and skills that were necessary to do the homework, having students correct each others' papers, and asking about points on which the students had difficulty or made errors. These reviews ensured that the students had a firm grasp of the skills and concepts that would be needed for the day's lesson.

Effective teachers also reviewed the knowledge and concepts that were relevant for that day's lesson. It is important for a teacher to help students recall the concepts and vocabulary that will be relevant for the day's lesson because our working memory is very limited. If we do not review previous learning, then we will have to make a special effort to recall old material while learning new material, and this makes it difficult for us to learn the new material.

Daily review is particularly important for teaching material that will be used in subsequent learning. Examples include reading sight words (i.e., any word that is known by a reader automatically), grammar, math facts, math computation, math factoring, and chemical equations. When planning for review, teachers might want to consider which words, math facts, procedures, and concepts need to become automatic, and which words, vocabulary, or ideas need to be reviewed before the lesson begins.

In addition, teachers might consider doing the following during their daily review:

- Correct homework.
- Review the concepts and skills that were practiced as part of the homework.
- Ask students about points where they had difficulties or made errors.
- Review material where errors were made.
- Review material that needs overlearning (i.e., newly acquired skills should be practiced well beyond the point of initial mastery, leading to automaticity).

Present new material in small steps with student practice after each step: Only present small amounts of new material at any time, and then assist students as they practice this material. Our working memory, the place where we process information, is small. It can only handle a few bits of information at once—too much information swamps our working memory. Presenting too much material at once may confuse students because their working memory will be unable to process it. Therefore, the more effective teachers do not overwhelm their students by presenting too much new material at once. Rather, these teachers only present small amounts of new material at any time, and then assist the students as they practice this material.

Only after the students have mastered the first step do teachers proceed to the next step. The procedure of first teaching in small steps and then guiding student practice represents an appropriate way of dealing with the limitation of our working memory.

The more successful teachers did not overwhelm their students by presenting too much new material at once. Rather, they presented only small amounts of new material at one time, and they taught in such a way that each point was mastered before the next point was introduced. They checked their students' understanding on each point and retaught material when necessary.

Some successful teachers taught by giving a series of short presentations using many examples. The examples provided concrete learning and elaboration that were useful for processing new material.

Teaching in small steps requires time, and the more effective teachers spent more time presenting new material and guiding student practice than did the less effective teachers. In a study of mathematics instruction, for instance, the most effective mathematics teachers spent about 23 minutes of a 40-minute period in lecture, demonstration, questioning, and working examples.

In contrast, the least effective teachers spent only 11 minutes presenting new material. The more effective teachers used this extra time to provide additional explanations, give many examples, check for student understanding, and provide sufficient instruction so that the students could learn to work independently without difficulty. In one study, the least effective teachers asked only nine questions in a 40-minute period. Compared with the successful teachers, the less effective teachers gave much shorter presentations and explanations, and then passed out worksheets and told students to solve the problems. The less successful teachers were then observed going from student to student and having to explain the material again.

Similarly, when students were taught a strategy for summarizing a paragraph, an effective teacher taught the strategy using small steps. First, the teacher modeled and thought aloud as she identified the topic of a paragraph. Then, she led practice on identifying the topics of new paragraphs. Then, she taught students to identify the main idea of a paragraph.

The teacher modeled this step and then supervised the students as they practiced both finding the topic and locating the main idea. Following this, the teacher taught the students to identify the supporting details in a paragraph. The teacher modeled and thought aloud, and then the students practiced. Finally, the students practiced carrying out all three steps of this strategy. Thus, the strategy of summarizing a paragraph was divided into smaller steps, and there was modelling and practice at each step.

Ask a large number of questions and check the responses of all students: Questions help students practice new information and connect new material to their prior learning. Students need to practice new material. The teacher's questions and student discussion are a major way of providing this necessary practice. The most successful teachers in these studies spent more than half of the class time lecturing, demonstrating, and asking questions.

Questions allow a teacher to determine how well the material has been learned and whether there is a need for additional instruction. The most effective teachers also ask students to explain the process they used to answer the question, to explain how the answer was found. Less successful teachers ask fewer questions and almost no process questions.

In one classroom-based experimental study, one group of teachers was taught to follow the presentation of new material with lots of questions. They were taught to increase the number of factual questions and process questions they asked during this guided practice. Test results showed that their students achieved higher scores than did students whose teachers did not receive the training.

Imaginative teachers have found ways to involve all students in answering questions. Examples include having all students:

- Tell the answer to a neighbor.
- Summarize the main idea in one or two sentences, writing the summary on a piece of paper and sharing this with a neighbor, or repeating the procedures to a neighbor.
- Write the answer on a card and then hold it up.
- Raise their hands if they know the answer (thereby allowing the teacher to check the entire class).
- Raise their hands if they agree with the answer that someone else has given.

Across the classrooms that researchers observed, the purpose of all these procedures was to provide active participation for the students and also to allow the teacher to see how many students were correct and confident. The teacher may then reteach some material when it was considered necessary. An alternative was for students to write their answers and then trade papers with each other.

Other teachers used choral responses to provide sufficient practice when teaching new vocabulary or lists of items. This made the practice seem more like a game. To be effective, however, all students needed to start together, on a signal. When students did not start together, only the faster students answered. In addition to asking questions, the more effective teachers facilitated their students' rehearsal by providing explanations, giving more examples, and supervising students as they practiced the new material.

Provide models: Providing students with models and worked examples can help them learn to solve problems faster.

Students need cognitive support to help them learn to solve problems. The teacher modelling and thinking aloud while demonstrating how to solve a problem are examples of effective cognitive support. Worked examples (such as a math problem for which the teacher not only has provided the solution but has clearly laid out each step) are another form of modelling that has been developed by researchers. Worked examples allow students to focus on the specific steps to solve problems and thus reduce the cognitive load on their working memory. Modelling and worked examples have been used successfully in mathematics, science, writing, and reading comprehension.

Many of the skills that are taught in classrooms can be conveyed by providing prompts, modelling use of the prompt, and then guiding students as they develop independence. When teaching reading comprehension strategies, for example, effective teachers provided students with prompts that the students could use to ask themselves questions about a short passage. In one class, students were given words such as "who," "where," "why," and "how" to help them begin a question. Then, everyone read a passage and the teacher modeled how to use these words to ask questions.

Many Examples Were Given

Next, during guided practice, the teacher helped the students practice asking questions by helping them select a prompt and develop a question that began with that prompt. The students practiced this step many times with lots of support from the teacher. Then, the students read new passages and practiced asking questions on their own, with support from the teacher when needed. Finally, students were given short passages followed by questions, and the teacher expressed an opinion about the quality of the students' questions.

This same procedure—providing a prompt, modelling, guiding practice, and supervising independent practice—can be used for many tasks. When teaching students to write an essay, for example, an effective teacher first modeled how to write each paragraph, then the students and teacher worked together on two or more new essays, and finally students worked on their own with supervision from the teacher.

Worked examples are another form of modelling that has been used to help students learn how to solve problems in mathematics and science. A worked example is a step-by-step demonstration of how to perform a task or how to solve a problem. The presentation of worked examples begins with the teacher modelling and explaining the steps that can be taken to solve a specific problem.

The teacher also identifies and explains the underlying principles for these steps.

Usually, students are then given a series of problems to complete at their desks as independent practice. But, in research carried out in Australia, students were given a mixture of problems to solve and worked examples. So, during independent practice, students first studied a worked example, then they solved a problem; then they studied another worked example and solved another problem. In this way, the worked examples showed students how to focus on the essential parts of the problems. Of course, not all students studied the worked examples. To correct this problem, the Australian researchers also presented partially completed problems in which students had to complete the missing steps and thus pay more attention to the worked example.

Guide Student Practice: Successful teachers spend more time guiding students' practice of new material.

It is not enough simply to present students with new material, because the material will be forgotten unless there is sufficient rehearsal. An important finding from information-processing research is that students need to spend additional time rephrasing, elaborating, and summarizing new material in order to store this material in their long-term memory. When there has been sufficient rehearsal, the students are able to retrieve this material easily and thus are able to make use of this material to foster new learning and aid in problem solving. But when the rehearsal time is too short, students are less able to store, remember, or use the material. As we know, it is relatively easy to place something in a filing cabinet, but it can be very difficult to recall where exactly we filed it. Rehearsal helps us remember where we filed it so we can access it with ease when needed.

A teacher can facilitate this rehearsal process by asking questions; good questions require students to process and rehearse the material.

Rehearsal is also enhanced when students are asked to summarize the main points, and when they are supervised as they practice new steps in a skill. The quality of storage in long-term memory will be weak if students only skim the material and do not engage in it. It is also important that all students process the new material and receive feedback, so they do not inadvertently store partial information or a misconception in long-term memory.

In one study, the more successful teachers of mathematics spent more time presenting new material and guiding practice. The more successful teachers used this extra time to provide additional explanations, give many examples, check for student understanding, and provide sufficient instruction so that the students could learn to work independently without difficulty. In contrast, the less successful teachers gave much shorter presentations and explanations, and then they passed out worksheets and told students to work on the problems. Under these conditions, the students made too many errors and had to be retaught the lesson.

The most successful teachers presented only small amounts of material at a time. After this short presentation, these teachers then guided student practice. This guidance often consisted of the teacher working the first problems at the blackboard and explaining the reason for each step, which served as a model for the students. The guidance also included asking students to come to the blackboard to work out problems and discuss their procedures. Through this process, the students seated in the classroom saw additional models.

Although most teachers provided some guided practice, the most successful teachers spent more time in guided practice, more time asking questions, more time checking for understanding, more time correcting errors, and more time having students work out problems with teacher guidance.

Teachers who spent more time in guided practice and had higher success rates also had students who were more engaged during individual work at their desks. This finding suggests that, when teachers provided sufficient instruction during guided practice, the students were better prepared for the independent practice (e.g., seatwork and homework activities), but when the guided practice was too short, the students were not prepared for the seatwork and made more errors during independent practice.

Check for Student Understanding: Checking for student understanding at each point can help students learn the material with fewer errors. The more effective teachers frequently checked to see if all the students were learning the new material. These checks provided some of the processing needed to move new learning into long-term memory. These checks also let teachers know if students were developing misconceptions.

Effective teachers also stopped to check for student understanding. They checked for understanding by asking questions, by asking students to summarize the presentation up to that point or to repeat directions or procedures, or by asking students whether they agreed or disagreed with other students' answers. This checking has two purposes: (a) answering the questions might cause the students to elaborate on the material they have learned and augment connections to other learning in their long-term memory, and (b) alerting the teacher to when parts of the material need to be retaught.

In contrast, the less effective teachers simply asked, "Are there any questions?" and, if there were no questions, they assumed the students had learned the material and proceeded to pass out worksheets for students to complete on their own.

Another way to check for understanding is to ask students to think aloud as they work to solve mathematical problems, plan an essay, or identify the main idea in a paragraph. Yet another check is to ask students to explain or defend their position to others. Having to explain a position may help students integrate and elaborate their knowledge in new ways, or may help identify gaps in their understanding.

Another reason for the importance of teaching in small steps, guiding practice, and checking for understanding comes from the fact that we all construct and reconstruct knowledge as we learn and use what we have learned. We cannot simply repeat what we hear word for word. Rather, we connect our understanding of the new information to our existing concepts or "schema," and we then construct a mental summary (i.e., the gist of what we have heard). However, when left on their own, many students make errors in the process of constructing this mental summary. These errors occur, particularly, when the information is new and the student does not have adequate or well-formed background knowledge. These constructions are not errors so much as attempts by the students to be logical in an area where their background knowledge is weak. These errors are so common that there is a research literature on the development and correction of student misconceptions in science. Providing guided practice after teaching small amounts of new material, and check-ing for student understanding, can help limit the development of misconceptions.

Obtain a High Success Rate: It is important for students to achieve a high success rate during classroom instruction.

In two of the major studies on the impact of teachers, the investigators found that students in classrooms with more effective teachers had a higher success rate, as judged by the quality of their oral responses during guided practice and their individual work.

In a study of fourth-grade mathematics, it was found that 82 percent of students' answers were correct in the classrooms of the most successful teachers, but the least successful teachers had a success rate of only 73 percent. A high success rate during guided practice also leads to a higher success rate when students are working on problems on their own.

The research also suggests that the optimal success rate for fostering student achievement appears to be about 80 percent. A success rate of 80 percent shows that students are learning the material, and it also shows that the students are challenged.

The most effective teachers obtained this success level by teaching in small steps (i.e., by combining short presentations with supervised student practice), and by giving sufficient practice on each part before proceeding to the next step. These teachers frequently checked for understanding and required responses from all students.

It is important that students achieve a high success rate during instruction and on their practice activities. Practice, we are told, makes perfect, but practice can be a disaster if students are practicing errors! If the practice does not have a high success level, there is a chance that students are practicing and learning errors.

Once errors have been learned, they are very difficult to overcome.

When we learn new material, we construct a gist of this material in our long-term memory.

However, many students make errors in the process of constructing this mental summary. These errors can occur when the information is new and the student did not have adequate or well-formed background knowledge. These constructions are not errors so much as attempts by the students to be logical in an area where their background knowledge is weak. But students are more likely to develop misconceptions if too much material is presented at once, and if teachers do not check for student understanding.

Providing guided practice after teaching small amounts of new material, and checking for student understanding, can help limit the development of misconceptions.

Unless all students have mastered the first set of lessons, there is a danger that the slower students will fall further behind when the next set of lessons is taught. So there is a need for a high success rate for all students. "Mastery learning" is a form of instruction where lessons are organized into short units and all students are required to master one set of lessons before they proceed to the next set. In mastery learning, tutoring by other students or by teachers is provided to help students master each unit.

Variations of this approach, particularly the tutoring, might be useful in many classroom settings.

Provide Scaffolds for Difficult Tasks: The teacher provides students with temporary supports and scaffolds to assist them when they learn difficult tasks.

Investigators have successfully provided students with scaffolds, or instructional supports, to help them learn difficult tasks. A scaffold is a temporary support that is used to assist a learner. These scaffolds are gradually withdrawn as learners become more competent, although students may continue to rely on scaffolds when they encounter particularly difficult problems. Providing scaffolds is a form of guided practice.

Scaffolds include modelling the steps by the teacher, or thinking aloud by the teacher as he or she solves the problem. Scaffolds also may be tools, such as cue cards or checklists, that complete part of the task for the students, or a model of the completed task against which students can compare their own work.

The process of helping students solve difficult problems by modelling and providing scaffolds has been called "cognitive apprenticeship." Students learn strategies and content during this apprenticeship that enable them to become competent readers, writers, and problem solvers. They are aided by a master who models, coaches, provides supports, and scaffolds them as they become independent.

One form of scaffolding is to give students prompts for steps they might use. Prompts such as "who," "why," and "how" have helped students learn to ask questions while they read. Teaching students to ask questions has been shown to help students' reading comprehension. Similarly, one researcher developed the following prompt to help students organize material.

1. Draw a central box and write the title of the article in it.
2. Skim the article to find four to six main ideas.
3. Write each main idea in a box below the central box.
4. Find and write two to four important details to list under each main idea.

Another form of scaffolding is thinking aloud by the teacher.

For example, teachers might think aloud as they try to summarize a paragraph. They would show the thought processes they go through as they determine the topic of the paragraph and then use the topic to generate a summary sentence. Teachers might think aloud while solving a scientific equation or writing an essay and at the same time provide labels for their mental processes.

Such thinking aloud provides novice learners with a way to observe "expert thinking" that is usually hidden from the student. Teachers also can study their students' thought processes by asking them to think aloud during problem solving.

One characteristic of effective teachers is their ability to anticipate students' errors and warn them about possible errors some of them are likely to make. For example, a teacher might have students read a passage and then give them a poorly written topic sentence to correct. In teaching division or subtraction, the teacher may show and discuss with students the mistakes other students have frequently made. In some of the studies, students were given a checklist to evaluate their work. Checklist items included "Have I found the most important information that tells me more about the main idea?" and "Does every sentence start with a capital letter?" The teacher then modeled use of the checklist.

In some studies, students were provided with expert models with which they could compare their work. For example, when students were taught to generate questions, they could compare their questions with those generated by the teacher. Similarly, when learning to write summaries, students could compare their summaries on a passage with those generated by an expert.

Require and Monitor Independent Practice: Students need extensive, successful, independent practice in order for skills and knowledge to become automatic.

In a typical teacher-led classroom, guided practice is followed by independent practice—by students working alone and practicing the new material. This independent practice is necessary because a good deal of practice (over learning) is needed in order to become fluent and automatic in a skill. When material is over learned, it can be recalled automatically and doesn't take up any space in working memory. When students become automatic in an area, they can then devote more of their attention to comprehension and application.

Independent practice provides students with the additional review and elaboration they need to become fluent. This need for fluency applies to facts, concepts, and discriminations that must be used in subsequent learning. Fluency is also needed in operations, such as dividing decimals, conjugating a regular verb in a foreign language, or completing and balancing a chemical equation.

The more successful teachers provided for extensive and successful practice, both in the classroom and after class. Independent practice should involve the same material as the guided practice. If guided practice deals with identifying types of sentences, for example, then independent practice should deal with the same topic or, perhaps, with a slight variation, like creating individual compound and complex sentences. It would be inappropriate if the independent practice asked the students to do an activity such as "Write a paragraph using two compound and two complex sentences," however, because the students have not been adequately prepared for such an activity. Students need to be fully prepared for their independent practice. Sometimes, it may be appropriate for a teacher to practice some of the seatwork problems with the entire class before students begin independent practice.

Using Role-Play as a Teaching Strategy

Role-playing refers to the changing of one's behaviour to assume a role, either unconsciously to fill a social role, or consciously to act out an adopted role. While the *Oxford English Dictionary* offers a definition of role-playing as "the changing of one's behaviour to fulfill a social role", in the field of psychology, the term is used more loosely in four senses:

- To refer to the playing of roles generally such as in a theatre, or educational setting;
- To refer to taking a role of an existing character or person and acting it out with a partner taking someone else's role, often involving different genres of practice;
- To refer to a wide range of games including role-playing video game, play-by-mail games and more;
- To refer specifically to role-playing games.

Amusement

Many children participate in a form of role-playing known as make believe, wherein they adopt certain roles such as doctor and act out those roles in character. Sometimes make believe adopts an oppositional nature, resulting in games such as cops and robbers.

Entertainment

Historical re-enactment has been practised by adults for millennia. The ancient Romans, Han Chinese, and medieval Europeans all enjoyed occasionally organising events in which everyone pretended to be from an earlier age, and entertainment appears to have been the primary purpose of these activities. Within the 20th century historical re-enactment has often been pursued as a hobby.

Improvisational theatre dates back to the Commedia dell'Arte tradition of the 16th century. Modern improvisational theatre began in the classroom with the "theatre games" of Viola Spolin and Keith Johnstone in the 1950s. Viola Spolin, who was one of the founders the famous comedy troupe Second City, insisted that her exercises were games, and that they involved role-playing as early as 1946. She accurately judged role-playing in the theatre as rehearsal and actor training, or the playing of the role of actor versus theatre roles, but many now use her games for fun in their own right.

Role-playing Games

A role-playing game is a game in which the participants assume the roles of characters and collaboratively create stories. Participants determine the actions of their characters based on their characterisation, and the actions succeed or fail according to a formal system of rules and guidelines. Within the rules, they may improvise freely; their choices shape the direction and outcome of the games.

Role-playing can also be done online in the form of group story creation, involving anywhere from two to several hundred people, utilizing public forums, private message boards, mailing lists, chatrooms, and instant-messaging chat clients (e.g., MSN, Yahoo!, ICQ) to build worlds and characters that may last a few hours, or several years. Message boards such as ProBoards and InvisionFree are popularly used for role-playing. Often on forum-based roleplays, rules, and standards are set up, such as a minimum word count, character applications, and "plotting" boards to increase complexity and depth of story.

There are different genres of which one can choose while role-playing, including, but not limited to, fantasy, modern, medieval, steam punk, and historical. Books, movies, or games can be, and often are, used as a basis for role-plays (which in such cases may be deemed "collaborative fan-fiction"), with players either assuming the roles of established canon characters or using those the players themselves create ("Original Characters") to replace—or exist alongside—characters from the book, movie, or game, playing through well-trodden plots as alternative characters, or expanding upon the setting and story outside of its established canon.

Training

Role-playing may also refer to role training where people rehearse situations in preparation for a future performance and to improve their abilities within a role. The most common examples are occupational training role-plays, educational role-play exercises, and certain military wargames.

Simulation

One of the first uses of computers was to simulate reality around its participants in order to role-play the flying of aircraft. As early as the 1940s, flight simulators used computers to solve the equations of flight and train future pilots. After World War II the army began full-time role-playing simulations with soldiers using computers both within full scale training exercises and for training in numerous specific tasks under wartime conditions. Examples include weapon firing, vehicle simulators, and control station mock-ups.

How to Teach Using Role-Playing

Role-playing exercises can be hard work for the instructor, both in preparation and in execution, but the work tends to pay off in terms of student motivation and accomplishment.

As with any big project, it's best to take it one step at a time:

Define Objectives

The details of what you need to do depend entirely on why you want to include role-playing exercises in your course.

- What topics do you want the exercise to cover?
- How much time do you and your class have to work on it?
- What do you expect of your students: research, reports, presentations?

- Do you want the students role-playing separately or together?
- Do you want to include a challenge or conflict element?

Choose Context & Roles

In order to prepare for the exercise:

- Decide on a problem related to the chosen topic(s) of study and a setting for the characters. It is a good idea to make the setting realistic, but not necessarily real. Consider choosing and adapting material that other instructors have prepared.
    - o For problems and settings with lots of detail, have a look at examples in the Starting Point Case Study Module. The module itself contains more information about using cases to teach.
- If the characters(s) used in the exercise are people, define his or her goals and what happens if the character does not achieve them.
- You should work out each characters' background information on the problem or, better yet, directions on how to collect it through research. If possible, prepare maps and data for your students to interpret as part of their background information rather than the conclusions upon which they would ordinarily base their decisions (especially if the characters are scientists).

Introducing the Exercise

Engage the students in the scenario by describing the setting and the problem.

- Provide them with the information you have already prepared about their character(s): the goals and background information. It needs to be clear to the student how committed a character is to his/her goals and why.
- Determine how many of your students have done role-playing before and explain how it will work for this exercise.
- Outline your expectations of them as you would for any assignment and stress what you expect them to learn in this lesson.
- If there is an inquiry element, suggest a general strategy for research/problem solving.

Student Preparation/Research

Even if there is no advance research assigned, students will need a few moments to look over their characters and get into their roles for the exercise. There may also be additional questions:

- Why they are doing this in character? Why did you decide to make this a role-playing exercise?
- Students may have reservations about the character that they have been assigned or about their motives. It is good for the instructor to find out about these before the actual role-play. It can be very difficult for a student to begin researching an issue from a perspective very different from their own because even apparently objective data tends to be reinterpreted as support for pre-existing world-views.
    - o With regards to environmental issues, many environmental groups have well-written, carefully researched, and nicely-engineered websites that will provide arguments as well as information for a student assigned a character to whom protecting the environment is very important.
    - o Similar websites representing the very common viewpoint of the worker, property owner, or industrialist whose future may be in conflict with environmental interests are hard to find. One site, Debate Central, has constructed arguments for characters promoting property rights and wary of government intervention. Their topic coverage is still limited, however. A poorer alternative is to send students to the websites of companies involved in an issue to read their PR material.
    - o Often, the best resource for understanding people is other people. Model UN encourages participants to call the embassy of the country they are to represent for advice. The same can be done with the PR divisions of mining firms and unions, environmental and taxpayer protection groups, etc.
- If there is an inquiry component (*i.e.* student-led research), the students may need help coming up with a research plan and finding resources.

The Role-Play

Depending on the assignment, students could be writing papers or participating in a Model-UN-style summit. For a presentation or interaction, props can liven up the event, but are not worth a lot of effort as they are usually not important to the educational goals of the project.

- Potential Challenges with Interactive Exercises

Large Classes

For large classes, split the group up, or use an etiquette like Robert's Rules of Order to ensure that people who have something to say can say it. A Model UN works well for large groups.

Good Vs. Evil

The students need to sympathize with their characters, so it is a bad idea to assign overtly evil ones. It's too much to ask of students to represent the interests of genocidal tyrants. These exercises are supposed to be fun! Likewise, the instructor should use situations without simple or obvious solutions or situations that are doomed. Because of issues in the students' own backgrounds, it is also generally good to choose settings and characters that are either fictitious or well removed from the students in space and time. Asking college students to role-play well-known Republican or Democratic politicians can be a recipe for trouble.

Not Letting Go

One reason that open-ended, problem-solving exercises are fun and somewhat realistic is that the students, in character, decide the outcome of the scenario. This can be damaged if the instructor decides on the "correct" ending or pushes the students to play characters a certain way.

Lack of Social Skills

A chronic problem with role-playing is that some students don't pay attention to others and that charismatic students can overwhelm less assertive ones. If the student is violating the rules you as the instructor have established for the role-play, do not hesitate to remove them from the exercise immediately. Disciplinary action may be appropriate depending on the student's behaviour.

However, within the limits of the rules, there will still be minor problems, which may actually become a useful part of the lesson. Bonnet's (2000) 10-year-old students reported that they were alienated by characters that came across as too angry about issues. These children may well recognize that courtesy and calmness are valuable tools for a debater.

Concluding Discussion

Like any inquiry-based exercise, role-playing needs to be followed by a debriefing for the students to define what they have learned and to reinforce it. This can be handled in reflective essays, or a concluding paragraph at the end of an individual written assignment, or in a class discussion. The instructor can take this opportunity to ask the students if they learned the lessons defined before the role-play began.

Assessment

Generally, grades are given for written projects associated with the role-play, but presentations and even involvement in interactive exercises can be graded. Special considerations for grading in role-playing exercises include:

- Playing in-character
    - Working to further the character's goals
    - Making statements that reflect the character's perspective
- In an interactive exercise, being constructive and courteous
- For many assignments, being able to step back and look at the character's situation and statements from the student's own perspective or from another character's perspective.

Using Case Study as a Teaching Strategy

A case study (or case report) is a descriptive, exploratory or explanatory analysis of a person, group or event. An explanatory case study is used to explore causation in order to find underlying principles. Case studies may be prospective (in which criteria are established and cases fitting the criteria are included as they become available) or retrospective (in which criteria are established for selecting cases from historical records for inclusion in the study).

Thomas offers the following definition of case study: "Case studies are analyses of persons, events, decisions, periods, projects, policies, institutions, or other systems that are studied holistically by one or more methods. The case that is the *subject* of the inquiry will be an instance of a class of phenomena that provides an analytical frame — an *object* — within which the study is conducted and which the case illuminates and explicates."

Another suggestion is that *case study* should be defined as a *research strategy*, an empirical inquiry that investigates a phenomenon within its real-life context. Case study research can mean single and multiple case studies, can include quantitative evidence, relies on multiple sources of evidence, and benefits from the prior development of theoretical propositions. Case studies should not be confused with qualitative research and they can be based on any mix of quantitative and qualitative evidence. Single-subject research provides the statistical framework for making inferences from quantitative case-study data. This is also supported and well-formulated in (Lamnek, 2005): "The case study is a research approach, situated between concrete data taking techniques and methodologic paradigms."

The case study is sometimes mistaken for the case method, but the two are not the same.

Case Selection and Structure

An average, or typical, case is often not the richest in information. In clarifying lines of history and causation it is more useful to select subjects that offer an interesting, unusual or particularly revealing set of circumstances. A case selection that is based on representativeness will seldom be able to produce these kinds of insights. When selecting a subject for a case study, researchers will therefore use information-oriented sampling, as opposed to random sampling. Outlier cases (that is, those which are extreme, deviant or atypical) reveal more information than the potentially representative case. Alternatively, a case may be selected as a key case, chosen because of the inherent interest of the case or the circumstances surrounding it. Or it may be chosen because of researchers' in-depth local knowledge; where researchers have this local knowledge they are in a position to "soak and poke" as Fenno puts it, and thereby to offer reasoned lines of explanation based on this rich knowledge of setting and circumstances.

Three types of cases may thus be distinguished:

1. Key cases
2. Outlier cases
3. Local knowledge cases

Whatever the frame of reference for the choice of the subject of the case study (key, outlier, local knowledge), there is a distinction to be made between the *subjestorical unity* through which the theoretical focus of the study is being viewed. The object is that theoretical focus – the analytical frame. Thus, for example, if a researcher were interested in US resistance to communist expansion as a theoretical focus, then the Korean War might be taken to be the *subject*, the lens, the case study through which the theoretical focus, the *object*, could be viewed and explicated.

Beyond decisions about case selection and the subject and object of the study, decisions need to be made about purpose, approach and process in the case study. Thomas thus proposes a typology for the case study wherein purposes are first identified (evaluative or exploratory), then approaches are delineated (theory-testing, theory-building or illustrative), then processes are decided upon, with a principal choice being between whether the study is to be single or multiple, and choices also about whether the study is to be retrospective, snapshot or diachronic, and whether it is nested, parallel or sequential. It is thus possible to take many routes through this typology, with, for example, an exploratory, theory-building, multiple, nested study, or an evaluative, theory-testing, single, retrospective study. The typology thus offers many permutations for case study structure.

A closely related study in medicine is the case report, which identifies a specific case as treated and/or examined by the authors as presented in a novel form. These are, to a differentiable degree, similar to the case study in that many contain reviews of the relevant literature of the topic discussed in the thorough examination of an array of cases published to fit the criterion of the report being presented. These case reports can be thought of as brief case studies with a principal discussion of the new, presented case at hand that presents a novel interest.

Generalizing from Case Studies

A critical case is defined as having strategic importance in relation to the general problem. A critical case allows the following type of generalization, 'If it is valid for this case, it is valid for all (or many) cases.' In its negative form, the generalization would be, 'If it is not valid for this case, then it is not valid for any (or only few) cases.'

The case study is also effective for generalizing using the type of test that Karl Popper called falsification, which forms part of critical reflexivity. Falsification is one of the most rigorous tests to which a scientific proposition can be subjected: if just one observation does not fit with the proposition it is considered not valid generally and must therefore be either revised or rejected. Popper himself used the now famous example of, "All swans are white," and proposed that just one observation of a single black swan would falsify this proposition and in this way have general significance and stimulate further investigations and theory-building. The case study is well suited for identifying "black swans" because of its in-depth approach: what appears to be "white" often turns out on closer examination to be "black."

Galileo Galilei's rejection of Aristotle's law of gravity was based on a case study selected by information-oriented sampling and not random sampling. The rejection consisted primarily of a conceptual experiment and later on of a practical one. These experiments, with the benefit of hindsight, are self-evident. Nevertheless, Aristotle's incorrect view of gravity dominated scientific inquiry for nearly two thousand years before it was falsified. In his experimental thinking, Galileo reasoned as follows: if two objects with the same weight are released from the same height at the same time, they will hit the ground simultaneously, having fallen at the same speed. If the two objects are then stuck together into one, this object will have double the weight and will according to the Aristotelian view therefore fall faster than the two individual objects. This conclusion seemed contradictory to Galileo. The only way to avoid the contradiction was to eliminate weight as a determinant factor for acceleration in free fall.

History of the Case Study

It is generally believed that the case-study method was first introduced into social science by Frederic Le Play in 1829 as a handmaiden to statistics in his studies of family budgets. (Les Ouvriers Europeens (2nd edition, 1879). The use of case studies for the creation of new theory in social sciences has been further developed by the sociologists Barney Glaser and Anselm Strauss who presented their research method, Grounded theory, in 1967.

The popularity of case studies in testing hypotheses has developed only in recent decades. One of the areas in which case studies have been gaining popularity is education and in particular educational evaluation.

Case studies have also been used as a teaching method and as part of professional development, especially in business and legal education. The problem-based learning (PBL) movement is such an example. When used in (non-business) education and professional development, case studies are often referred to as *critical incidents*.

Ethnography is an example of a type of case study, commonly found in communication case studies. Ethnography is the description, interpretation, and analysis of a culture or social group, through field research in the natural environment of the group being studied. The main method of ethnographic research is through observation where the researcher observes the participants over an extended period of time within the participants own environment.

When the Harvard Business School was started, the faculty quickly realized that there were no textbooks suitable to a graduate program in business. Their first solution to this problem was to interview leading practitioners of business and to write detailed accounts of what these managers were doing. Cases are generally written by business school faculty with particular learning objectives in mind and are refined in the classroom before publication. Additional relevant documentation (such as financial statements, time-lines, and short biographies, often referred to in the case as “exhibits”), multimedia supplements (such as video-recordings of interviews with the case protagonist), and a carefully crafted teaching note often accompany cases.

Case Study as a Teaching Tool

Case studies are stories. They present realistic, complex, and contextually rich situations and often involve a dilemma, conflict, or problem that one or more of the characters in the case must negotiate.

A Good Case Study, According to Professor Paul Lawrence is: “the vehicle by which a chunk of reality is brought into the classroom to be worked over by the class and the instructor. A good case keeps the class discussion grounded upon some of the stubborn facts that must be faced in real life situations.”

Although they have been used most extensively in the teaching of medicine, law and business, case studies can be an effective teaching tool in any number of disciplines. As an instructional strategy, case studies have a number of virtues. They “bridge the gap between theory and practice and between the academy and the workplace” (Barkley, Cross, and Major 2005, p.182). They also give students practice identifying the parameters of a problem, recognizing and articulating positions, evaluating courses of action, and arguing different points of view.

Case studies vary in length and detail, and can be used in a number of ways, depending on the case itself and on the instructor’s goals.

- They can be short (a few paragraphs) or long (e.g. 20+ pages).
- They can be used in lecture-based or discussion-based classes.
- They can be real, with all the detail drawn from actual people and circumstances, or simply realistic.
- They can provide all the relevant data students need to discuss and resolve the central issue, or only some of it, requiring

students to identify, and possibly fill in (via outside research), the missing information.

- They can require students to examine multiple aspects of a problem, or just a circumscribed piece.
- They can require students to propose a solution for the case or simply to identify the parameters of the problem.

Finding or Creating Cases

It is possible to write your own case studies, although it is not a simple task. The material for a case study can be drawn from your own professional experiences (e.g., negotiating a labour dispute at a local corporation or navigating the rocky shoals of a political campaign), from current events (e.g., a high-profile medical ethics case or a diplomatic conundrum), from historical sources (e.g., a legal debate or military predicament), etc. It is also possible to find published cases from books and on-line case study collections. Whatever the source, an effective case study is one that, according to Davis (1993):

- tells a "real" and engaging story
- raises a thought-provoking issue
- has elements of conflict
- promotes empathy with the central characters
- lacks an obvious or clear-cut right answer
- encourages students to think and take a position
- portrays actors in moments of decision
- provides plenty of data about character, location, context, actions
- is relatively concise

Using Case Studies

How you use case studies will depend on the goals, as well as on the format, of your course. If it is a large lecture course, for example, you might use a case study to illustrate and enrich the lecture material. (An instructor lecturing on principles of marketing, for example, might use the case of a particular company or product to explore marketing issues and dilemmas in a real-life context.) Also in a large class you might consider breaking the class into small groups or pairs to discuss a relevant case. If your class is a smaller, discussion-format course, you will be able to use more detailed and complex cases, to explore the perspectives introduced in the case in greater depth, and perhaps integrate other instructional strategies, such as role playing or debate.

Regardless of the format in which you employ case studies, it is important that you, as the instructor, know all the issues involved in the case, prepare questions and prompts in advance, and anticipate where students might run into problems. Finally, consider who your students are and how you might productively draw on their backgrounds, experiences, personalities, etc., to enhance the discussion.

While there are many variations in how case studies can be used, these six steps provide a general framework for how to lead a case-based discussion:

1. Give students ample time to read and think about the case. If the case is long, assign it as homework with a set of questions for students to consider (e.g., What is the nature of the problem the central character is facing? What are some possible courses of action? What are the potential obstacles?)
2. Introduce the case briefly and provide some guidelines for how to approach it. Clarify how you want students to think about the case (e.g., "Approach this case as if you were the presiding judge" or "You are a consultant hired by this company. What would you recommend?") Break down the steps you want students to take in analyzing the case (e.g., "First, identify theconstraints each character in the case was operating under and the opportunities s/he had. Second, evaluate the decisions each character made and their implications. Finally, explain what you would have done differently and why."). If you would like students to disregard or focus on certain information, specify that as well (e.g., "I want you to ignore the political affiliation of the characters described and simply distinguish their positions on stem-cell research as they are articulated here.")
3. Create groups and monitor them to make sure everyone is involved. Breaking the full class into smaller groups gives individual students more opportunities for participation and interaction. However, small groups can drift off track if you do not provide structure. Thus, it is a good idea to make the task of the group very concrete and clear (e.g., "You are to identify three potential courses of action and outline the pros and cons of each from a public relations standpoint"). You may also want to designate roles within each group: for example, one individual might be charged with keeping the others on

task and watching the time; a second individual's role might be to question the assumptions or interpretations of the group and probe for deeper analysis; a third individual's role might be to record the group's thoughts and report their decision to the class. Alternatively, group members could be assigned broad perspectives (e.g., liberal, conservative, libertarian) to represent, or asked to speak for the various "stake-holders" in the case study.

4. Have groups present their solutions/reasoning: If groups know they are responsible for producing something (a decision, rationale, analysis) to present to the class, they will approach the discussion with greater focus and seriousness. Write their conclusions on the board so that you can return to them in the discussion that follows.
5. Ask questions for clarification and to move discussion to another level. One of the challenges for a case-based discussion leader is to guide the discussion and probe for deeper analysis without over-directing. As the discussion unfolds, ask questions that call for students to examine their own assumptions, substantiate their claims, provide illustrations, etc.
6. Synthesize issues raised. Be sure to bring the various strands of the discussion back together at the end, so that students see what they have learned and take those lessons with them. The job of synthesizing need not necessarily fall to the instructor, however; one or more students can be given this task.

Some variations on this general method include having students do outside research (individually or in groups) to bring to bear on the case in question, and comparing the actual outcome of a real-life dilemma to the solutions generated in class.

Using Writing as a Teaching Strategy

Writing is A Multifaceted Task That involves the use and coordination of many cognitive processes. Due to its complexities, many students find writing challenging and many teachers struggle to find methods to effectively teach the skill.

Gathering Evidence for Effectively Teaching Writing

Advice from professional writers and the experiences of successful writing teachers offer some guidance in developing sound writing practices. However, these accounts are frequently based on testimonials involving the writing development of an individual or a single classroom.

This makes it difficult to understand how or why a writing strategy was effective and what elements of the strategy would be essential to make it work in new situations.

Scientific studies of writing interventions provide a more trustworthy approach for identifying effective methods for teaching writing; they supply evidence of the magnitude of the effect of a writing intervention, how confident one can be in the study's results, and how replicable the writing strategy is in new settings with new populations of students.

What Does the Research Show?

The list of recommendations presented below is based on scientific studies of students in grades 4–12. The strategies for teaching writing are listed according to the magnitude of their effects. Practices with the strongest effects are listed first. However, the effects of some writing interventions differ minimally from the effects of others. Therefore, one should not assume that only the first several strategies should be implemented. All of the strategies are potentially useful, and we encourage teachers to use a combination of strategies to best meet the needs of their students.

Evidence of the effectiveness of each strategy or technique was compiled from research studies that met several criteria. First, a recommendation was not made unless there was a minimum of four studies that showed the effectiveness of a writing intervention. Second, in each study reviewed, the performance of one group of students was compared to the performance of another group of students receiving a different writing intervention or no intervention at all. This permitted conclusions that each intervention listed below resulted in better writing performance than other writing strategies or typical writing teaching in the classroom. Third, each study was reviewed to ensure it met standards for research quality and that study results were reliable (reducing the chance that error in assessment contributed to the results). Fourth, studies were only included if students' overall writing quality was assessed post-intervention. This criterion was used to identify strategies that had a broad impact on writing performance, as opposed to those with a more limited impact on a specific aspect of writing such as spelling or vocabulary.

Effective Writing Practices

- Writing strategies: Explicitly teach students strategies for planning, revising, and editing their written products. This may involve teaching general processes (e.g., brainstorming or editing) or more speci?c elements, such as steps for writing a persuasive essay. In either case, we recommend that teachers model the strategy, provide assistance as students practice using the strategy on their own, and allow for independent practice with the strategy once they have learned it.

- Summarizing text: Explicitly teach students procedures for summarizing what they read. Summarization allows students to practice concise, clear writing to convey an accurate message of the main ideas in a text. Teaching summary writing can involve explicit strategies for producing effective summaries or gradual fading of models of a good summary as students become more proficient with the skill.
- Collaborative writing: Allow students to work together to plan, write, edit, and revise their writing. We recommend that teachers provide a structure for cooperative writing and explicit expectations for individual performance within their cooperative groups or partnerships. For example, if the class is working on using descriptive adjectives in their compositions, one student could be assigned to review another's writing. He or she could provide positive feedback, noting several instances of using descriptive vocabulary, and provide constructive feedback, identifying several sentences that could be enhanced with additional adjectives. After this, the students could switch roles and repeat the process.
- Goals: Set specific goals for the writing assignments that students are to complete. The goals can be established by the teacher or created by the class themselves, with review from the teacher to ensure they are appropriate and attainable. Goals can include (but are not limited to) adding more ideas to a paper or including specific elements of a writing genre (e.g., in an opinion essay include at least three reasons supporting your belief). Setting specific product goals can foster motivation, and teachers can continue to motivate students by providing reinforcement when they reach their goals.
- Word processing: Allow students to use a computer for completing written tasks. With a computer, text can be added, deleted, and moved easily. Furthermore, students can access tools, such as spell check, to enhance their written compositions. As with any technology, teachers should provide guidance on

proper use of the computer and any relevant software before students use the computer to compose independently.

- Sentence combining: Explicitly teach students to write more complex and sophisticated sentences. Sentence combining involves teacher modelling of how to combine two or more related sentences to create a more complex one. Students should be encouraged to apply the sentence construction skills as they write or revise.
- Process writing: Implement flexible, but practical classroom routines that provide students with extended opportunities for practicing the cycle of planning, writing, and reviewing their compositions. The process approach also involves: writing for authentic audiences, personal responsibility for written work, student-to-student interactions throughout the writing process, and self-evaluation of writing.
- Inquiry: Set writing assignments that require use of inquiry skills. Successful inquiry activities include establishing a clear goal for writing (e.g., write a story about conflict in the playground), examination of concrete data using specific strategies (e.g., observation of students arguing in the playground and recording their reactions), and translation of what was learned into one or more compositions.
- Prewriting: Engage students in activities prior to writing that help them produce and organize their ideas. Prewriting can involve tasks that encourage students to access what they already know, do research about a topic they are not familiar with, or arrange their ideas visually (e.g., graphic organizer) before writing.
- Models: Provide students with good models of the type of writing they are expected to produce. Teachers should analyze the models with their class, encouraging students to imitate in their own writing the critical and effective elements shown in the models.

What we Know

- Evidence-based practices for teaching writing include:
- Teaching strategies for planning, revising, and editing
- Having students write summaries of texts
- Permitting students to write collaboratively with peers
- Setting goals for student writing

- Allowing students to use a word processor
- Teaching sentence combining skills
- Using the process writing approach
- Having students participate in inquiry activities for writing
- Involving students in prewriting activities
- Providing models of good writing

Additional Suggestions

With any combination of teaching strategies a teacher chooses to use, students must be given ample time to write. Writing cannot be a subject that is short-changed or glossed over due to time constraints. Moreover, for weaker writers, additional time, individualized support, and explicit teaching of transcription skills (i.e., handwriting, spelling, typing) may be necessary. For all students, teachers should promote the development of self-regulation skills. Having students set goals for their writing and learning, monitoring and evaluating their success in meeting these goals, and self-reinforcing their learning and writing efforts puts them in charge, increasing independence and efficacy.

Teachers should supplement their current writing practices and curricula with a combination of evidence-based practices that best meets the needs of their students.

A Combination of Effective Writing Practices

No single strategy for teaching writing will prove effective for all students. Furthermore, the above strategies do not constitute a writing curriculum. Teachers should aim to supplement their current writing practices and curricula with a mix of the aforementioned evidence-based writing practices. The optimal mixture of practices should be tailored to best meet the writing needs of the class, as well as the needs of individual students. It is especially important to monitor the success of each technique implemented to be sure that it is working as intended, and to make adjustments as needed.

Writing Teaching Strategies

Affinity Diagram

The affinity diagram is a business tool used to organize ideas and data. It is one of the Seven Management and Planning Tools. The tool is commonly used within project management and allows large numbers of ideas stemming from brainstorming to be sorted into groups, based on their natural relationships, for review and analysis. It is also frequently used in contextual inquiry as a way to organize notes and insights from field interviews. It can also be used for organizing other freeform comments, such as open-ended survey responses, support call logs, or other qualitative data.

People have been grouping data into groups based on natural relationships for thousands of years; however the term affinity diagram was devised by Jiro Kawakita in the 1960s and is sometimes referred to as the KJ Method.

Process

1. Record each idea on cards or notes.
2. Look for ideas that seem to be related.
3. Sort cards into groups until all cards have been used.

Once the cards have been sorted into groups the team may sort large clusters into subgroups for easier management and analysis. Once completed, the affinity diagram may be used to create a cause and effect diagram. In many cases, the best results tend to be achieved when the activity is completed by a cross-functional team, including key stakeholders. The process requires becoming deeply immersed in the data, which has benefits beyond the tangible deliverables.

Biopoems

Bio-Poems can be used at the beginning of school as an opening activity for the first week of school. They can also be used anytime throughout the year when introductions are necessary (e.g. change of semester class, new students, etc.). This activity ensures success and builds self-esteem.

A Biopoem is a poem that describes a person in 11 lines. There is a specific formula to use when writing a bio poem.

(First name)-

(Four adjectives that describe the person)

Son or Daughter of (your parents names)

Lover of (three different things that the person loves)

Who feels (three different feelings and when or where they are felt)

Who gives (three different things the person gives)

Who fears (three different fears the person has)

Who would like to see (three different things the person would like to see)

Who lives (a brief description of where the person lives)

-(last name)

For Example:

Darice

Adventurous, curious, earthy, and caring

Daughter of Marge and Seth

Lover of climbing, fishing, biking

Who feels relaxed with friends, happy on holidays, and energetic when outdoors

Who gives love, patience, and encouragement

Who fears large exams, big black hairy spiders, and mice

Who would like to see Alaska, the Black Sea,and India.

Who lives in Chicago, Illinois

Ali

6

Book Clubs and Peer Discussion Groups

Book clubs – groups of readers who meet on a regular basis to discuss books – appeal to readers because they combine book discussions with an opportunity to engage with reading peers. Vibrant online reading communities connect readers around the world. Students involved in positive reading experiences such as book clubs report more motivation and interest in reading both inside and outside of school. Book clubs provide avid readers a community of other readers who share their enthusiasm, while the social nature of book clubs can engage developing readers who lack positive reading experiences.

Cause and Effect Chain

This strategy helps students recognize cause and effect relationships. The cause and effect chain may be used to look at a series of events that are a result of one another or are caused by one another, like a chain reaction. The cause and effect chain graphic organizer reinforces the idea that each CAUSE brings about a related EFFECT, that in turn each EFFECT becomes a

CAUSE for the next effect, and that all CAUSES lead to the final EFFECT. The example of a trail of dominoes being knocked over often helps students visualize this relationship. If one domino does not fall, the final effect will change.

1. Distribute the Cause and Effect Chain graphic organizer.
2. Students begin the chain by writing the initial cause in the first box labeled "C." Students continue filling in effects and causes until the chain is complete.

3. Students may be directed to enter signal words on the lines provided between the boxes

Clustering

Clustering is similar to another process called Brainstorming. Clustering is something that you can do on your own or with friends or classmates to try to find inspiration in the connection between ideas. The process is similar to freewriting in that as you jot down ideas on a piece of paper or on the blackboard, you mustn't allow that ugly self-censor to intrude and say that your idea (or anyone else's) is dumb or useless. Write it down anyway. In Clustering, you jot down only words or very short phrases. Use different colored pens as ideas seem to suggest themselves in groups. Use printing or longhand script to suggest that ideas are main thoughts or supportive ideas. Don't bother to organize too neatly, though, because that can impede the flow of ideas. Don't cross anything out because you can't tell where an idea will lead you. When you get a few ideas written down, you can start to group them, using colored circles or whatever. Draw linking lines as connections suggest themselves.

Below is a finished example of Clustering. It is printed here with permission of the aforementioned Thruston Parry. The assignment was to write a Cause and Effect Paper on the weather phenomenon known as El Niño. If you have a very fast modem connection or you're working in a computer lab, you can click HERE or on the image below for an animated sequence showing how the clustering might have happened. (A large image file —532 kb — is involved, and we don't encourage you to download it without a fast connection; if the download stalls, you can return to this page by clicking on the RETURN link below the image, or you can click on STOP and then BACK.)

Points to Ponder:

- Do you think you could write an essay based on the ideas clustered here?
- Can you draw additional links between concepts?
- Are there ideas listed above that you'd reject as irrelevant or too much to deal with?
- Can you think of some ideas (or a whole set of ideas) that should have been included but weren't?
- What about the *causes* of El Niño? Should they be included in this essay?

- Can you come up with a Thesis Statement that would be appropriate for an essay based on this clustering of ideas?

Creating a Classroom Magazine

Classroom Magazines are often overlooked and under-utilized as a valuable resource in an effective reading program. Here's how to make the best use of this source of high-interest non-fiction text across the curriculum!

Multiple Readings

Usually, these magazines are a one-time read-through, and then they are sent home. You can get more "bang for your buck" if they are used multiple times for different reasons. In my classroom, my students keep their individual copy in a folder. This way they are easily accessible to the children when needed. I also keep laminated copies (of current and past issues) in a browsing box that is located in my classroom library. Students can read and reread their magazines during independent reading or they can be used during a guided reading session to demonstrate a strategy.

Using Snippets and Lifting the Text

Classroom magazines are a great piece of high-interest nonfiction text that is written on a level accessible to your students. Often I used to find myself searching for this type of short text to share with my students on the overhead to quickly and effectively demonstrate a strategy or a skill, without getting lost in the length of the text. I also found it difficult to find well-written nonfiction that wasn't too far above my students. By "lifting" the text from the classroom magazines, I no longer waste time searching for pieces of such text.

Comprehension Strategies Lessons

The lessons that follow are examples of comprehension strategies and writing lessons. The lessons are numbered for organizational purposes only. They are not meant to be taught one directly after another. In Debbie Miller's book *Reading With Meaning*, she cites an article written by David Pearson (and researchers Dole, Duffy, and Roehler.) From that article, "Developing Expertise in Reading Comprehension: What Should be Taught and How Should It Be Taught?" Debbie summarizes that "Teachers need to teach strategies explicitly and for surprisingly long periods of time, using well-written literature and nonfiction." Teaching this way works well when using the Reader's Workshop Approach. More information about Reader's

Workshop and explicit strategy instruction can be found in two wonderful books: *Strategies That Work* by Stephanie Harvey and Anne Goudvis and *Reading With Meaning* by Debbie Miller.

Activating-Building-Revising Schema

Classroom magazines are a wonderful way to supplement your science and social studies curriculum with current up-to-date information. It also helps students understand how to activate, build, and revise their schema. Schema is what you already know. Before reading an article, have students "activate" their schema by talking about what they already know about the subject.

Record this information on a chart. Tell the students that they are going to build their schema by reading the article. After reading, record new information that they have now built into their schema. Then tell the students that they are going to "revise" their schema, by going back and crossing off any information that was incorrectly activated at the beginning.

Questioning

Explain to students that we naturally have many questions that we ask because we want to better understand topics. Using a classroom magazine article, model first how you would read and ask many questions.

Choose another article to be read with the students. Plan for several stopping points throughout the article for students to stop and tell a partner or group questions that they are wondering so far. Lastly, have the students read an article independently and record their questions on sticky notes. You may want to have the students come together as a group to share their questions.

Visualizing

When reading nonfiction texts, students will encounter the text feature of comparisons or similes. Explain to your students that nonfiction writers use these to help you get a better understanding or visual of what they are trying to convey. For example, instead of saying that the Goliath spider is 7 inches in diameter, students would be able to picture how big they are if they were being compared with something they are familiar with, such as a dinner plate.

Give students examples of comparisons and have them illustrate by visualizing. Then, use your Time For Kids magazine to search for examples of comparisons.

Inferring

Inference is a strategy that naturally goes hand in hand with science and social studies. When teaching inference the important thing for students to understand is that we take what we already know (our background knowledge and schema) and put it with clues from the text to make a good inference. To practice inferring, it's good to start simple with riddles. Give the students short Who Am I? or What Am I? riddles to solve. After they solve the riddle, have them highlight the clues that helped them figure it out. Once they become comfortable with inferring, choose a classroom magazine article to read. Model how you can take the information that you gained to create your own riddle for someone else to solve. Then read a new article together and have your students try to write their own.

Students can also apply the strategy during independent reading. As they read an article they can make inferences and record them on sticky notes. During a sharing time, students can then share their inferences.

Determining Importance/summarizing with Poetry

Use *Time for Kids* to create a poem that actually hones in on the skills of summarizing and determining importance. The article, Animals on the Move, was used to model how to create a poem by using the most important details. Read the article with the students. After each section ask them to use a few words or a sentence to tell mainly what each section was about or what was most important about the section.

The Steps

Identify a Strategy worth Teaching

Identifying strategies worth teaching means looking for strategies that will be genuinely helpful. In the case of struggling writers, strategies worth teaching are the ones which will help them overcome their writing difficulties. In our research we have decided that the best way to identify such strategies is by talking with struggling writers, asking them about how they write, what they think about while writing, and what they see as difficulties. Additional insight can be gained by studying student papers to infer where writers are having difficulty and by observing writers at work.

Introduce the Strategy by Modelling it.

Introducing strategies by modelling them generally means some form of composing out loud in front of students. Many of the teachers in our studies prefer to do this for groups or whole classes by writing at an overhead projector. They speak their thoughts while writing, calling particular attention to the strategy they are recommending for students. Sometimes they ask students to contribute to the writing the teacher is doing, to copy the writing for themselves, or to compose a similar piece of writing in connection with the writing the teacher is doing. Teachers in our studies also frequently model writing strategies during individual conferences with students.

Scaffold Students' Learning of the Strategy.

Scaffolding the learning of a writing strategy means helping students to try the strategy with teacher assistance. This is best done in a writing workshop. The workshop setting is ideal for giving varying degrees of assistance according to individual needs. It is also ideal for conferring with individuals and for setting up partnerships and peer groups so that students can assist each other in the learning of strategies. Even when a writing workshop is not used, some amount of in-class writing with teacher assistance is necessary to make sure that writers practice using the strategy being taught.

Repeated Practice and Reinforcement.

Helping students to work toward independent mastery of the strategy through repeated practice and reinforcement means giving them opportunities to use the strategy many times with decreasing amounts of assistance each time. The idea here is that it is better to teach a few key writing strategies well than it is to teach many of them insufficiently. Students value and master the things we have them do repeatedly. In a way, this gets back to identifying strategies worth teaching — look for ones that are crucial to writing processes, such as strategies for planning particular types of writing, or for structuring texts certain ways. Then model, practice and repeat.

Monitoring and Evaluating Student Learning

Monitoring competence or self-monitoring can be described as awareness of what one knows. A high level of monitoring competence means one can make accurate assessments of one's skill or knowledge, while a low level means the opposite. The body of educational research literature which has come to be known as the effective schooling research identifies the practice of monitoring student learning as an essential component of high-quality education. The careful monitoring of student progress is shown in the literature to be one of the major factors differentiating effective schools and teachers from ineffective ones.

Indeed, those analyses which have sought to determine the relative effect sizes of different instructional practices have identified monitoring student progress as a strong predictor of student achievement. What does "monitoring student learning" involve?

The American Heritage dictionary defines monitoring as KEEPING WATCH OVER; SUPERVISING and also gives another more specific meaning: To Scrutinize Or Check Systematically With A View To Collecting Certain Specified Categories Of Data.

As the term is used in educational settings, monitoring takes in both these meanings and is closely connected with the related functions of record keeping, reporting, and decision making.

Definition

For our purposes here we shall define monitoring as activities pursued by teachers to keep track of student learning for purposes of making instructional decisions and providing feedback to students on their progress.

When educators speak of classroom monitoring, they generally refer to the following teacher behaviors: Questioning students during classroom discussions to check their understanding of the material being taught. Circulating around the classroom during seatwork and engaging in one-to-one contacts with students about their work. Assigning, collecting, and correcting homework; recording completion and grades. Conducting periodic reviews with students to confirm their grasp of learning material and identify gaps in their knowledge and understanding

Administering and correcting tests; recording scores. Reviewing student performance data collected and recorded and using these data to make needed adjustments in instruction. Defined this way, monitoring obviously includes many kinds of activities, but it is important to note that the present analysis does not address issues relating to schoolwide or district-level monitoring of student learning. It is not concerned, except incidentally, with monitoring students' behaviour. And it provides only cursory information on such matters as teacher training in monitoring and assessment practices or the processes teachers follow in putting monitoring information to use.

Instead, the focus here is classroom-level monitoring of student learning progress and what research says about the relationships between such monitoring and the student outcomes of achievement, attitudes and social behaviour.

The Research on Monitoring Student Learning

Several dozen documents were reviewed in preparation for this report. Of these, 23 are studies or reviews which clearly indicate a relationship between one or more forms of monitoring student learning and student outcomes—usually achievement. Fifteen documents are reviews and eight are studies. Five involve elementary students, three involve secondary students, and fifteen are concerned with the entire K-12 range. Fourteen have general achievement as the dependent variable. Language arts is the outcome focus of three documents. Others include: mathematics—3, science—2, social studies—1, and student attitudes—5. Some investigations were concerned with more than one outcome area. Nineteen of the studies concern regular education students of various races, socioeconomic groups, and ability levels.

Three have special education subjects, and one focuses on Chapter 1 participants. Of the kinds of monitoring functions investigated, teacher questioning to check student understanding is the focus of three reports. Others include: monitoring seat work4, assigning/collecting/grading homework—2, conducting periodic reviews in class—2, formative testing—2, and reviewing records—3.

Nine of the reports focused on two or more of these functions. Findings pertaining to each of these kinds of classroom monitoring—and to monitoring in general—are cited in the sections which follow.

Questioning and Other Learning Probes

The term "learning probe" refers to a variety of ways that teachers can ask for brief student responses to lesson content so as to determine their understanding of what is being taught. Questions to the class, quizzes, and other means of calling upon students to demonstrate their understanding are methods used by teachers to find out if their instruction is "working" or if it needs to be adjusted in some way.

Does the use of learning probes have a beneficial effect on student achievement? The research indicates that this approach can indeed produce achievement benefits. Particularly effective techniques include: Keeping questions at an appropriate level of difficulty; that is, at a level where most students can experience a high degree of success in answering. Paying close attention to who is answering questions during classroom discussion and calling upon non volunteers

Asking students to comment or elaborate on one another's answers. Using information on students levels of understanding to increase the pace of instruction whenever appropriate. (There is a strong positive relationship between content covered and student achievement. Monitoring can alert teachers to situations where they can profitably pick up the instructional pace and thus cover more material.)

Monitoring Seatwork

Research comparing the behaviour of effective teachers (i.e., those whose students achieve highly. or higher than would be expected given background variable) with that of less effective teachers has clearly revealed the importance of monitoring the class during seatwork periods. Such monitoring involves teachers moving around the classroom, being aware of how well or poorly students are progressing with their assignments, and working with students one-to-one as needed.

The most effective teachers:

- Have systematic procedures for supervising and encouraging students while they work.
- Initiate more interactions with students during seatwork periods, rather than waiting for students to ask for help
- Have more substantive interactions with students during seatwork monitoring, stay task- oriented, and work through problems with students.
- Give extra time and attention to students they believe need extra help.
- Stress careful and consistent checking of assignments and require that these be turned in

Monitoring Homework

The assignment of homework, like many educational practices, can be beneficial, neutral, or detrimental depending upon he nature and context of the homework tasks.

The use of homework assignments bears a significant and positive relationship to achievement when the homework is carefully monitored, as well as serving the function of increasing students' learning time.

- Homework confers the most beneficial results when assignments are:
- Closely tied to the subject matter currently being studied in the classroom
- Given frequently as a means of extending student practice time with new material

- Appropriate to the ability and maturity levels of students
- Clearly understood by students and parents
- Monitored by parents; i.e., when parents are aware of what needs to be done and encourage homework completion
- Quickly checked and returned to students
- Graded and commented on
- The research also indicates that homework which meets these criteria is positively related to student attitudes.

Students may say they don't like homework, but research shows that those who are assigned regular homework have more positive attitudes toward school, toward the particular subject areas in which homework is assigned, and toward homework itself, than students who have little or no homework. the research also indicates that homework which meets these criteria is positively related to student attitudes.

Students may say they don't like homework, but research shows that those who are assigned regular homework have more positive attitudes toward school, toward the particular subject areas in which homework is assigned, and toward homework itself, than students who have little or no homework.

Monitoring As A Part of Classroom Reviews

Research has established a link between integrating monitoring methods into periodic classroom reviews and the later achievement of students involved in the review sessions. Daily, weekly, and monthly reviews can all enhance the learning of new material and, if they incorporate questioning and other learning probes, can call attention to areas where reteaching is needed. The effectiveness of using review sessions to monitor student learning is clearly revealed in the research on the effects of teacher training: teachers trained in methods for conducting periodic classroom reviews which include the use of learning probes had students whose achievement was higher than it was before the teachers had been trained and higher than the achievement of students of untrained teachers.

In addition, including monitoring activities in periodic reviews is a built-in feature of such successful programs as Distar and the Exemplary Centre for Reading instruction (ECRI) system, as well as being a function carried out by the effective teachers in several comparative observational studies.

Classroom Testing

Those who study assessment and evaluation techniques are quick to point out that the role of standardized testing has received considerably more research attention than have classroom testing and other classroom-level assessment methods. The existing research does indicate, however, that well-designed classroom testing programs bear a positive relationship to later student achievement.

Beneficial effects are noted when tests are: Administered regularly and frequently An integral part of the instructional approach (i.e., well-aligned with the material being taught) Collected, scored, recorded and returned to students promptly so that they can correct errors of understanding before these become ingrained

When attitudes toward testing are studied, students who are tested frequently and given feedback are found to have positive attitudes toward tests.

They are generally found to regard tests as facilitating learning and studying, and as providing effective feedback—an outcome which has surprised some researchers, who had anticipated finding more negative student attitudes toward testing.

Reviewing Student Performance Data

While it is beyond the scope of this paper to describe the various systems teachers can use for recording and interpreting student performance data, it is worthwhile to note the importance of having and using such a system. Research comparing effective and ineffective teachers cites the existence and use of a systematic procedure for keeping and interpreting data on student performance as a notable difference between these groups.

Monitoring Methods Used In Combination

Research findings on the discrete effects of various classroom monitoring methods comprise only part of the story of applying classroom monitoring techniques. Research also indicates that using these methods in combination is superior to using only one or two of them. One researcher identifies five of the six monitoring methods above in his list of effective teaching behaviors. Another cites all of them as important components of a student accountability system. And in the comparative research on effective and ineffective teachers, the effective teachers were found to have implemented all or most of these monitoring functions in their classrooms.

Common Elements Across Monitoring Methods

Looking at the range of research on monitoring student learning, several attributes of effective monitoring are cited repeatedly across the different investigations:

Setting High Standards.

When students' work is monitored in relation to high standards, student effort and achievement increase. Researchers caution, however, that standards must not be set so high that students perceive them as unattainable; if they do, effort and achievement decrease.

The definition of "high standards" differs across studies, but generally, researchers indicate that students should be able to experience a high degree of success (on assignments, during classroom questioning, etc.) while continually being challenged with new and more complex material.

Holding Students Accountable For Their Work: Establishing expectations and guidelines for students' seatwork, homework, and other functions and following through with rewards/sanctions facilitates learning and enhances achievement.

Frequency and Regularity: Whether the topic is teacher monitoring of seatwork, administration of tests, checking homework, or conducting reviews, researchers cite frequency and regularity in carrying out monitoring activities as a major reason they are effective.

Clarity

Clarity about expectations, formats, and other aspects of direction-giving bears a positive relationship to the achievement of the students doing the homework, participating in the classroom questioning session, etc.

Collecting, Scoring, and Recording Results of Classwork,

Homework, Tests, and So On: These activities are positively related to achievement, because they produce useful information to teachers and students and because they communicate to students that teachers are serious about effort and completion of assignments.

Feedback: Providing feedback to students lets them know how they are doing and helps them to correct errors of understanding and fill in gaps in knowledge. Some researchers focus on the ways in which feedback is provided, pointing out that students who are having learning difficulties require support, encouragement, and attention to their success if the feedback is to foster achievement of learning goals.

Teachers' Skills in Monitoring Student Learning

Given the strong connection between teachers' monitoring of students' learning progress and those students' academic performance, it would be ideal if teachers received thorough training in monitoring and were highly skilled in classroom monitoring practices. Unfortunately, this is not the case.

The Eesearch on Classroom-level Monitoring and Assessment Reveals That: While standardized achievement test results are the main focus of assessment/evaluation efforts, nearly all important decisions about student placement, instructional pacing and so on are made on the basis of teachers' ongoing classroom monitoring.

Many Teachers do Not: assign homework frequently or regularly, record completion assignments, monitor seatwork and check on students' progress, or conduct the kind of questioning that helps to monitor learning.

Teachers do not receive adequate pre-service training in conducting formal or informal assessments. Administrative support for and inservice training in the skills associated with assessment and monitoring are extremely inadequate. Many teachers are aware that their monitoring skills are inadequate and desire training to expand their capabilities; many others are unaware of the importance of close monitoring of student progress and of their own need for skill development in this area.

The research on teachers' decision-making processes confirms this lack of monitoring on the part of many teachers. According to this research, a great many teachers are reluctant to make. changes in the instructional strategy or pacing of lessons once these are planned, even when instruction and learning are progressing poorly. To a considerable degree, this improves with experience.

Experienced teachers are found to vary teaching strategies in response to student. performance cues much more than do novices. Still, monitoring/assessment skills remain an area of inadequate preparation for many teachers.

Effective Monitoring Practices

Since there are so many methods of monitoring student learning, descriptions of only a few will be given here. These are offered as examples of approaches used by successful teachers. Using learning probes is the subject of the following question-and-answer exchange with practitioners (Excerpted from EDUCATIONAL PSYCHOLOGY:

Theory Into Practice by Robert E. Slavin. Englewood Cliffs, NJ: Prentice-Hall, 1986) How do you monitor students' comprehension and work during a lesson? Teachers say they monitor students by: Asking them to interpret or summarize material presented to them in the lesson.

Thinking about the questions that students are asking and noting what parts of the lesson don't seem to be understood. Asking questions from various levels of Bloom's taxonomy of learning objective. Asking students to act things out or draw them.

Walking around the class and checking worksheets, calling attention to errors and noting good work being done having students do quick problems on individual chalkboards encouraging children to listen to each other by summarizing comments of others and calling on children who don't seem to be listening.

In the following paragraphs, a researcher reports on the differences between the monitoring behaviors of effective and less effective junior high school English and mathematics teachers. (Excerpted from STUDENT.

Accountability For Written Work in Junior

HIGH SCHOOL CLASSES by Murray E. Worshan. Austin, TX: Research and Development Centre for Teacher Education, 1981. (ED 203 387)) Both effective English and math teachers were extremely consistent in efficient monitoring techniques. They did more than just circulate among students during seatwork periods. these teachers were systematic in noting individual students while moving or looking around the classroom, and they addressed individuals frequently, usually privately, to keep students accountable and on-task.

These teachers were concerned that students work steadily on classwork as well as on tests, and their careful monitoring enabled them to address students immediately who were not working as expected. The nature and process of effective monitoring—of both behaviour and academic work— appeared to be highly salient in both math and English classes to keeping students on-task and responsible for their work.

More effective math and English teachers were extremely consistent in checking assignments regularly. Homework was assigned virtually every day, and a daily routine in most teachers' classes involved students' exchanging papers and checking them in class as directed by the teacher.

Usually the more effective teachers had students sign papers they graded, and at least one effective math teacher cautioned her students to grade papers with care. Two key actions on the part of the more effective teachers in both math and English classes followed the checking period. First, these teachers asked students for their grades and recorded them immediately as the class watched and listened.

Next, these teachers always took up papers to check themselves. They were thus holding students accountable for doing their work, for doing it well, and for checking it accurately. A further step noted in classes of several more effective math teachers was their individually questioning students who made low grades or zeros.

These teachers determined whether students were having difficulty and needed extra help or were not doing their assignments at all. These teachers told students that they noted such grades resulting from lack of effort in their garde book. When checking daily assignments in class, more effective math and English teachers provided feedback to students as to content as well as a review or further explanation of concepts and processes.

By explaining how to figure grades and having grades announced for recording purposes, teachers enabled students to hear how they stood in relation to the rest of the class and gave evidence of the fact that the teachers took seriously the work they assigned. By taking up, checking, and returning papers, teachers provided additional feedback by means of written comments and possible modification on student grading.

The advisability of using these effective monitoring practices is further underscored in the following guidelines concerning seat work and homework. (Excerpted from "Teacher behaviour and Student Achievement," by Jere E. Brophy and

Thomas L. Good. In Handbook of Research on Teaching (Third Ed.), edited by Merlin C. Wittrock.

New York: Macmillan Publishing Co., 1985) . . .seat work (and homework) assignments provide needed practice and application opportunities. Ideally, such assignments will be varied and interesting enough to motivate student engagement, new or challenging enough to constitute meaningful learning experiences rather than pointless busywork, and yet easy enough to allow success with reasonable effort. . . . Student success rates, and the effectiveness of seat work assignments generally, are enhanced when teachers explain the work and go over practice examples with the students before releasing them to work independently. Furthermore, once the students are released to work independently, the work goes more smoothly if the teacher (or an aide) circulate to monitor progress and provide help when needed. If the work has been well chosen and well explained, most of these "Helping" interactions will be brief, and at any given time, most students will be progressing smoothly through the assignment rather than waiting for help. Students should know what work they are accountable for, how to get help when they need it, and what to do when they finish.

Performance should be monitored for completion and accuracy, and students should receive timely and specific feedback. When the whole class or group has the same assignment, review of the assignment can be part of the next day's lesson. Other assignments will require more individualized feedback. Where performance is poor, teachers should provide not only feedback but reteaching and follow-up assignments designed to insure that the material is mastered.

Teacher competence in assessing students' skill levels and monitoring their learning progress is essential for effective instruction to take place. "Imagine," writes researcher Robert Slavin," an archer who shoots an arrow at a target but never finds out how close to the bull's-eye the arrows fall.

The archer wouldn't be very accurate to begin with, and would certainly never improve in accuracy. Similarly, effective teaching requires that teachers be constantly aware of the effects of their instruction." Improvements in preservice and inservice training in assessment and monitoring skills can both increase teachers' awareness of these effects and help them to make instructional changes as called for by the information they collect. This is vital for, as noted by writers Howell and McCollum-Gahley, "the most important part of continuous monitoring is not taking data, but making decisions

Monitoring, Evaluating and Reporting on Underachievement

Monitoring, evaluating and reporting student outcomes and programme effectiveness are key elements in a school's management of students at risk of not achieving. These processes are critical for the way information about progress is gathered and analysed and for the use made of this information to raise achievement levels and improve outcomes.

Overall, ERO found that schools were far less effective at monitoring, evaluating and reporting the outcomes for students at risk of not achieving than they were at identifying them or implementing programmes to support them.

Use of Achievement Information

Senior managers, teachers and staff varied in their ability to use achievement information to identify learning needs and to plan appropriate interventions. Schools were generally more able at gathering and collating student achievement information than they were at interpreting the results and determining which intervention would benefit individual students.

ERO did find examples of achievement information being used well to support students at risk of not achieving. These included principals and senior staff:

- setting meaningful targets to raise the achievement of at-risk students, particularly in reading and mathematics;
- helping teachers develop and resource effective classroom programmes matched to the needs of at-risk students;
- identifying the most effective support personnel to address the needs of these students based on assessment data;
- informing trustees about the best way of resourcing provision for students at risk of not achieving; and
- focusing primarily on student achievement as part of the annual planning cycle and decision-making processes.

Achievement information was used most effectively when school boards and senior managers were able to use the data to set school priorities and develop plans for reaching targets related to low achievement. In the best instances boards and managers saw the quality of teaching based on sound assessment as more important than the purchase and use of externally developed programme packages.

In one urban, decile 4 secondary school, addressing underachievement was a school-wide focus based on the analysis of achievement information. The analysis of achievement information helped the board to understand that there were specific literacy issues at the school. In light of this information, the board, principal and teachers developed a shared commitment to ensuring that low achievement in literacy was addressed. The school's charter plans, and strategic and annual plans were specifically devoted to improving levels of literacy at the school.

The strategic plan set goals and directions related to school-wide literacy achievement. The annual plan identified specific objectives for improving literacy and student achievement especially at the classroom level. All school planning clearly set out required actions, people responsible, timelines for completion and expected outcomes.

Monitoring and Evaluating Underachievement Initiatives

In just under half the schools reviewed, ERO found that schools had yet to evaluate the extent to which their programmes resulted in improved outcomes for at-risk students. This finding was consistent with ERO's 2007 report *The Collection and Use of Assessment Information in Schools* which also noted that assessment data needed to be better analysed to identify students' learning needs and to provide more useful, timely information for school reports.

Monitoring and evaluation of school initiatives should be outcomes based. It must ask and answer the question about what difference programmes or interventions have made to students' learning. Monitoring and evaluation should also consider other associated factors such as the effectiveness of the teaching strategies employed, the efficacy of links between what is being taught and learnt in withdrawal programmes and classroom programmes, and whether or not the board's investment in particular programmes or initiatives is yielding the benefits expected for the students they serve.

Most schools use commercially produced readymade learning materials to support instruction or as part of an intervention programme. Where this is the case senior managers should monitor the effectiveness of these packages in meeting the learning needs of individuals or groups of students. The Ministry of Education has produced a set of guidelines for integrating readymade packages into teaching programmes. These guidelines are based on research that identifies effective teacher practice for integrating commercially produced readymade learning materials into classrooms to meet students' learning needs. The research focused on practice related to the use of literacy packages but the findings could well influence school choices in other curriculum areas. These guidelines form a useful tool for school monitoring and review.

Sound monitoring and evaluation evidence can lead to revised views about the worth of a programme. Teachers in one school used achievement data to confirm that a reading programme they were using was not helpful in improving students' achievement levels. The programme was discontinued. In this instance the school put the students first by using internal evaluation to good effect. The following examples show the effective use of monitoring and evaluation practices when considering student achievement.

In a small decile 1 primary school, the school made achievement matters visible. They analysed student achievement information and discussed it with all staff to raise awareness of issues that needed to be addressed. Collated trends from the year were recorded on a graph (carefully ensuring there were no student names) so all teachers, support staff, even visitors to the staff room, were aware of how the school was confronting achievement issues, and the progress they were making to address these matters.

In an urban, decile 8 school, the teachers found through standardised testing that students' inferential reading skills were unacceptably low and had been for a while. They realised that something needed to be done and set about modifying their teaching practice to improve these levels.

In a small, semi-rural, decile 2 primary school, the principal and teacher in charge of reading programmes discovered that the students' reading levels across the school had not met expectations. They reported this to trustees, who recognised that programmes needed to change. As a result the board approved the release of the deputy principal to support teachers in improving levels of reading achievement as part of classroom teaching.

What is Important

Good classroom assessment and teaching is the first point of intervention for most students at risk of not achieving. Student achievement information is of most use when senior leaders and classroom teachers use data analyses to identify the particular learning needs of students and to determine what will work best to improve achievement for individuals or groups of students.

Sound monitoring and evaluation is important in determining the effectiveness of class and school-based interventions, programmes and initiatives. Evidence from well-structured monitoring and evaluation can provide school leaders and trustees with valuable information about what interventions work best for students and whether they need to decide on other options. Without outcomes-based information valuable time and resources can be lost for supporting the needs of students at risk of not achieving.

Effective Use of Staffing

Schools used a variety of approaches for employing teachers or additional staffing to assist students at risk of not achieving.

ERO found that boards and schools generally had a limited knowledge of the impact of additional staffing on improving the achievement of at-risk students. Schools need to know that staff are being used in the most effective way to meet the targets they have set, and to be assured that this resource is used to support educational outcomes. The rationale for employing additional staff should be carefully thought through as part of an overall staffing strategy for the school. For boards, principals and senior leaders, asking which staff member or combinations of staff will be most effective in meeting the needs of students is a critical first step.

In this evaluation, schools found different ways to resource their programmes and interventions. They had to attract qualified teachers and teacher aides as part of meeting their programme commitments and, in some cases, the successful implementation of support programmes depended on the availability of suitable staff. Where schools stressed the importance of effective classroom teaching as the first point of intervention, most used teacher aides as support personnel for the teacher. In other instances schools chose to withdraw students and the resource required to set up and sustain initiatives for a small number of students led to some improvisation in the use of staffing. In smaller schools, the principal often provided additional regular support by teaching small groups of at-risk students. In larger primary schools, the deputy and assistant principals often ran such programmes.

Boards often employed additional staff to work with groups or individual students. In most schools, additional staffing was met through teacher aides. These staff were appointed to operate particular programmes under the supervision of a teacher or, in some cases, to reduce class sizes. Teacher aides took on a range of roles in the school's overall provision for students.

Good practice involved training teacher aides for their specific roles. Training was usually ongoing and was done under the supervision of the SENCO or teacher-in-charge. Sometimes an RTLB from the local school cluster trained them or they attended specific training sessions provided by advisory staff. Teacher aides particularly benefited training by RTLB. This was usually done at the school and reinforced on a regular basis with meetings to discuss the effectiveness of their instructional and monitoring strategies.

Teacher aides, who have had relevant training, assist in teaching students under the guidance of the SENCO. They participate in professional development so they can be more effective in assisting students who underachieve or who have English as second language.

Teacher aides work alongside students in classrooms as well as facilitating withdrawal groups. They are well trained in a range of tasks including the use of self-pacing boxes, reading programmes, speech-language programmes and ESOL strategies. Teacher aides are also trained in physiotherapy and specific disability techniques. Some schools preferred to use teacher aides to support more able students as part of the classroom programme. The benefit of this approach was to free the teacher to work with the students most at risk of not achieving. This may be the most effective use of the teacher aide resource given that students at risk of not achieving require high quality, focused teaching.

Reporting to the Board

ERO found that the quality of reporting to the board varied between high quality reports based on student outcome data, to descriptions of activities and programmes with little reference to the progress achieved by students. High quality board reports give trustees essential information for making decisions about the staffing and resourcing of programmes to meet the needs of students at risk of not achieving. They help trustees to understand how effective their school's provision is, and alert them to any emerging trends in school achievement.

Examples of useful board reporting in this evaluation included information about the numbers of students who were at risk of not achieving. Reports informed trustees about systemic or curriculum factors contributing to low achievement, such as the quality of numeracy or literacy programmes or the resourcing to support improved student performance. Effective reports included information about the range and nature of learning support programmes and interventions, and about their impact on student learning. In effective schools, information given to boards was clearly presented and contributed to systematic self-review processes.

In an urban, decile 10 primary school, the board requested reports that tracked student achievement and progress in literacy. The trustees were interested in the effectiveness of the school's work in this area, where improvements were necessary and how they as board members could help.

The school's teaching staff subsequently prepared reports about student literacy including information on reading, oral language, writing and spelling. These included relevant information on student achievement expectations, priority areas for targeting, and the results of testing at the end of the year. They also reviewed the "where to next" aims from the previous year and identified next steps for the following year.

In a small decile 1 primary school, the principal prepared for the board a detailed report on reading, using the results of a standardised test for students in Years 4, 5 and 6. The board was given an explanation of the test, what the results showed and how teachers would use these. The concept of 'stanines' was explained so the board could understand the test results. Results were well presented, giving clear information on the performance of students at each class level, and by ethnicity and gender.

The report indicated the number of children who were achieving below national norms and gave eight recommendations to help address these concerns. The board used these to decide the on the best interventions and resources to raise the achievement of this group of students.

Eight Problems in Indian Education

Historically, three systems have served the educational needs of Indians: Bureau of Indian Affairs schools, parochial or mission schools and public schools. Recently, through the Office of Economic Opportunity, the tribes themselves established a fourth school system, primarily in the Headstart Program.

These systems—still involved in attempting to better the lot of the Indian—have had much experience in providing programs to meet Indians' needs and have been in the business of education on and off reservations for many years. In spite of what they have attempted and of what contributions they have made, acute problems exist in the Indian education field. And Indian education will not progress, develop or evolve into a dynamic field unless the problems inherent in it are identified and solved. In an analysis of the situation, I have categorized these problems into eight broad areas, from "lack of money" to "too many instant Indian experts."

Lack of Money

By far one of the most pressing problems is the unavailability of money or inadequate funding of Indian education programs or systems.

The demand far exceeds the supply, and available monies are only for the most basic educational needs of the students . . . "the traditional curriculum." Very small amounts, if any, are available for innovative programs and ideas. Without adequate funding, the ideology and philosophy of Indian education become so many words. The concept of Indian education faces a bleak future characterized by stagnation, insensitivity, inadequate facilities and personnel. Is this what we educators wish to be contented with?

The irrelevant curricula. just what do we mean by the often-repeated phrase, irrelevant curricula? My definition is that it is schools not doing their job in meeting the needs of their students—especially Indian students. This area encompasses four necessary corrections.

An Indian student presently is subjected to an educational system geared to the needs of the non-Indian student without any concern to unique problems and background of the Indian. Yes, the Indian must live in the white man's world, but if he is to become a productive member of the human race, the schools must develop programs to meet his needs.

The American school curricula stresses values in direct contrast with the values held, in varying degrees, by the Indian. Such highly esteemed values as agressiveness, competition, individual personal gain, out-smarting your fellow man, and verbal ability and agility are taught the non-Indian youngster from the time he is able to comprehend. These values become the foundations of the American educational system. Thus, the Indian student is thrown into a foreign situation—he has no experiential background comparable to it and consequently, retardation is "built into" the educational program as far as the Indian is concerned.

Another aspect is the stress of the English language in the system. If educators would recognize that the English language is not the mother tongue of most Indian students, educational programming could become more relevant, meaningful and rewarding to the Indian student.

If curriculum experts would include courses reflecting the positiveness of the Indians' contributions to the greater society, another correction would be made. It is not difficult to understand why the average Indian student has a negative self-concept: he is taught in a foreign classroom, by a teacher who is literally a foreigner, and in a foreign language that he comes from a people who were bloodthirsty, marauding killers, and that the only good Indian is a dead Indian.

Correct this image by eliminating these teachings, and replacing them with more positive characteristics.

Education has directly contributed to the destruction of the institution of the family among Indians: To illustrate this engulfment rather than bridgment of parent and child, let me give the following example.

Fifth graders are studying the atom or atom bomb and its effect on society as a whole. If the Indian child seeks to understand the concept of the atom more fully in an inquiry at home, he will discover that his parents are unable to help him gain that understanding because there is no concept paralleling the atom in the Indian language. Instead of help or clarification, the child may receive some type of scolding. In the case of the non-Indian child, the parents may not know the answer, but they have other resources to which to turn—a neighbor, a set of reference books, a nearby library. Thus, the Indian child begins to question the intelligence of his parents, and when this happens, the parental role is threatened and weakened. This weakening continues as the child progresses through school because the parent falls further behind, as he is not keeping up with his child. Destruction of the family institution is therefore hastened.

Lack of Qualified Indians in Indian Education.

By far the most glaring problem is the acute shortage of qualified Indians in Indian education. Materialistic gains, incentives and opportunities entice the qualified Indian educator away from this challenging field. There is much hard work and many challenges in Indian education: isolation, poor or inadequate facilities, eager but academically deprived students, but one's ingenuity, creativity, patience and forbearance are put to a real test in facing these and other challenges. If Indian education is to meet the needs of the students, if it is to have the sensitivity required, if it is to be dynamic and viable, it must have more qualified Indian educators—it must reach the stage wherein it will challenge the Indian educator to take up arms to join its ranks and to improve its lot.

Insensitive School Personnel.

It is tragic that this exists in the 20th Century. Too many administrators and teachers are not knowledgeable about the American Indian. Whether it is attributable to apathy, indifference or design does not lessen the problem. If school personnel are truly educators, it behooves them to learn about the people they are teaching: To fail in this task is to fail to educate. The burden of this responsibility rests squarely on the shoulders of the educator, and the exercise of that responsibility is long overdue.

Differing Expectations of Education Programs.

The American educational system is foreign in concept, principle and objective to the Indian student. The thinking, attitudes and experiences of the non-Indian are the base of the value structure rather than the aspects of Indian culture. Thus the educational perspectives of the Indian are not considered. The Indian views education as providing him with immediate practical skills and tools, not a delayed achievement of goals or as means for a future gain.

Lack of Involvement in and Control of Educational Matters.

The Indian has not been able to express his ideas on school programming or educational decision-making. When they have been expressed, his participation has been limited and restricted. If problems in Indian education are to be resolved, the Indian citizen must become involved. He needs to have more control in the programs to which his children are exposed, to have a say in what types of courses are in the curriculum, to help hire teachers, to establish employment policies and practices, and all of the other responsibilities vested in school administration—that of being on a Board of Education. There are working examples of Indian-controlled school boards. These dynamic systems point up the fact that Indians can handle school matters. It is time that more Indians became involved in such control.

Difficulties of Students in Higher Education.

Colleges and universities need to establish programs which can deal effectively with the problems and needs of the Indian student—if he is to remain in school. In general, the Indian student has an inadequate educational background as he may have been looked upon as less than college material in high school. He has unusual adjustment problems and usually inadequate financial help. It is time that more colleges and universities attempt to solve these development factors and provide a more successful educational experience for the Indian student.

Too Many Instant-Indian Education Experts.

To the detriment of Indian education and its growth, each day sprouts more "instant Indian education experts," who do more damage than good. Usually, these experts have all the answers: they have completely identified the problems and have formulated solutions, but they leave it to the Indian to implement. Again, the Indian is given something to implement which he has had no part in formulating. These experts usually depend on superficial, shallow studies done in one visit to a reservation or school, or they depend on one or two conferences with Indians who have little or no knowledge of the critical problems confronting the Indian generally. Indian education can well do without these experts who cannot be reasoned with or who feel they know what is best for the Indian.

There may be other factors which contribute to the problems of Indian education, but these eight areas are, I think, contributing to the situation wherein Indian education is not realizing its full development.

Non-formal Education in Technology

Non-formal learning is a distinction in learning between formal and informal learning. It is learning that occurs in a formal learning environment, but that is not formally recognised. It typically involves workshops, community courses, interest based courses, short courses, or conference style seminars. The learning takes place in a formal setting such as an educational organisation, but is not formally recognised within a curriculum or syllabus framework.

Learning is not restricted to the time spent in school. It begins at birth and continues all your life.

The present pattern in which we have education at the beginning of our lives, then work in one field until an extended retirement period, is changing. Lifelong learning is becoming part of modern life. This is because rapid technological change and growth in information require ongoing learning.

Given the importance of learning foundations, currently those who miss out on basic education suffer exclusion. However, ongoing learning throughout life enables people to take advantage of new opportunities that arise as society changes. It also provides opportunities for those who are unemployed to re-enter the workforce.

Every kind of learning that happens outside the traditional school setting can be called non-formal. However, defining non-formal education is not easy, it has been described variously as an educational movement, a setting, a process and a system.

The projects and programmes implemented under the label of 'non-formal education' are very diverse in scope. What they usually have in common is an organised, systematic, educational activity, carried on outside the framework of the formal education system, to provide different types of learning to particular groups in the population, both adults and children.

Thus non-formal education is different from the institutionalised, chronologically graded and hierarchically structured nature of the formal education system However, the boundaries between formal and non-formal education can sometimes be blurred, especially when certification enters into a non-formal education programme.

Radio, television, computers and the Internet are modern delivery tools for education. However, in low-income communities the cost of these tools and the need for skills in installing, using and maintaining these tools poses obstacles to widespread adoption of computers and the Internet.

One solution has been the establishment of Community Learning Centres (CLCs) and Multimedia Community Telecentres. These centres, many of which are run by the communities themselves, aim to enhance basic education, train teachers, develop local businesses, strengthen municipal administration and civil society organisations, and provide health care information for populations in small villages.

By equipping these centres with ICT tools, these centres provide connectivity and communication mechanisms to all. The debate over the relative value of formal and informal learning has existed for a number of years. Traditionally formal learning that takes place in a school or university and has a greater value placed upon it than informal learning, such as learning within the workplace. This concept of formal learning being the socio-cultural accepted norm for learning was first challenged by Scribner and Cole in 1973, who claimed most things in life are better learnt through informal processes, citing language learning as an example. Moreover, anthropologists noted that complex learning still takes place within indigenous communities that had no formal educational institutions.

It's the acquisition of this knowledge or learning which occurs in everyday life that has not been fully valued or understood. This led to the declaration the by OECD educational ministers of the "life-long learning for all" strategy in 1996. This includes 23 countries from five continents, who have sort to clarify and validate all forms of learning including formal, non-formal and informal. This has been in conjunction with the European Union which has also developed policies for life-long learning which focus strongly on the need to identify, assess and certificate non-formal and informal learning, particularly in the workplace.

***Table:** Countries involved in recognition of non-formal learning (OECD 2010)*

Austria	*Denmark*	*Italy*	*South Africa*
Australia	Germany	Korea	Spain
Belgium	Greece	Malta	Slovenia
Canada	Hungary	Mexico	Switzerland
Chile	Iceland	Netherlands	United Kingdom
Czech Republic	Ireland	Norway	

Formal, Informal and non-Formal Learning

Although all definitions can be contested this article shall refer to the European Centre for the Development of Vocational Training (Cedefop) 2001 communication on 'lifelong learning: formal, non-formal and informal learning' as the guideline for the differing definitions. Formal Learning: learning typically provided by an education or training institution, structured (in terms of learning objectives, learning time or learning support) and leading to certification. Formal learning is intentional from the learner's perspective. (Cedefop 2001)

Informal Learning: learning resulting from daily life activities related to work, family or leisure. It is not structured (in terms of learning objectives, learning time or learning support) and typically does not lead to certification. Informal learning may be intentional but in most cases it is not-intentional (or "incidental"/random)(Cedefop 2001))

Contested Definitions

If there is no clear distinction between formal and in-formal learning where is the room for non formal learning. It is a contested issue with numerous definitions given. The following are some the competing theories.

Similarly, Hodkinson et al. (2003), conclude after a significant literature analysis on the topics of formal, informal, and non-formal learning, that "the terms informal and non-formal appeared interchangeable, each being primarily defined in opposition to the dominant formal education system, and the largely individualist and acquisitional conceptualisations of learning developed in relation to such educational contexts."(Hodkinson et al., 2003, p. 314) Moreover, he states that "It is important not to see informal and formal attributes as somehow separate, waiting to be integrated. This is the dominant view in the literature, and it is mistaken. Thus, the challenge is not to, somehow, combine informal and formal learning, for informal and formal attributes are present and inter-related, whether we will it so or not. The challenge is to recognise and identify them, and understand the implications. For this reason, the concept of non-formal learning, at least when seen as a middle state between formal and informal, is redundant."(p. 314)

Eraut's classification of learning into formal and non-formal:

This removes informal learning from the equation and states all learning outside of formal learning is non-formal. Eraut equates informal with connotations of dress, language or behaviour that have no relation to learning. Eraut defines formal learning as taking place within a learning framework; within a classroom or learning institution, with a designated teacher or trainer; the award of a qualification or credit; the external specification of outcomes. Any learning that occurs outside of these parameters is non-formal.(Ined 2002)

The EC (2001) Communication on Lifelong Learning: formal, non-formal and informal learning:

The EU places non-formal learning in between formal and informal learning. This has learning both in a formal setting with a learning framework and as an organised event but within a qualification. "Non-formal learning: learning that is not provided by an education or training institution and typically does not lead to certification. It is, however, structured (in terms of learning objectives, learning time or learning support). Non-formal learning is intentional from the learner's perspective." (Cedefop 2001)

Livingstone's adults formal and informal edu ation, non-formal and informal learning:

This focuses on the idea of adult non-formal education. This new mode, 'informal education' is when teachers or mentors guide learners without reference to structured learning outcomes. This informal education learning is gaining knowledge without an imposed framework, such as learning new job skills. (Infed, 2002)

Billett (2001): there is no such thing as informal learning:

Billet's definition states there is no such thing as non-formal and informal learning. He states all human activity is learning, and that everything people do involves a process of learning. "all learning takes place within social organisations or communities that have formalised structures." Moreover he states most learning in life takes place outside of formal education. (Ined 2002)

Validation

Cedefop has created European guidelines to provide validation to a broad range of learning experiences, thereby aiding transparency and comparability across its national borders. The broad framework for achieving this certification across both non-formal and informal learning is outlined in the Cedefop European guidelines for validating non-formal and informal learning; Routes from learning to certification.

Different Countries Approaches

There are different approaches to validation between OCED and EU countries, with countries adopting different measures. The EU, as noted above, through the Cedefop -released European guidelines for validating non-formal and informal learning in 2009 to standardise validation throughout the EU. Within the OCED countries, the picture is more mixed.

Table: *Countries with the existence of recognition for non-formal and informal learning (Feutrie, 2007)*

	Full Program	*Partial Program*	*Limited Program*	*No program*
Austria			x	
Australia	x			
Belgium		x		
Canada	x			
Chile				x
Czech Republic			x	
Denmark	x			
Germany		x		
Greece				x
Hungary			x	
Iceland			x	
Ireland		x		
Italy			x	
Korea			x	
Malta			x	
Mexico		x		
Netherlands		x		
Norway	x			
South Africa		x		
Spain			x	
Slovenia			x	
Switzerland			x	
United Kingdom		x		

Importance of Technologies in Education in Non-Formal Education

Technology is a scientific way of developing new techniques and a systematic way of evolving and applying these techniques. Education Technology is an application of scientific knowledge about learning and condition of learning to improve the effectiveness and efficiency of education system. It can be considered as the systematic use of scientific method to plan realize and evaluate effective teaching learning process in informal, non- informal and formal education. It is comparatively a new idea that is grown as a result of the integration of technological devices in the use of practice in education.

Electronic devices such as film projectors, tape recorder, television sets and micro computers are mostly practiced and used as teaching tools in education. Non electronic instrumental materials such as books, photograph, poster, charts are also used.

Technological devices are now used in large proportion. It has occupied a critically important role in the field of education and almost in the non-formal education. Its application is needed to an individual and society as an effective information tool to support educational development. Now a days educational technology can be used effectively for non- formal system whatever level it may be. Different instrumental materials such as audio visual media are used to communicate the needed factual information to the learners. These materials can be capable more accurately and efficiently than the teacher. Thinks seen are mightier than things heard. Visual aids - pictures, charts, maps, graphs, photographs, cartoon etc are served through the sense of vision.

These materials should provide to adult women's environment. It enhances the adult thinking capacity and help them to reason things with proper understanding. These materials are usually pleasure to the eye. They help them to think and express new idea. It motivates the class also and added atmosphere to the situation, attention by some attractive features and conveyed the message quickly. Educational Technology requires a lot of change on the part of the instructors. They should be properly trained to participate in the teaching learning activities. Much specialized training is needed especially in non formal teaching method for successful program. Use of media such as puppet show street drama, role play, songs, dance visualization method etc are free games used in non-formal education classes. Since the adults get bored with traditional teaching, the literacy instructor have to use audio visual materials to attract and sustain learners interest in the teaching/ learning program.

The main aims of Education Technology of NFE program are :

i. To provide appropriately designed situations for learning and teaching.

ii. To modify the learners environment by presentation of materials by arranging the different learning activities and by organizing the physical and social surrounding of the learner.

The program should be locally planned as often as possible, target group should be included. Target groups are benefited from Educational Technology. Educational Technology for adult education is targeted to those who are working and do not have time go to literacy class. It is particularly important in reaching women who are cultural or religious regions can not go to literacy class. People who wants additional information that will improve their quality of education. Some innovative programs for self learning environment in reaching Neo-literate with appropriate learning programs.

Different New Techniques for Reaching Learner

There are many Educational Technology Programs that have sought creative for reaching learners that are compatible with the demands on learners lives.

7

Non-formal Education through Distance Education

Different educational systems are also changing with expansion of Education. Technology. Everybody realizes that there is inadequacy of face to face system of education. Due to the growing needs of the society, Distance Education Systems came into being. In this system learning is not through a teacher but learning process through Instrumental materials and electronic messages that emanate from the teacher. Teacher and Taught are separated by distance. There is not personal face to face contact on the part of teaching and learning process. Mass media is utilized. This kind of methodology would be important to the Non-Formal Education where many youth and adult have got a chance to acquire knowledge and skill from distance education. Employed adult also have got chance to acquire knowledge from it. Their aspire remains unfulfilled due to lack of time to go regular institution.

Here come Distances Education to help such people. It caters to the needs of such classes of society. Thus, Distance Education complements the adult classes of Non-Formal Education. Corresponding materials of distance education are self instrumental. Radio broadcasts, audio and video cassettes provides academic support to the learner. Thus, teaching and learning through electronic devices is an effective alternative to the non formal literacy classes The techniques of distance education has been accepted by community. This systems of education as viable alternative to search the deprived region also. It would help to bring change in the disadvantaged peoples. Distance Education would support to non formal learner.

Information Technology (IT) in Adult Learning

Information technology (IT) will certainly play a greater role at all levels and in all kinks of education in the future. The use of computers in schools is already common in several countries, and computers are also being used in some adult education programmes. The user of computers probably needs some basic literacy skills, and thus IT will be most relevant for semi-literates, neo-literates and others who want to expand their reading / writing skills and knowledge base. The use of personal computer will either include the application of software for training purposes, such as continuing education software for neo-literates, or the use of the Internet for gathering information and learning abut relevant topics. One advantage of the Personal computer is that it is interactive and can "respond" to the inputs of the learner. The learning process can also be made more interesting and varied with the use of computers, compared to books. Technical expertise is also needed to address the problems which inevitably come with the use of computers. The use of Information Technology should be integrated into the teaching/ learning process and in programmes for capacity building.

Use of Computer in Literacy Training In some countries computers in particular Personal Computers (PC) have become more common and widespread in most of the countries in the region .The distribution of computers very widely, both between countries and within one country people in the urban areas usually have more readily access to computers than a rural areas. Computer s used to be very expensive and therefore, out of reach for most education programmes for the poor such as literacy programmes.

The utilization of computers for literacy training has also been hampered by lack of adequate software. The situation however, is changing prices for both hardware and software have fallen and more user-friendly software is within reach. The new focus on computers for literacy training can be seen in two areas. The first is the introduction and use of Internet, and the second is the utilization of computers for training of literacy instructors and learners at local level. Internet Internet was introduced to the public in 1994, and its use has since then grown exponentially (very fastly) in many countries. The users of Internet have mostly been in urban areas since Internet requires connection to reliable telephone lines through modems and an Internet Service Provider (ISP).Access is rather limited in certain geographic areas and the service also requires regular payments to the ISP.

Access is rather limited in certain geographic areas, and the services also requires regular payments to the ISP. However, Internet has in short time proved to be an invaluable source of information for those institutions and persons who are able to access and utilize this new resource.

Computer Software for Literacy Training

Computer software for literacy training has great potentials where computers are available. There is, unfortunately, limited computer software available for literacy training. This is a rather sad fact since computers may be valuable tools both for literacy instructors and particularly for the learners. People often have the attitude that computers are difficult to handle and that users have to be not only literate but necessary to study the computer's operating system or advanced word processing tools to be able to interact with the computer in a simple way. If the soft ware is user-friendly (easy to use) and easy to understand, then it may be sufficient to teach a learner for a few minutes how to use the mouse before she/he starts to play with the computer. Computer games are very popular among children and playing in an interactive way with the computer can also be utilized by adult learners. The computer will give feedback to the user/learner through text, pictures and sound.

The learning process can then be more fun and varied than using traditional methods such as textbooks, writing pads and pencils. Another advantage is that locally developed software may be easily copied from one diskette to another at very low cost and widely disseminated.

Computer Assisted Instruction (CIA) is already a part of formal education in many developed countries. Computer Assisted Language Learning (CALL) is being applied in some countries to teach language skills. Software can be developed in local language s using existing programmes, such as Toolbox, Authoware and Director. The development of software for CIA in most countries in Asia- Pacific has just started, but will probably prove important for literacy training in the future.

Mobile Technology Initiatives for Non-Formal Education

There is a wide and growing interest in the use of mobile telephony to improve education service

Out-comes. This interest is by bilateral and multilateral donors, private foundations, non-governmental organisations, academic researchers and private companies, many of whom are associated with the Mobiles for Education (mEducation) Alliance. This Alliance aims to "reduce barriers to access appropriate, scalable, and low-cost mobile technologies to help improve learning outcomes in formal and non-formal education across all levels, especially in low-resource and developing country contexts".

Mobile telephony in education is often associated with the wider use of electronic technology in education, and in some projects mobile phones are used in conjunction with other technology systems. Mobile telephones have been used to assist in teaching students and keeping students and parents informed about school information. As well as directly helping with learning, they can be useful for education-related payments, especially in environments with poor financial infrastructure.

Use of Information and communication Technology (ICT) is the way through which large population of India can be reached. During the Gyandoot project as a case of empowerment to people using ICT, it was found that it helped in reducing harassment of people, corruption with increasing awareness among the people. ICT has become a buzzword while talking about technology and its implications. The hardware, software, the methods and know how required or used in acquiring, storing, processing and displaying data and information is collectively known as Information Technology (IT). There is no use in gathering and rapidly processing information that can not be transmitted as fast. Also high capacity channels are of no use if they can not be used to full capacity. Convergence of IT and CT these two technologies gave birth to ICT. Mainly education system is categorized in two categories namely formal and informal. The traditional regular teaching in schools and colleges is in the purview of formal Education. Other ways of getting education are included in the category of informal education.

There are various claims and measures regarding how people learn.

These claims and measures are usually based on average results from a large group. Large size of classes is also challenge particularly regarding course delivery, evaluation and assignment design.

Passive learning occurs when students use their senses to take in information from a lecture, reading assignment, or audiovisual. This is the mode of learning most commonly present in classrooms whereas active learning involves the student through participation and investment of energy in all three phases of the learning process (input, operations, and feedback). This type of learning is more apt to stimulate higher cognitive processes and critical thinking.

Teacher has key role in the whole process whereas in case of Mobile phone based education various applications of these new tools are supplemented to make the teaching-learning process effective.

Mobile Phones can play an important role in imparting education and improving the skills of both pre-service and in-service teacher professionals. In this paper how learning through mobiles can be made easier and effective for both formal and non-formal forms of education.

Mobile Application For Formal Education

Mobile Phone applications are becoming indispensable parts of contemporary culture, spreading across the globe through traditional and vocational education. In India the education system can be formally divided into three parts namely primary (including nursery and preprimary), High school or secondary level (High and senior secondary levels) and the college or higher level (including college, university levels) In all these levels of education Mobile phone can be utilized for better teaching learning process. Using multimedia applications available in Mobile phones can result in the increasing retention rates, because people remember 20% of what they see, 40% of what they see and hear, but about 75% of what they see and hear and do simultaneously.

The use of the mobile devices in Teaching-learning process gives opportunity for students to interact with each other and with the teacher using the mobile devices. Mobile learning is new in education hence it is important for educators, researchers, and practitioners to share what works and what does not work in mobile learning so that the field of mobile learning can be implemented in a more timely and effective manner. Mobile devices are changing constantly with increasing capabilities and there is not enough time for everyone to conduct research and complete projects to learn about the best practices in mobile learning.

Mobile phone has the potential to remove the barriers that are causing the problems of low rate of education in any country. It can be used as a tool to overcome the issues of cost, less number of teachers, and poor quality of education as well as to overcome time and distance barriers.

There are various types of Mobile phones and applications available which can be utilized for the knowledge creation and dissemination in the modern world. Mobile phones having Radio, T.V, Internet and many other hardware and software applications can be utilised.

The use of Mobile Phones in education not only improves classroom teaching learning process, but also provides the facility of M-learning.

Primary Level

Government of India has announced 2010-2020 as decade of innovation. Reasoning and critical thinking skills are necessary for innovation . Foundation of these skills can be laid only at primary level of education.

Students who enter school are very curious, creative, and capable of learning many things.

At this level, statement 3Picture is worth than thousand of words 3is very much true in case of teaching –learning process.

Students studying at this level take much interest in cartoons. They understand more through animated pictures. Hence if the same environment is created in schools for teaching kids at primary level may bring drastic changes in the education scenario. Nursery students can be taught by showing pictures, animals, fruits etc. With the help of Mobile and its peripheral devices, like T.V screen and computer students at this level are able to grasp a lot by hearing voices or sounds and animated motion of various animals. Language learning is also taught at this level. To know a new language at this age is easier as compared to other levels. Mobile phones can be used to teach phonetics and pronunciation.

Lessons, poems & lectures by eminent scholars stored in computers or mobiles can easily be shown to the students time and again. Parents also can store good & useful lectures in any field in their mobile phones and can show those to their children. Such type of teaching and learning retains for long time in the minds of the children. Infrastructure needed for such environment is only a computer capable of mobile attachment and with T.V tuner card for running cable T.V programmes on the computer. A latest mobile or smart phone with latest educational applications is required for it.

High Level

At high school level subjects like History, Geography, Political science, Physics, Chemistry, Biology, Physical education etc are taught. Lessons in these subjects can easily be taught by showing small movie related with the subject to create interest among the students. Internet is basic tool which can be utilized by teachers and students to find any information on any topic. Instead of showing complete movie, serial or programme, relevant part of that may be stored in mobiles and can be shown to the students of a class by attaching that mobile with the computer or Television. Such teaching –learning makes the environment very interactive and is liked by students.

College Level: At college level various facilities like computers, Multi Media (MM) Electronic Board, MM projector and other peripheral devices related with teaching learning process are easily available. Now easy availability of 3Aakash' tablet will help in providing and getting more education for teachers and students respectively. Various programs running on Edusat are also very helpful and provide good knowledge to the students.

Soft skill recorded program on Edusat can help students in improving their English and communication skill so that they can be placed well in reputed Multi National Companies (MNCs). Certain lectures of eminent personalities are also delivered through Edusat. All such important and relevant lectures must be stored and must be available in format that can be accessible through mobile phones to teachers and students of affiliated Higher Education Institutes (HEIs). Mobile phone/tablet is connected to repository through Internet and utilized by the students and teachers for Improvement. The use of mobile technology is good for informal learning where learners can access information and learning materials from anywhere and at any time. It includes distance education and other open learning systems. There are so many universities and institutes providing facility of distance education.

As mobile technology becomes more ubiquitous, there will be more use of mobile technology for informal learning. As soon as events happen around the world, users of mobile technology will be able to get up-to-date information on these events using mobile devices. Once the students are enrolled, a unique number is generated called reference number and it is provided to the particular students. In such an environment Mobile number of all the students is must. And for providing information to the concerned students regarding its second installment of fees, Personal Contact Programme (PCP) details, dare sheet, fee details etc can be provided immediately to the students with the help of mobile phone. Once the database having mobile number is created many of these functions can be done instantly. Short message service (SMS) of Mobile phone may be utilized for this purpose.

After fees for admission is deposited the SMS must ensure the students that his fees have been deposited at right place for the particular course. With the help of such practices a lot of paper work can be saved and helps the environment making it pollution free. Moreover the enrolled students can be given username and password for using various online services through mobile phones. Instead of providing hard copy of study material, online study material in mobile readable form must be provided to enrolled students. Fees payment through mobile system must also be available on the portal of concerned University or Institute. All these activities will

help in making the environment green. Exam results in such cases may be provided online on the same day as same is happening in case of online exams and entrance tests. This would help to sort out the problem of the delay in declaration of results of various exams by various universities. But all this must be the case for the informal education system.

Challenges of M-learning

Use of Mobile phones in education requires major shift in the way content is designed and delivered. New technologies cannot be imposed without enabling teachers and learners to understand these fundamental shifts. M-learning is any educational interaction delivered through mobile phones and can be accessed as per students' convenience from anywhere. Certain in built softwares in mobile phones like dictionary, geo-location, geography, data access, readers and maps can be utilized and adapted for educational purposes.

M-learning hardware may include mobile phones, handheld PCs, tablets, the iPad, and otebooks, as well as devices such as the iPod touch that are able to run mobile applications. Ongoing training is necessary for the trainers in institutions and organizations who are engaged in the design of curriculum, teaching materials and delivery of ICT-enabled education .

At this time Mobile phone is not utilized fully due to various challenges. Successful ICT initiatives meet three intertwined objectives: availability, access, and demand .

Mobile must be available and it must be accessible at demand. In the present scenario the following are the major challenges in the m-learning.

1. The access to ICT facilities whether by students or by teachers is of great concern in India. There are limited resources for

buying Mobile phone, books, stationery, furniture and other classroom materials.

2. Teachers lack adequate qualification, training and their lesson plans are most often outdated or irrelevant. In many of the HEIs certain new ICT tools like Multimedia board and visualiser are available but these are not in use.
3. All teachers are not willing to introduce new technologies to themselves first and subsequently to their students.

Another barrier is lack of trained teachers to exploit ICT proficiently.

4. Rural population may not be able to pay hefty amount to utilize such ICT resources for education.
5. Mobile phones are designed for talking and hence one of the major challenges in the implementation of ICT in education is the initial thinking that is based on the technology.
5. One first thinks about the available technology and then a try is being made to apply it into education field.
6. Major challenge for educators and trainers is how to develop learning materials for delivery on mobile devices.
7. A lot of information available online may dissuade student learning. Students can feel isolated in absence of classroom like environment.
8. Low bandwidth available for mobile phone is not going to serve the purpose.
9. Compatibility and interoperability of software and educational applications is also of great concern.
10. Implementation of RTE , in that case General Enrolment Ratio (GER) must be increased, how mobile phone can help in making aware about the RTE and enrolment of their children in school.
11. Cost of smart phones and data plans is out of reach for some students.
12. Small screen size and keys are difficult to use effectively, also there is additional strain on battery life imposed by mobile apps can be frustrating.
13. Inbuilt M-learning softwares are rarely available.

Reproducing the existing applications in mobile format can increase the workload of faculty.

Proposed Solutions

The first and foremost solution is the need to change the mind setup. As the word mobile is heard every one starts thinking about its facilities except its educational utility and tools.

Mobile phone is thought just as medium of communication, for listening phone calls, songs and viewing and capturing photos.

(1) Accessibility issue can be resolved due to diminishing cost of mobiles and increasing number of applications in the education field.

(2) In this age of ICT, teachers also have to compete for getting latest knowledge and various new ICT tools and applications. Teachers must be trained well on various mobile learning applications to utilize such applications and their features in a well defined way.

(3) Proper motivation to the teachers is must because they are the ultimate implementers. Monetary incentives can be offered as means of motivation for teachers to practice Mobile phone.

(4) A nominal fees must be taken from students to use the Resources.

(5) Cost is no longer an issue as prices of mobile phone and smart phones are decreasing at great speed and number of services are increasing day by day.

(6) Specifically education purpose oriented mobile phones can be designed and low cost devices like 3Aakash tablet‘ and such tools are made available with the largest telecommunication company BSNL can be more useful option.

(7) Learning material must be developed in format that may be easily displayed on mobile phones.

(8) Authenticity of online material can be increased by putting certain checks on the publishing the abusive and low standard material. GOI has already taken care of this issue and has asked major giants in this sector like yahoo, Google have been informed about the checks and legal frameworks to be designed in the certain timeframe.

(9) Bandwidth must be increased by governments.

(10) Accessibility of device to every citizen who need it for getting education must be increased.

(11) One educational application designed for NOKIA mobile phone may not properly for SAMSUNG or other company device.

Application developer software developer for mobile phone must keep in mind its general application so that an application designed for Mobile X may run properly for Mobile Y also and vice versa.

(12) Different components in smart phones degrade from use, their functionalities, available resources and power supplies are still able to satisfy the requirement of educational applications. Hence some smart phones may be used for education purpose even after these are discarded by their users.

Second hand phones have some features which may be utilized for education purpose in developing countries.

(13) New Mobile devices have compatibility to attach with LCD, T.V and computer hence screen size at the important times for showing to whole class would not be a great problem.

(14) Stakeholders must stress on preparing new softwares and educational applications which can be used on the present and future coming smart phones.

Modular Instruction in Technology and Home

Modules are increasingly being used in many countries as a way of organising a language curriculum. As a consequence, many coursebooks are now structured on the basis of "modules" rather than "units", and most teachers, when faced with this innovation, wonder whether this is really a new development, opening up new paths for learning and teaching, or whether it might not just be "old wine in new bottles".

Modular teaching is one of the most widespread and recognizes teaching learning techniques in United States, Australia and many other Western countries including Asian region. Modular is used in almost all subjects like *natural science*, especially in *biology* and *medical education* and even in *social sciences* as well as in *computers education*. All kinds of subjects are being taught through modules. It is a recent development based on *programmed learning*; a well established and universally recognized phenomenon. It considering the individual differences among the learners which necessitate the planning for adoption of the most appropriate teaching techniques in order to help the individual grow and develop at her/his own pace.

Such curricula can't be fixed once and forever – rather, they should be so flexible as to allow different language needs to be met at different ages and school levels. This, in turn, implies describing language objectives so that they are recognisable, comparable across educational systems, and clearly amenable to assessment and evaluation.

- A "module" is a portion of such a curriculum:
- It is a *relatively autonomous* portion, since it is based on a limited number of objectives which the learner is expected to achieve and the school is expected to be able to assess and certify. This certification can be used as part of a unit-credit system, so that at each stage of the curriculum (at school, as well as after school) one should be able to demonstrate what sort of language competence she/he has actually achieved.
- Modules are *relatively* autonomous, because, especially in the early stages of language learning, one cannot give up the ideas of a *sequence* of learning steps and of a *spiral* , *recursive* approach to language. So it is legitimate to talk about the *integration* of basic, intermediate, and advanced modules. However, the basic idea of modularity is that at all levels there should be the opportunity to *choose* and *combine* modules in different ways according to the context of each particular teaching situation.
- Modules are not limited to the "core" language syllabus. It is possible to envisage and implement, for example, *cross-curricular* modules (involving several school subjects), *project* modules (aimed at carrying out a particular project) as well as *remedial* or *development* modules.

What's the Difference, Then, Between a "Module" and a "Unit"?

- A module aims at developing a clearly identifiable and certifiable portion of the curriculum, expressed in terms of *competence objectives.*
- These objectives should be achieved within a clear and realistic time limit (language modules usually range between 20 and 30 hours). This time limit is an important feature of the modular organisation, since the whole curriculum is built around the idea that time and human and material resources should be spent to achieve foreseeable results. This, of course, may introduce an element of rigidity – this is why a modular organisation implies constant *monitoring* and *feedback* to ensure that learning is really *work-in-progress.*
- Units, too, are generally based on clearly defined objectives (often described in terms of grammar, vocabulary, functions,

skills, etc.). Modules, however, seem to be aiming higher – to enable learners to achieve a level of competence which should be described in terms other than just grammar, vocabulary or functions. Units often remain a sub-division of modules (although they may also be called in different ways: stages, steps, etc.), but the *focus* of modules – their overall organising principle - should be of a different kind.

So What Should Modules Focus on?

Many alternatives are possible - here are just a few. Modules could be focussed on

- *...spheres of experience* : the family ... jobs ... school life ...
- *macrofunctions* : describing ... narrating ... discussing ...
- *communicative activities* : reading ... oral interaction ... mediating (e.g. interpreting, translating ...)
- *topics* : racism ... advertising ... new technologies ...
- *vocational competences* : giving instructions ... talking on the phone ... using the Internet ...
- *textual genres* : novels ... plays ... poetry ...
- *areas of linguistic investigation* : lexis ... syntax ... verbal vs non-verbal language ...
- *or any combination of the above* .

The point to make here is that purely linguistic choices (e.g. in terms of grammar, vocabulary, *microfunctions* like "asking for advice") should come as a *consequence* of having chosen a particular *focus* – not as the starting point.

What Should we Assess in a Module?

This is perhaps where one of the distinctive features of modules vs units comes into play. If at the end of each "unit" within a module we can test learners on *discrete* items (though not necessarily limiting ourselves to structures and vocabulary ...), at the end of a module learners should be put in a position to demonstrate their *overall competence*, as defined in the module objectives.

This also means that *unit tests* belong to the *formative* area of evaluation, while *module tests* belong to the *summative* area. It goes without saying that even at the end of a module learners who have *not* achieved the module objectives should have the opportunity to "balance out" their weaknesses through the provision of appropriate remedial work.

Designing Modules for Learning

During the past fifty years third level education has expanded and diversified and the demands and expectations being placed on Higher Education Institutions are now formidable, with changes in the student body and increased pressure from government on costs, procedures and results. For academic staff, there are increased pressures through increased teaching loads, growing reporting and administrative requirements and pressure to develop and strengthen their research profile. Amongst academic staff surveys consistently report that teaching is a source of reward but staff say that they are working longer hours and dealing with a more diverse student group (McInnis 2000). At the same time, they still wish to improve and innovate their practice by designing and delivering effective courses and modules. The increased size and diversity of the student group has impacted on the process of course design. Biggs (1999) offers valuable suggestions for course design strategies in the context of a growing student population and Knight (2002) argues for courses in higher education to be designed in order to maximize the chance that learners will experience coherence, progression and deep learning.

Barnett et al. (2004) argue that the curriculum receives scant regard in current debates about teaching and learning in higher education but suggest that this may change in the context of quality assurance mechanisms and benchmarking. Knight (2002) points out that material on design work for teachers planning programmes in higher education is insubstantial. He suggests that there is a need for advice on programme design and argues for texts to be developed to target specific national markets. Thus, this chapter has been written to guide teachers in higher education who are currently involved in module design and would benefit from a practical manual that will steer them through the process of designing a module for the first time. It will also be of benefit to teachers who are redesigning existing modules, and wish to bring an awareness of current thinking to the task.

The focus of this chapter is the design of modules which form part of programmes in higher education. In the context of this chapter, we are taking a module to be a self contained, formally structured learning experience with a coherent and explicit set of learning outcomes and assessment.

Modules are not developed in isolation, but within a course or programme structure, and the process is informed by the external national qualifications framework and where relevant, professional body requirements. Thus, internal and external factors must be taken into account at the planning stage. In terms of designing modules, we would argue that there is a need for a planned integrated approach to the process with the focus on the learning of the student. We would suggest that academic staff can begin the process not by focusing on the content of the module and how they intend to teach it, rather by focusing on the quality of learning that can be achieved by their students.

The aim of the chapter is to support the reader in becoming a logical module planner, aware of the important decisions to be made, and the variety of possibilities available. Planning a module is a process that requires time, commitment and a thoughtful, systematic approach. We guide you through the process of structuring learning into modules and by working through the chapter, you will be facilitated to design a module that supports your students' learning. We would intend that the material presented would be adapted and modified to suit your professional context.

The chapter will bridge theory and practice in module design and deepen your understanding of the process, regardless of subject matter or institutional setting. The focus is on higher education, although much of what is suggested has application in other areas of education. Key issues in the process of module design will be explored and the relationship between educational philosophy, learner needs and the module design process itself will be analysed to ensure that they work in harmony and maximize the learning.

The chapter is structured in a number of sections, each including a practical activity entitled 'Action Trigger' for you to complete. The aim of these activities is to provide you with a hands-on opportunity to work through the design of your module of choice and to ensure that the time you invest will be productive in terms of the process and product.

Context

The traditional curriculum focused on the teacher rather than the learner. However, in recent years there has been a paradigm shift taking place, moving the emphasis from teaching to learning and a more student-centred curriculum. This change has impacted on the curriculum design process with a greater emphasis on the learning in terms of knowledge, skills and competencies within courses and modules. The focus is on how learners learn and the design of effective learning environments. Alongside this change in pedagogy, the Bologna Agreement has emphasized the need for reform to modernise European higher education.

This chapter recognizes that many countries have national qualifications frameworks and that each institution has its own realities of quality assurance procedures with which to engage. However, we will outline a generic model of module design that academic staff can take and adapt within the realities of their own institutional and national contexts.

The standpoint is taken that although modularity is 'a good thing', it does not come without problems and whilst being cognizant of these, the focus of this work is to help teachers to gain educationally sound ideas and strategies for improving learning, teaching and assessment in a modularised context.

The Module Design Process

There are a variety of models for the design of courses in higher education (Toohey 1999; Biggs 1999) and many of the same issues are relevant in the context of designing modules. In the process of devising a module, the key is to forge educationally sound and logical links between learner needs, aims, learning outcomes, resources, learning and teaching strategies, assessment criteria and evaluation.

Framework Towards Designing Modules for Learning

A Framework for Module Design and Development is outlined. This provides an overview of the process, highlighting the important variables in module design and illustrating the relationships between them; however it is important to stress that it is not a linear process.

A Place to Start

Any systematic approach to module design must be considered within the context of a theoretical framework.

Applying Relevant Theory

The question remains when designing modules for learning, why is it important to be aware of the theories that underpin learning? We would argue that a theory should make explicit the underlying psychological dynamics of events related to learning. Each one is based on different assumptions about the nature of learning and we are suggesting that you identify your own theory of learning because the strategies one might use to enhance learning will direct follow from one's orientation.

It could be argued that teachers bring to the classroom or lecture theatre an inbuilt informal theory of teaching. This theory, which may be either consciously stated or implicit in what the teachers do, has implications for the way in which students learn. It is outside the scope of this chapter to go into depth on learning theories. Further discussion of these theories can be found in Carlile and Jordan (2005).

In addition to taking cognizance of different learning theories, it is also important o take into account that there is no universal way of learning. Brown and Atkins (1991) state that differing students will use different strategies on different tasks. They stress the importance of 'learning-for-understanding' and 'learning-for-knowledge' orientations, with learning being a continuous process of development back and forth between the two.

When designing modules, we would argue that it is important for teachers to be aware of concepts of deep and surface approaches to learning. Much research has previously been conducted on the relationship between courses and the approach students take to learning (Marton and Saljo 1976; Entwistle 1981; Gibbs 1992; Ramsden 1992; Biggs 1999). Arising from these studies, there are implications in terms of module design. Seeking to incorporate the following to your module design can offer a greater likelihood of fostering a deep approach to learning:

- sustained interaction with content and others;
- relating new ideas to previous knowledge;
- providing explicit explanations and a clear knowledge base to students;
- structuring in a reasonable student workload;
- providing opportunities for students to pursue topics in depth so that they can understand the material for themselves;
- ensuring an appropriate formative and summative assessment strategy.

These ideas resonate with teachers in today's higher education environment and have implications both for our choice of learning and teaching strategies and how we assess learning. An awareness of these approaches to learning is fundamental to the entire module design process.

Constructive Alignment: the Importance of Coherence

Constructive alignment is an approach to curriculum design that maximises the conditions for quality learning by ensuring alignment throughout the process, from the forming of learning outcomes, to the choice of teaching methods to assessment.

> *"The fundamental principle of constructive alignment is that a good teaching system aligns teaching method and assessment to the learning activities stated in the objectives so that all aspects of this system are in accord in supporting appropriate student learning."*
>
> *(Biggs 1999:25)*

There are three elements involved in the process of constructively aligning your module:

1. Defining the learning outcomes;
2. Choosing the learning and teaching methods that can lead to attainment of outcomes;
3. Assessing student learning outcomes.

This is a design for learning which is most likely to encourage deep engagement from students but setting up an aligned system requires time and some thought on the part of the academic. However, we argue that a well designed module depends for its success on the interrelationship between these elements and should inform your thinking at all stages as you work through the process.

We now begin by identifying the areas that need to be addressed as this gives a clear focus to the design activity. We are not suggesting an approach in which each step needs to be completed before the next is begun. Rather, one can move back and forth as required. It is often easier to think productively about abstract topics such as values only after thinking about more concrete issues such as curriculum content and learning and teaching strategies. A series of steps are now outlined to take you through the module design process and in the forthcoming sections of the chapter, each will be dealt with in some detail.

- Thinking through a rationale for your module
- Deciding on aims and learning outcomes for the module
- Thinking about the module content
- Exploring learning and teaching strategies and the appropriate learner support
- Focusing on assessment
- Considering learner support
- Planning a module evaluation strategy

Developing a Module Rationale

The purpose of a rationale is to serve as a broad value system for the learning in your module. However, seldom will a module be designed in isolation but rather it is more likely to form part of a programme of study and it is important to give consideration to the underlying values and beliefs about the purposes of education. The opportunity to think through and discuss such issues through the process of module design can support teachers to highlight the values that they hold as educators. We would content that your module should do more than add information to students' stock of knowledge but should be seeking to encourage a deep approach to learning.

The activity below can assist you in developing a coherent rationale statement for your module.

Action Trigger

- What are the educational goals for your module?
- What conceptions do you have of your learners?
- Why is the subject matter important?
- What are your beliefs and values about learning and teaching?

Aims and Learning Outcomes

The aim of your module indicates the general direction or orientation of a module in terms of its content and sometimes its context within a programme. An aim tends to be written in terms of the teaching intentions:

- The aim of the module is to provide an introduction to the application of statistical theory in general insurance.
- The module aims to provide an effective and common grounding in written and interpersonal skills.

The traditional way of describing modules and programmes in Higher Education has been to write in terms of the content with academics defining courses in terms of what is taught. However, recent development have encouraged a move to an outcomes based approach to course design with learning being defined in terms of what the students can do at the end of a module or programme. There is continuing debate in the literature about the value of defining learning in terms of outcomes and the effect that this may have on student learning but it is not the purpose of this chapter to enter into the debate. Although many academics have misgivings about the outcomes based approach, many of us are now required to define modules and courses in these terms. The use of learning outcomes is a means of describing the contents of a module or course in terms of the learning that is intended to happen.

A learning outcome is a statement of what the learner is expected to know, understand and / or be able to do at the end of a period of learning. Learning outcomes focus on learning rather than teaching and are not about what the teacher can provide but what the learner can demonstrate at the end of a module or course. Learning outcomes should be written taking into account level descriptors relevant to the level of study, and if relevant professional body requirements. They can support students to better understand what they can expect to know and be able to do at the end of a module. Some examples of learning outcomes follow:

On completion of the module the learner will be expected to able to: explain the role of accounting information in organisations

Successful students will typically be able to: identify and critically evaluate the strategic options available to enterprises

The phrases used to start the sentence lead to the use of action verbs and to a focus on how students will demonstrate their learning. You need to think about how you will ask your students to demonstrate their understanding. When they are being assessed students may be asked to discuss a concept, analyse a situation, describe a process or evaluate some data.

These are the tasks the student actually does in order to demonstrate understanding and so these terms can be used to express the learning outcome. Bloom's Taxonomy developed in 1956 still remains one of the best aids to writing good learning outcomes There are no rules on how many outcomes per module or course but some guidelines have been given on the literature in learning outcomes in the U.K. It has been suggested that a module should have between four and eight learning outcomes and an entire programme should have up to twenty five (Moon 2002).

Teaching for Learning

Here, we are going to explore a range of teaching methods and will focus on the methods and combinations of methods that can best realize the sort of constructive engagement with learning activities that leads to understanding (Ramsden 1992). Even the best designed modules, with very worthwhile defined learning outcomes, can fail if the teaching strategies employed are inappropriate to encourage and support the learners towards meeting the desired learning outcomes. It is useful to reflect on what we mean by a teaching strategy? Toohey (1999:152) offers the following definition:

> *"A teaching strategy is ... a plan for someone else's learning, and it encompasses the presentations which the teacher might make, the exercises and activities designed for students, materials which will be supplied or suggested for students to work with, and ways in which evidence of their growing understanding and capability will be collected."*

This definition is very helpful as it emphasizes that a teaching strategy is fundamentally about supporting your student's learning. In giving consideration to how, as academics, we can teach in order to ensure that our students are engaging with the learning process, it is necessary to focus on the type of teaching strategies we can employ to achieve this end.

The following approach will help you to think through and decide on appropriate teaching strategies for your module. First, take time to read over your module aims, learning outcomes and content material. Then, focus on how best you can involve students in making sense of the material through active engagement and application.

Action Trigger:

- Who are your learners? E.g. undergraduate, postgraduate, adult, international students
- What kinds of learning are you trying to achieve? E.g. knowledge, skills, attitudes.
- How are you going to deliver the content? E.g. lectures, tutorials, seminars, practicals
- What learning activities can be organized to meet the learning outcomes? E.g case studies, problem-solving, role play, group discussions
- What resources are available to you? E.g. handouts, worksheets, OHPs, visuals
- Does your teaching strategy support the learner to meet the desired learning outcomes? The matrix in Table 1 provides an opportunity for you to review a range of popular teaching strategies in higher education and the type of learning which each strategy best supports.

Learning Outcomes		***Teaching Strategy***	***Learner Activity***
	Transmit / Inform	Lecture Reading Tutorial Researching	Reproduce learning Linking to theory Clarify and expand Self-directed learning
Knowledge	Engage	Discussion Question and Answer Peer Teaching/Learning Web-based Teaching	Interpreting knowledge Clarify knowledge providing multiple perspectives; self insight exploring learning; Providing multiple perspectives;
	Practice	Seminar Class Presentation Field Trip	Clarify knowledge Presentation skills Experiential
Skills	Application	Laboratory Demonstration Games Problem solving Case Study Group work	Apply theory to practice Deepen understanding Exploring learning Transform knowledge Appraising; synthesing Transform knowledge

The table above is not a comprehensive summary of all possible teaching strategies and more detail can be found in Higgs and McCarthy (2005). The reality is that there is no shortage of teaching strategies. However, the key issue for module designers is selecting the strategies that are most likely to support the achievement of learning outcomes and are suitable for use in your teaching context taking into account the resources available to you.

Assessing Your Learners

In relation to assessment, we would suggest that the fundamental principles are that the assessment methods should be in accord with the learning outcomes of the module and should foster a deep approach to learning.

Assessment is generally considered in terms of either being Formative and/or Summative. Formative assessment is used to inform both student and teacher as to how the learner is progressing. Integral to this process is the feedback that students receive from the teacher and this should be used to improve both the learning of students and the teaching practice. Summative assessment is used to grade students at the end of a module or to accredit them at the end of a programme.

Formative assessment may be used to contribute to continuous assessment but we would argue that in order for students to have the maximum opportunities to learn in a module, then there must be some option for a formative assessment which does not contribute to the final grade. Students can then obtain feedback which will allow them to address any gaps in their knowledge or skills.

Action Trigger:

- What knowledge do you want to assess? Refer to your learning outcomes.
- What skills do you want to test?
- Have you built in provision for formative and summative assessment?
- What weighting do you want to give to the final exam and other forms of continuous assessment?

Despite the fact that there are a variety of assessment methods available, Brown (1999:8) notes 'that the range of ways that students are assessed is extremely limited with around 80% of assessments being in the form of exams, essays and reports of some kind.' We would encourage you to give consideration to a wide range of possible assessment methods.

Table will outline a range of assessment methods to assist you in choosing an appropriate assessment taking into account the link between learning outcomes and assessment, within the context of modularity.

Learning Outcomes		***Teaching Strategy***	***Learner Activity***	***Assessing for Learning***
	Transmit / Inform	Lecture Reading Tutorial Researching	Reproduce learning Linking to theory Clarify and expand Self-directed learning	Essay exam; Open Book exam Reflective Journal Assignment
Knowledge Skills	Engage	Discussion Question and Answer Peer Teaching/Learning Web-based Teaching	Interpreting knowledge Clarify knowledge providing multiple perspectives; self insight exploring learning; Providing multiple perspectives;	Interview; Presentation; Viva Quiz Self and peer assessment; Portfolio; Project Computer Assisted Assessment
	Practice	Seminar Class Presentation Field Trip	Clarify knowledge Presentation skills Experiential	Presentation; Project Presentation Project
	Application	Laboratory Demonstration Games Problem solving Case Study Group work	Apply theory to practice Deepen understanding Exploring learning Transform knowledge Appraising; synthesing Transform knowledge	Practical Assessment; Lab Reports Practical Assessment Set problems in Exam Case Study Assessment Group Project

Assessment should be given serious consideration and reflection and the choice of assessment methods should clearly relate to the learning outcomes. There will rarely be one method of assessment which satisfies all learning outcomes for a module and we would recommend that in devising your assessment strategy, a variety of methods is included. It is also important for module designers to think about how modularity may impact upon assessment practices and give consideration to some of the pitfalls associated with assessment within modular structures. In designing or redesigning modules, it is vital to bear in mind which parameters of assessment do you need to agree on as a group, and which can be left to individual teachers or subject coordinators. In a modular system, it is important to guard against over-assessing students based on the unit of study. Also there is a tendency in a modular curriculum to crowd the assessments with the result that students are handing in multiple assessments at the mid way point and at the end. This is an unacceptable burden for students and it is therefore vitally important that within a programme of study, the timetable of assessment is planned thoroughly in advance so the students do not face this problem.

Supporting Your Learners

In designing modules consideration should be given to the type of learner support which will be required for the achievement of the learning outcomes. There are administrative issues around module design: scheduling of teachers, students, teaching activities, assessment time and module resources. Many modules are over ambitious and require more time on the part of students for their completion than is reasonable. Modules depend for their success on the careful allocation of resources, whether this is teaching rooms, laboratories, library facilities and equipment.

Whether you are teaching a module alone, or are adopting a team-teaching approach, you will find a need for support, whether it be technically subject-specific, audio-visual, information skills or information technology, and it is important to think through the issues around support.

Action Trigger:

- Have you considered the implications of the likely background, qualifications and experience of students?
- Have you considered a learner support policy?
- Have you ideas for producing a student guide for the module?

Evaluation Mechanisms

Module design and development is an ongoing process and this will look at the kind of evaluation mechanisms that might be used to elicit meaningful information to assist you in reviewing and improving your module. This should be based upon criteria that are co-operatively developed and concerned with gathering information about the quality and effectiveness of the module. Evaluation is not just a retrospective process, but can be an integral part of the module development, informing you before, during and after the process.

When designing your evaluation strategy it is important to consider the following:

Action Trigger:

- Are you designing into the module opportunities for feedback and evaluation?
- Are you using feedback and evaluative processes throughout the year not just as part of annual monitoring and review?
- Who is the evaluation for?
- Why are you carrying out the evaluation?
- What will your evaluation do?
- What kind of information do you want to collect?
- What do you plan to do with the information once collected?

Before selecting your evaluation methods within the strategy, the key thing to consider is your evaluation question i.e. what do you want to know? Your selection of methods will be determined by considering, for example, who the evaluation is for, the scale of your evaluation, the necessity for authenticity within the data collection and levels of resources available to you.

When designing your evaluation strategy it is important to consider when you will collect your data and how you will select your student and/or stakeholder sample. It is also recommended that something is done with any data collected and if students have been involved in the data collection, try and feedback any data and make changes as appropriate.

Teaching the Extension Classes

It is the process of arranging situations in which the important things learned are called to the attention of the learners, their interest developed, desire aroused, and action promoted.

Principles of Extension Teaching

The principles which need to be followed for making the extension teaching effective are discussed here:

Extension Teaching Requires Specific and Clearly Defined Objectives. While deciding the objectives of teaching, following aspects are to be considered:

a. People to be taught.

b. Behavioural changes to be developed in people.

c. Content or subject matter to bring the desired change in behaviour.

d. The life situation in which the action is going to take place.

1. Extension Teaching Requires a Suitable Learning Situation:

The learning situation consists of the following five inter-related elements:

a. Instructor (Extension Worker)

b. Learners (Farmers, Women, Youth)

c. Subject Matter (i.e. Agriculture, Horticulture, Social Forestry)

d. Teaching Materials (Seeds, Plants, Audio-visual aids).

2. Extension Teaching Requires Effective Communication:

Extension teaching, to the effective, must take into consideration proper functioning of the elements of communication process.

a. Communicator

b. Message

c. Channel

d. Treatment

e. Audience

Effective communication can motivate people to act.

Extension as an Educational Process

Teaching-learning is one of the most delicate, significant, and complex of all social processes because it changes the way people think and act. Extension workers must skillfully provide learning experiences effectively.

Extension Teachers and Teaching

Emphasis on the educational aspect of extension programs stems from the belief that education helps people learn how to do things for themselves, whereas Service consists of doing things for the people. Education makes people self-reliant; service makes them dependent on others. Education is more than imparting information or supplying answers; it also helps develop the ability to understand and reason, to think through problems, and arrive at wise solution.

Can teaching be learned? Yes. The ability of individuals engaged in teaching varies. There are no born teachers as there are no born lawyers, doctors, engineers, fishermen, or carpenters. Everyone is gifted by nature. Anyone with good intelligence and the will to study, practice, plan, and revise ways of doing the job can gain the skill to do effective teaching. Hence, there is no mystery about learning how to be a good extension teacher. It is simply a matter of hard work, practice, concentration and the will to achieve proficiency. This is the price one must pay for acquiring real skill in any profession.

Requirements of extension teaching

Good extension teaching requires carefully planned programs, procedure, and technique. Designing good teaching plans is a highly professional job, and one that pays well as an achievement. A number of conditions must be met and actions must be taken to make extension teaching procedures and methods effective.

Extension teaching requires specific and clearly defined objectives. All purposeful teaching has specific objectives derived from the broader program objectives. Before extension teaching can attain maximum effectiveness, changes desired in the behaviour of people must be identified.

Teaching objectives properly stated, contain four different aspects: people to be taught, behavioural changes to be developed in people, content or subject matter to which the behaviour is related, and life situation in which the action is to take place. For example: the teaching objective in a training program may be to develop the skill (behaviour) of extension workers (persons) in conducting method demonstrations (content) before groups of fish farmers (life situation). Another objective may be to impart knowledge (behaviour) among fishfarmers (people) the benefits gained from applying the right amount of fertilizer (content) through demonstrations (life situation). Still another objective may be to develop interest (behaviour) among fishfarm families (people) in fishery cooperatives (content) through community meetings (life situation).

It can be seen from these examples that well stated teaching objectives are specific in the behaviour changes desired, the people who are to make the change, the content to be dealt with, and the life situation in which teaching and learning are to take place. The examples also show that the elements are different in each objective. Teaching objectives stated in this manner give direction and guidance to both teachers and learners as well.

It is true that one can accomplish some favourable results without a clear definition of what he is trying to do, but if improvements will result from the total program, extension workers must have well-defined teaching objectives. Achievements, therefore, can be adequate only in terms of some standard, and that standard can only be derived from one's concept of the objectives he wishes to attain through teaching effort.

Extension teaching must accomplish certain kinds of educational changes in relation to the subject matter taught. Among these are:

Changes in knowledge, or things known, amount of knowledge, and kinds of knowledge. Examples: stocking rate (by farm size), kinds and amounts of fertilizer to use, kinds and amounts of pesticide to use. Changes in skills, or ability to do things. How easily and effectively one can do a specified task, and the number of things one can do, are all reflections of skill.

Changes in attitude or feelings, for or against things and issues, points of view, beliefs, reactions and the like. Attitudes are important in determining what a person does and how he does it. They must become strongly positive (favorable) before desired changes in behaviour will give him satisfaction if the interest is met.

Changes in interest: Interest is a specific form of attitude, but educational interest may be defined as a desire to learn, or to gain information, or to understand, or to gain skill, pertaining to some object in one's environment that he believes will give him satisfaction if the interest is met.

Changes in understanding: Understanding has to do with gaining insight into the relationship of facts and issues, usually involving cause and effect. It has to do with the development of a deeper and broader vision of how various elements, important facts and principles operate in a situation. To gain understanding requires knowledge and thinking skill.

Extension teaching usually requires a combination of teaching methods. Because not all extension methods will reach the people or influence them, a combination of various teaching methods must be considered. By and large, the changes people make on their farms, in their homes, and in their communities are in proportion to the number of times they are exposed to information through personal visits, meetings, demonstrations, and the like. Obviously, if wide response is desired, rural people must be exposed to changes.

Extension teaching requires careful evaluation of results. Evaluation is useful in guiding teaching effort and educational programs. Extension teaching is complex because observation alone cannot be a basis for evaluation. Pretesting is more precise than casual observation in determining the outcome of an educational activity.

Learning Experience and Learning Situations

Learning experience is the core of the educational process. It is the mental and/or physical reaction of a learner to seeing, hearing, or doing the things to be learned.

An effective learning situation consists of five essential elements:

1. An effective instructor or leader
2. Learners who want and need to learn
3. Content or subject matter that is useful to learners
4. Appropriate instructional equipment and materials
5. An appropriate physical environment

There is a constant reaction by the learners with each of the other four major elements in the learning situation. For example, a learner may at one time be reacting to the dress of the instructor, to his mannerisms, or to his voice; at another time to his teaching equipment, or to the manner in which he handles the subject matter; later to some aspect of the physical facilities such as the hard chair, or poor light, or excessive heat. In addition to the mental focus on these elements, and many others not mentioned here, learners react to such items as outside obstructions, individual interpretation, members of the group, and personal problems. The great task of the extension worker is to minimize the almost infinite number of possible distractions to the mental process. The effectiveness of a learning experience is therefore, related directly to the manner and extent of mental concentration on the subject matter.

There are a number of things an instructor can do that would help assure a good learning situation. Some of the important ones are given below:

1. Have in mind that teaching objectives are clearly significant to# the learners, and are attainable through the educational process within the mental and physical limitations of the learners.

2. Have a thorough knowledge of significant subject matter related to the learner's needs.
3. Be personable, enthusiastic, and interested in the subject matter.
4. Use democratic instructional procedures and approaches.
5. Be prepared, prompt, and courteous in every teaching-learning session.
6. Arrange and manage the learning situation to prevent or minimize distractions within and outside the learning situation.
7. Be skillful in the use of teaching material and equipment such as blackboard, visual equipment and other reading materials.
8. Always prepare and use a carefully developed teaching plan.

To become a proficient extension teacher one must constantly work at analyzing his teaching procedures, motivating his audience, research of new technology to extend, gaining further understanding of the teaching-learning process, and developing greater skill in selecting, combining, and using the methods of extension education.

Communication

Communication is the process of imparting or exchanging information. As we have seen people learn in many ways. The transfer of modern technology to effect change from traditional to scientific aquaculture is the aim. To be able to teach these better skills they must know how to communicate effectively. The extension worker becomes the bridge between researchers and fishfarmers. This is concerned with the skills of communicating knowledge to the fishfarmer. Unless extension workers communicate effectively, they fail as teachers. The communication process (SMCR) consists of four essential elements:

1. Sender/Communicator of ideas/information
2. Message to be sent/transmitted
3. Channels/means of communication
4. Receiver of information/audience

When an extension worker goes to the fishfarmer, the extension worker must start the conversation. Therefore, he is the sender; what he says is the message; the spoken word is the channel; and the fishfarmer is the receiver. When the fishfarmer replies, the roles are temporarily reversed. The fishfarmer is the sender and extension worker becomes the receiver. Fishfarmer's response is the feedback.

The Communicator (sender) is the originator of the communication. As an extension worker, he must take the initiative to establish communication with the fishfarmer and keep it functioning. As a communicator the extension worker must be credible. He should gain the confidence of his clientele. Credibility can be improved by learning to communicate effectively.

A good communicator must:

- know his clientele, their wants and needs
- know his message, its content and how to present it
- know effective channels of communication for his message to get across and know his own abilities and limitations
- be interested in his clientele and their welfare and how his message can help
- be interested in improving his skills in communication
- prepare his message carefully, using appropriate materials to elicit interest from the clientele
- speak clearly
- use simple words to be easily understood
- realize the mutual understanding between extension workers and the fishfarmer is mostly the worker's responsibility
- be time conscious.

The Message: Extension workers have important information and ideas which he hopes will be received and interpreted by the clientele as he intended. Oftentimes, this is not the case due to incomplete information, poor presentation, and other reasons. To avoid these difficulties, extension workers should be prepared to reiterate the information. The purpose or objective should be clear in mind. What change in behaviour do you want to bring about? It can be a change in knowledge, attitude, skills, or in what you expect the clientele to do.

The content of the message should be of interest to him. It must be related to something he understands, feels or thinks, something he can accept. The treatment of the message is important to make it acceptable and understandable to the receiver (fishfarmer). It should be organized in terms he understands. It should conform to accepted social standards. Treatment can make a message interesting or boring.

The Channels of Communication: Extension methods are channels of communication. These methods may be classified as visual, spoken, or written or a combination of both.

Spoken methods include field and home visits, office calls, meeting of all kinds, radio, television and telephone calls. Except for radio and television, the rest are a two-way communication. Differences of opinion can be cleared up on the spot. There are also disadvantages and obstacles to be overcome. Since an oral message is not always recorded, the receiver may remember it differently than the sender wants. Where premise statements are only spoken, the receiver has no way to refer back to what was said. In spite of its problems, spoken communication when supplemented with visual aids is the best method of extension work.

Written communication is indispensable in day-to-day activities of extension. Records and reports must be prepared, kept available for use, and submitted to superiors. The clientele must be kept informed of activities and accomplishments.

Written communications have greater status and carry more authority than oral communication. Letters, bulletins, circulars, announcements of events and magazines contribute to extension in literate societies. They provide a low-cost method to disseminate information to a large number of people, but this is only a one-way communication. Few people will change their methods of fishfarming only because they read about it. An effective extension worker will adapt his extension methods to the subject, to the communication skills of the clientele and to the facilities available.

The Receiver (audience): The receivers are the acceptors. If the receiver did not accept, there was no communication at all. The significant thing to remember is this: while some may agree on some aspect, they may also differ in thousands of ways. Often, some of these differences block communication.

Differences in education mean different abilities to understand a difficult concept and other technicalities. For this reason, communication often fails because of a gap or language barrier.

In communication there are what we call filters. Filter in this sense is anything that prevents a message from getting through to the intended audience. Filters may be fear, prejudice, inability to grasp the idea, or any possible barriers.

The point is that a good communicator anticipates and tries to prevent filters if he can; he is ready with every means to overcome barriers in any case. Communication failure may also occur when the idea being communicated is contrary to the accepted local customs and beliefs. This too is filter. Recognizing this danger, alternative approaches to the problem should be used. The process by which a sender can convey his message to the audience often affects the transfer of an idea. If he is sincere and respectable, he is more likely to succeed in transmitting his idea to his audience.

Diffusion

Two interrelated processes help bring new ideas from their source of initial development to acceptance by fishfarmers. These processes are called diffusion and adoption. The diffusion process refers to the spread of new ideas from the original source to the ultimate users. In the case of aquaculture, it is the process by which new farm practices or innovations are communicated from sources of origin, usually researchers and practices adopted from advanced countries. The adoption process is a mental process through which an individual passes from first hearing about a new idea to its final adoption. The five stages in the adoption process commonly accepted today are:

Awareness Stage. At the awareness stage the individual is exposed to the innovation but lacks complete information about it. The individual is aware of the innovation, but is not yet motivated to seek further information. The primary function of the awareness stage is to initiate the sequence of later stages that lead to eventual adoption of the innovation.

Interest Stage. At the interest stage the individual becomes interested in the new idea and seeks additional information about it. The individual favours the innovation in a general way, but he has not yet judged its utility in terms of his own situation. The function of the interest stage is mainly to increase the individual's information about the innovation. The cognitive of "knowing" component of behaviour is involved at the interest stage. The individual is more psychologically involved with the innovation at the interest stage than at the awareness stage. Previously, the individual listened or read about the innovation; at the interest stage he actively seeks information about the idea. His personality and value, as well as the norms of his social system or groups may affect where he seeks information, as well as how he interprets this information about the innovation.

Evaluation Stage. At the evaluation stage the individual mentally applies the innovation to his present and anticipated future situation and then decides whether or not to try it. A sort of "mental trial" occurs at the evaluation stage. If the individual feels the advantages of the innovation outweight the disadvantages, he will decide to try the innovation. The trial itself, however, is conceptually distinct from the decision to try the new idea. The evaluation is probably least distinct of the five adoption stages, and one of the most difficult from which to question respondents. The innovation carries a subjective risk to the individual. He is unsure of the results, and for this reason, a reinforcement effect is needed at the evaluation stage to convince the individual that his thinking is on the right path. Information and advice from peers is likely to be sought at this point.

Trial Stage. At the trial stage the individual uses the information on a small scale in order to determine its utility in his own situation. The main function of the trial stage is to demonstrate the new idea in the individual's own situation and determine its usefulness for possible complete adoption. It is thus a validity test or "dry run"; the decision to use the ideas on a trial basis was made at the evaluation stage. The individual may seek specific information about the method of using the innovation at the trial stage.

Adoption Stage. At the adoption stage the individual decides to continue the full use of the innovation. The main function of the adoption stage are considerations of the trial results and the decision to ratify sustained use of the innovation. Adoption implies continued use of the innovation in the future. These then are the stages in the mental process of accepting new ideas and practices. Individuals may go through these stages at the different rates depending upon the practice itself. The complexity of the practice seems to be a major factor in determining the rate and manner with which people go through these mental stages.

An innovation may be rejected at any stage in the adoption process. The individual may decide at the evaluation stage that the innovation will not apply to his situation and mentally reject it. Or, the innovation may be rejected at the trial stage, where the individual decides that the rewards expected from adoption will not outweigh the cost and effort of doing so. Rejection may occur for less rational reasons.

Factors Affecting Adoption

The relative speed with which a new idea is adopted depends partially upon the characteristics of the new idea. Some factors affecting the rate of adoption are:

1. Cost and economic return. New practices that are high in cost generally tend to be adopted more slowly than do the less costly ones. However, regardless of cost, practices which produce

high returns for money invested tend to be adopted more rapidly than those which yield lower returns. Also, practices producing quick returns on investment tend to be more rapidly adopted than those which produce deferred returns or returns over a long period of time

2. Complexity. New ideas that are relatively simple to understand and use will generally be accepted more quickly than more complex ideas. For example, increased fertilizer application is likely to be more readily accepted than an innovation in fertilizer application methods.
3. Visibility. Practices also vary in the extent to which their operation and results are easily seen or demonstrated. The more visible the practice and its results, the more rapid is its adoption.
4. Divisibility. Practices such as fertilizer application, different fertilizer analysis, feed additives, weed sprays, or seed varieties may be tried by sample basis and the results compared with those from previous practice. A practice that can be tried on a limited basis will generally be adopted more rapidly than one that cannot.
5. Compatibility. A new idea or practice that is consistent with existing beliefs will be accepted more rapidly than one that is not.

Other factors such as prestige may affect the speed of adoption. In some areas, it may be considered a mark of social prestige to have a farm plan. The demand for farm planning may be considerable although the degree to which the farmers put their plans into effect may vary considerably.

In any community, the readiness to accept new ideas and to put them into practice vary from farmer to farmer. We can classify them according to their readiness to accept new ideas.

Innovators. These are farmers who are eager to accept new ideas. Usually there are only a few people in this class in the normal farming community. In village societies, innovators are often looked on with suspicion and jealousy. Yet, they are important to the success of an extension program for they can be persuaded to try new methods and thereby create awareness in the communities where they live. However, the extension worker should exercise tact and caution and avoid individual preferences publicly which could result in rejection of the idea as a whole.

Early adopters. These are farmers who are more cautious, and want to see the idea tried and proven first under local conditions. They express early interest but must be convinced by result of demonstrations of the direct benefit to them. Usually this group of people includes local leaders and others who are respected in the community. Their support is vital to the process of acceptance by the community.

The majority. The rest of the farming community adopts a new idea slowly and often less completely. They differ in the speed of adoption. Some may never adopt the idea at all and may continue to oppose it. The majority are more likely to be influenced by the opinions of local leaders and neighbors than by the extension workers.

The main purpose of studying this classification is to understand how people can accept the new ideas that are being taught to them and be able to select leaders who can help program their objective and follow-up actions. If farmers in an area are not aware of the new idea, the innovators and early adopters must help demonstrate the accepted results for the benefit of the community.

8

E-learning and Vocational Education

E-learning refers to the use of electronic media and information and communication technologies (ICT) in education. E-learning is broadly inclusive of all forms of educational technology in learning and teaching. E-learning is inclusive of, and is broadly synonymous with multimedia learning, technology-enhanced learning (TEL), computer-based instruction (CBI), computer-based training (CBT), computer-assisted instruction or computer-aided instruction (CAI), internet-based training (IBT), web-based training (WBT), online education, virtual education, virtual learning environments (VLE) (which are also called learning platforms), m-learning, and digital educational collaboration. These alternative names emphasize a particular aspect, component or delivery method.

E-learning includes numerous types of media that deliver text, audio, images, animation, and streaming video, and includes technology applications and processes such as audio or video tape, satellite TV, CD-ROM, and computer-based learning, as well as local intranet/extranet and web-based learning. Information and communication systems, whether free-standing or based on either local networks or the Internet in networked learning, underly many e-learning processes.

E-learning can occur in or out of the classroom. It can be self-paced, asynchronous learning or may be instructor-led, synchronous learning. E-learning is suited to distance learning and flexible learning, but it can also be used in conjunction with face-to-face teaching, in which case the term blended learning is commonly used. It is commonly thought that new technologies make a big difference in education. Many proponents of e-learning believe that everyone must be equipped with basic knowledge of technology, as well as use it as a vehicle for reaching educational goals. E-learning refers to the use of technology in learning and education. There are several aspects to describing the intellectual and technical development of e-learning, which can be categorized into discrete areas.

These are addressed in turn in the sections of this article:

1. e-learning as an educational approach or tool that supports traditional subjects;
2. e-learning as a technological medium that assists in the communication of knowledge, and its development and exchange;
3. e-learning itself as an educational subject; such courses may be called "Computer Studies" or "Information and Communication Technology (ICT)";
4. e-learning administrative tools such as education management information systems (EMIS).
5. e-learning is a Study Medium without Teacher and Physical Classroom.
6. e-learning is beneficial Economically because of no use of Paper & Pencil.

Background

E-learning is a broadly inclusive term that describes educational technology that electronically or technologically supports learning and teaching. Bernard Luskin, a pioneer of e-learning, advocates that the "e" should be interpreted to mean "exciting, energetic, enthusiastic, emotional, extended, excellent, and educational" in addition to "electronic." This broad interpretation focuses on new applications and developments, and also brings learning and media psychology into consideration. Parks suggested that the "e" should refer to "everything, everyone, engaging, easy".

Depending on whether a particular aspect, component or delivery method is given emphasis, a wide array of similar or overlapping terms has been used. As such, e-learning encompasses multimedia learning, technology-enhanced learning (TEL), computer-based training (CBT), computer-assisted instruction (CAI), internet-based training (IBT), web-based training (WBT), online education, virtual education, virtual learning environments (VLE) which are also called learning platforms, m-learning, digital educational collaboration, distributed learning, computer-mediated communication, cyber-learning, and multi-modal instruction. Every one of these numerous terms has had its advocates, who point up particular potential distinctions. In practice, as technology has advanced, the particular "narrowly defined" aspect that was initially emphasized has blended into "e-learning." As an example, "virtual learning" in a narrowly-defined semantic sense implies entering the environmental simulation within a virtual world, for example in treating PTSD. In practice, a "virtual education course" refers to any instructional course in which all, or at least a significant portion, is delivered by the Internet. "Virtual" is used in that broader way to describe a course that not taught in a classroom face-to-face but through a substitute mode that can conceptually be associated "virtually" with classroom teaching, which means that people do not have to go to the physical classroom to learn. Accordingly, virtual education refers to a form of distance learning in which course content is delivered by various methods such as course management applications, multimedia resources, and videoconferencing. Students and instructors communicate via these technologies.

The worldwide e-learning industry is economically significant, and was estimated in 2000 to be over $48 billion according to conservative estimates. Developments in internet and multimedia technologies are the basic enabler of e-learning, with consulting, content, technologies, services and support being identified as the five key sectors of the e-learning industry. Information and communication technologies (ICT) are used extensively by young people.

E-learning expenditures differ within and between countries. Finland, Norway, Belgium and Korea appear to have comparatively effective programs.

History

In 1960, the University of Illinois initiated a classroom system based in linked computer terminals where students could access informational resources on a particular course while listening to the lectures that were recorded via some form of remotely-linked device like television or audio device.

In the early 1960s, Stanford University psychology professors Patrick Suppes and Richard C. Atkinson experimented with using computers to teach math and reading to young children in elementary schools in East Palo Alto, California. Stanford's Education Program for Gifted Youth is descended from those early experiments. In 1963, Bernard Luskin installed the first computer in a community college for instruction, working with Stanford and others, developed computer assisted instruction. Luskin completed his landmark UCLA dissertation working with the Rand Corporation in analyzing obstacles to computer assisted instruction in 1970.

Educational institutions began to take advantage of the new medium by offering distance learning courses using computer networking for information. Early e-learning systems, based on Computer-Based Learning/Training often attempted to replicate autocratic teaching styles whereby the role of the e-learning system was assumed to be for transferring knowledge, as opposed to systems developed later based on Computer Supported Collaborative Learning (CSCL), which encouraged the shared development of knowledge.

Computer-based learning made up many early e-learning courses such as those developed by Murray Turoff and Starr Roxanne Hiltz in the 1970s and 80s at the New Jersey Institute of Technology, and the ones developed at the University of Guelph in Canada. In 1976, Bernard Luskin launched Coastline Community College as a "college without walls" using television station KOCE-TV as a vehicle. By the mid-1980s, accessing course content become possible at many college libraries.

Cassandra B. Whyte researched about the ever increasing role that computers would play in higher education. This evolution, to include computer-supported collaborative learning, in addition to data management, has been realized. The type of computers has changed over the years from cumbersome, slow devices taking up much space in the classroom, home, and office to laptops and handheld devices that are more portable in form and size and this minimalization of technology devices will continue.

The Open University in Britain and the University of British Columbia (where Web CT, now incorporated into Blackboard Inc. was first developed) began a revolution of using the Internet to deliver learning, making heavy use of web-based training and online distance learning and online discussion between students. Practitioners such as Harasim (1995) put heavy emphasis on the use of learning networks.

With the advent of World Wide Web in the 1990s, teachers embarked on the method using emerging technologies to employ multi-object oriented sites, which are text-based online virtual reality system, to create course websites along with simple sets instructions for its students. As the Internet becomes popularized, correspondence schools like University of Phoenix became highly interested with the virtual education, setting up a name for itself in 1980. In 1993, Graziadei described an online computer-delivered lecture, tutorial and assessment project using electronic mail. By 1994, the first online high school had been founded. In 1997, Graziadei described criteria for evaluating products and developing technology-based courses include being portable, replicable, scalable, and affordable, and having a high probability of long-term cost-effectiveness.

By 1994, CALCampus presented its first online curriculum as Internet becoming more accessible through major telecommunications networks. CALCampus is where concepts of online-based school first originated, this allowed to progress real-time classroom instructions and Quantum Link classrooms. With the drastic shift of Internet functionality, multimedia began introducing new schemes of communication; through the invention of webcams, educators can simply record lessons live and upload them on the website page. There are currently wide varieties of online education that are reachable for colleges, universities and K-12 students. In fact, the National Centre for Education Statistics estimate the number of K-12 students enrolled in online distance learning programs increased by 65 percent from 2002 to 2005. This form of high learning allowed for greater flexibility by easing the communication between teacher and student, now teachers received quick lecture feedbacks from their students. The idea of Virtual Education soon became popular and many institutions began following the new norm in the education history.

The emergence of e-learning is arguably one of the most powerful tools available to the growing need for education. The need to improve access to education opportunities allowed students who desire to pursue their education but are constricted due to the distance of the institution to achieve education through "virtual connection" newly available to them. Online education is rapidly increasing and becoming as a viable alternative for traditional classrooms. According to a 2008 study conducted by the U.S Department of Education, back in 2006-2007 academic year, about 66% of postsecondary public and private schools began participating in student financial aid programs offered some distance learning courses, record shows only 77% of enrollment in for-credit courses being for those with an online component. In 2008, the Council of Europe passed a statement endorsing e-learning's potential to drive equality and education improvements across the EU.

Recent studies show that the effectiveness of online instruction is considered equal to that of face-to-face classroom instructions but not as effective as the combination of face-to-face and online methods.

Educational Approach

The extent to which e-learning assists or replaces other learning and teaching approaches is variable, ranging on a continuum from none to fully online distance learning. A variety of descriptive terms have been employed (somewhat inconsistently) to categorize the extent to which technology is used. For example, 'hybrid learning' or 'blended learning' may refer to classroom aids and laptops, or may refer to approaches in which traditional classroom time is reduced but not eliminated, and is replaced with some online learning. 'Distributed learning' may describe either the e-learning component of a hybrid approach, or fully online distance learning environments. Another scheme described the level of technological support as 'web enhanced', 'web supplemented' and 'web dependent'.(Sloan Commission)

Synchronous and Asynchronous

E-learning may either be synchronous or asynchronous. Synchronous learning occurs in real-time, with all participants interacting at the same time, while asynchronous learning is self-paced and allows participants to engage in the exchange of ideas or information without the dependency of other participants involvement at the same time. Synchronous learning involves the exchange of ideas and information with one or more participants during the same period of time. A face-to-face discussion is an example of synchronous communications. In e-learning environments, examples of synchronous communications include online real-time live teacher instruction and feedback, Skype conversations, or chat rooms or virtual classrooms where everyone is online and working collaboratively at the same time.

Asynchronous learning may use technologies such as email, blogs, wikis, and discussion boards, as well as web-supported textbooks, hypertext documents, audio video courses, and social networking using web 2.0. At the professional educational level, training may include virtual operating rooms. Asynchronous learning is particularly beneficial for students who have health problems or have child care responsibilities and regularly leaving the home to attend lectures is difficult. They have the opportunity to complete their work in a low stress environment and within a more flexible timeframe. In *asynchronous* online courses, students proceed at their own pace. If they need to listen to a lecture a second time, or think about a question for a while, they may do so without fearing that they will hold back the rest of the class. Through online courses, students can earn their diplomas more quickly, or repeat failed courses without the embarrassment of being in a class with younger students. Students also have access to an incredible variety of enrichment courses in online learning, and can participate in college courses, internships, sports, or work and still graduate with their class. Both the asynchronous and synchronous methods rely heavily on self-motivation, self-discipline, and the ability to communicate in writing effectively.

Linear Learning

Computer-based learning or training (CBT) refers to self-paced learning activities delivered on a computer or handheld device such as a tablet or smartphone. CBT often delivers content via CD-ROM, and typically presents content in a linear fashion, much like reading an online book or manual. For this reason, CBT is often used to teach static processes, such as using software or completing mathematical equations. Computer-based training is conceptually similar to web-based training (WBT), the primary difference being that WBTs are delivered via Internet using a web browser.

Assessing learning in a CBT is often by assessments that can be easily scored by a computer such as multiple choice questions, drag-and-drop, radio button, simulation or other interactive means. Assessments are easily scored and recorded via online software, providing immediate end-user feedback and completion status. Users are often able to print completion records in the form of certificates.

CBTs provide learning stimulus beyond traditional learning methodology from textbook, manual, or classroom-based instruction. For example, CBTs offer user-friendly solutions for satisfying continuing education requirements. Instead of limiting students to attending courses or reading printed manuals, students are able to acquire knowledge and skills through methods that are much more conducive to individual learning preferences. For example, CBTs offer visual learning benefits through animation or video, not typically offered by any other means.

CBTs can be a good alternative to printed learning materials since rich media, including videos or animations, can easily be embedded to enhance the learning.

However, CBTs pose some learning challenges. Typically the creation of effective CBTs requires enormous resources. The software for developing CBTs (such as Flash or Adobe Director) is often more complex than a subject matter expert or teacher is able to use. In addition, the lack of human interaction can limit both the type of content that can be presented as well as the type of assessment that can be performed. Many learning organizations are beginning to use smaller CBT/WBT activities as part of a broader online learning program which may include online discussion or other interactive elements.

Collaborative Learning

Computer-supported collaborative learning (CSCL) uses instructional methods designed to encourage or require students to work together on learning tasks. CSCL is similar in concept to the terminology, "e-learning 2.0".

Collaborative learning is distinguishable from the traditional approach to instruction in which the instructor is the principal source of knowledge and skills. For example, the neologism "e-learning 1.0" refers to the direct transfer method in computer-based learning and training systems (CBL). In contrast to the linear delivery of content, often directly from the instructor's material, CSCL uses blogs, wikis, and cloud-based document portals (such as Google Docs and Dropbox). With technological Web 2.0 advances, sharing information between multiple people in a network has become much easier and use has increased. One of the main reasons for its usage states that it is "a breeding ground for creative and engaging educational endeavours."

Using Web 2.0 social tools in the classroom allows for students and teachers to work collaboratively, discuss ideas, and promote information. According to Sendall (2008), blogs, wikis, and social networking skills are found to be significantly useful in the classroom. After initial instruction on using the tools, students also reported an increase in knowledge and comfort level for using Web 2.0 tools. The collaborative tools also prepare students with technology skills necessary in today's workforce.

Locus of control remains an important consideration in successful engagement of e-learners. According to the work of Cassandra B. Whyte, the continuing attention to aspects of motivation and success in regard to e-learning should be kept in context and concert with other educational efforts. Information about motivational tendencies can help educators, psychologists, and technologists develop insights to help students perform better academically.

Classroom 2.0

Classroom 2.0 refers to online multi-user virtual environments (MUVEs) that connect schools across geographical frontiers. Also known as "eTwinning", computer-supported collaborative learning (CSCL) allows learners in one school to communicate with learners in another that they would not get to know otherwise, enhancing educational outcomes and cultural integration. Examples of classroom 2.0 applications are Blogger and Skype.

E-learning 2.0

E-learning 2.0 is a type of computer-supported collaborative learning (CSCL) system that developed with the emergence of Web 2.0. From an e-learning 2.0 perspective, conventional e-learning systems were based on instructional packets, which were delivered to students using assignments. Assignments were evaluated by the teacher. In contrast, the new e-learning places increased emphasis on social learning and use of social software such as blogs, wikis, podcasts and virtual worlds such as *Second Life.* This phenomenon has also been referred to as Long Tail Learning. E-learning 2.0, in contrast to e-learning systems not based on CSCL, assumes that knowledge (as meaning and understanding) is socially constructed. Learning takes place through conversations about content and grounded interaction about problems and actions. Advocates of social learning claim that one of the best ways to learn something is to teach it to others.

In addition to virtual classroom environments, social networks have become an important part of E-learning 2.0. Social networks have been used to foster online learning communities around subjects as diverse as test preparation and language education. Mobile Assisted Language Learning (MALL) is the use of handheld computers or cell phones to assist in language learning. Traditional educators may not promote social networking unless they are communicating with their own colleagues. Virtual worlds for e-Learning have been amongst the first applications being deployed in clouds in order to exploit the characteristics of Cloud computing with respect to on-demand provision of resources during runtime.

Technology

Various technologies are used to facilitate e-learning. Most e-learning uses combinations of these techniques, including blogs, collaborative software, ePortfolios, and virtual classrooms.

Audio

The radio has been around for a long time and has been used in educational classrooms. Recent technologies have allowed classroom teachers to stream audio over the internet. There are also webcasts and podcasts available over the internet for students and teachers to download. For example, iTunes has various podcasts available on a variety of subjects that can be downloaded for free.

Video

Videos allow teachers to reach students who are visual learners and tend to learn best by seeing the material rather than hearing or reading about it. Teachers can access video clips through the internet instead of relying on DVDs or VHS tapes. Websites like YouTube are used by many teachers. Teachers can use messaging programs such as Skype, Adobe Connect, or webcams, to interact with guest speakers and other experts. Interactive video games are being integrated in the curriculum at both K-12 and higher education institutions.

Research on the use of video in lessons is preliminary, but early results show an increased retention and better results when video is used in a lesson. Creating a systematic video development method holds promise for creating video models that positively impact student learning.

Computers, Tablets and Mobile Devices

Computers and tablets allow students and teachers access to websites and other programs, such as Microsoft Word, PowerPoint, PDF files, and images. Many mobile devices support m-learning.

Blogging

Blogs allow students and teachers to post their thoughts, ideas, and comments on a website. Blogging allows students and instructors to share their thoughts and comments on the thoughts of others which could create an interactive learning environment.

Webcams

The development of webcams and webcasting has facilitated the creation of virtual classrooms and virtual learning environments. Virtual classrooms supported by such technology are becoming more and more popular, especially since they are contributing as a main solution to solving problems with travel expenses. Virtual classrooms with such technology also provide the benefits of being easy to set up.

Whiteboards

Interactive whiteboards ("smartboards") allow teachers and students to write on the touch screen, so learning becomes interactive and engaging.

Screencasting

Screencasting is a recent trend in e-learning. There are many screencasting tools available that allow users to share their screens directly from their browser and make the video available online so that the viewers can stream the video directly. The advantage of such tools is that it gives the presenter the ability to show his ideas and flow of thoughts rather than simply explain them, which may be more confusing when delivered via simple text instructions. With the combination of video and audio, the expert can mimic the one-on-one experience of the classroom and deliver clear, complete instructions. From the learner's point of view this provides the ability to pause and rewind and gives the learners the advantage of moving at their own pace, something a classroom cannot always offer.

Combining Technology

Along with the terms *learning technology*, *instructional technology*, the term educational technology refers to the use of technology in learning in a much broader sense than the computer-based training or *Computer Aided Instruction* of the 1980s. It is also broader than the terms *Online Learning* or *Online Education* which generally refer to purely web-based learning. In cases where mobile technologies are used, the term M-learning has become more common. E-learning, however, also has implications beyond just the technology and refers to the actual learning that takes place using these systems.

In higher education especially, the increasing tendency is to create a virtual learning environment (VLE) (which is sometimes combined with a Management Information System (MIS) to create a Managed Learning Environment) in which all aspects of a course are handled through a consistent user interface standard throughout the institution. A growing number of physical universities, as well as newer online-only colleges, have begun to offer a select set of academic degree and certificate programs via the Internet at a wide range of levels and in a wide range of disciplines. While some programs require students to attend some campus classes or orientations, many are delivered completely online. In addition, several universities offer online student support services, such as online advising and registration, e-counseling, online textbook purchases, student governments and student newspapers.

E-learning can also refer to educational websites such as those offering learning scenarios, worksheets and interactive exercises for children. The term is also used extensively in the business sector where it generally refers to cost-effective online training.

Virtual Classroom

Virtual Learning Environments (VLE), also known as learning platforms, utilize virtual classrooms and meetings which often use a mix of communication technologies. One example of web conferencing software that enables students and instructors to communicate with each other via webcam, microphone, and real-time chatting in a group setting, are GoToTraining, WebEx Training or Adobe Connect, which are sometimes used for meetings and presentations. Participants in a virtual classroom can raise hands, answer polls or take tests. Students are able to 'write on the board' and even share their desktop, when given rights by the teacher. Other communication technologies available in a virtual classroom include text notes, microphone rights and mouse control.

The virtual classroom also provides the opportunity for students to receive direct instruction from a qualified teacher in an interactive environment. Students have direct and immediate access to their instructor for instant feedback and direction. The virtual classroom also provides a structured schedule of classes, which can be helpful for students who may find the freedom of asynchronous learning to be overwhelming. In addition, the virtual classroom provides a social learning environment that replicates the traditional "brick and mortar" classroom. Most virtual classroom applications provide a recording feature. Each class is recorded and stored on a server, which allows for instant playback of any class over the course of the school year. This can be extremely useful for students to review material and concepts for an upcoming exam. This also provides students with the opportunity to watch any class that they may have missed, so that they do not fall behind. It also gives parents the ability to monitor any classroom to ensure that they are satisfied with the education their child is receiving.

Administrative Tools

Learning Management System: A learning management system (LMS) is software used for delivering, tracking and managing training and education; for example, tracking attendance, time on task, and student progress. Educators can post announcements, grade assignments, check on course activity, and participate in class discussions. Students can submit their work, read and respond to discussion questions, and take quizzes. An LMS may allow teachers, administrators, students, and permitted additional parties (such as parents if appropriate) to track various metrics. LMSs range from systems for managing training/educational records to software for distributing courses over the Internet and offering features for online collaboration. The creation and maintenance of comprehensive learning content requires substantial initial and ongoing investments of human labour. Effective translation into other languages and cultural contexts requires even more investment by knowledgeable personnel.

Two widely used internet-based learning management systems tools for e-learning are Blackboard Inc. and Moodle. Blackboard Inc. has over 20 million users daily. Offering six different platforms: Blackboard Learn, Blackboard Collaborate, Blackboard Mobile, Blackboard Connect, Blackboard Transact, and Blackboard Analytics; Blackboard's tools allow educators to decide whether their program will be blended or fully online, asynchronous or synchronous. Blackboard can be used for K-12 education, Higher Education, Business, and Government collaboration.

Moodle is an Open Source Course Management System. It is free to download and provides blended learning opportunities as well as platforms for distance learning courses. The Moodle website has many tutorials for creating a program or becoming a Moodle student.

Learning Content Management System

A learning content management system (LCMS) is software for author content (courses, reusable content objects). An LCMS may be solely dedicated to producing and publishing content that is hosted on an LMS, or it can host the content itself. The Aviation Industry Computer-Based Training Committee (AICC) specification provides support for content that is hosted separately from the LMS.

A recent trend in LCMSs is to address this issue through crowd-sourcing (cf.SlideWiki).

Computer-aided Assessment

Computer-aided assessment (also but less commonly referred to as e-assessment), ranging from automated multiple-choice tests to more sophisticated systems is becoming increasingly common. With some systems, feedback can be geared towards a student's specific mistakes or the computer can navigate the student through a series of questions adapting to what the student appears to have learned or not learned.

The best examples follow a formative Assessment structure and are called "Online Formative Assessment". This involves making an initial formative assessment by sifting out the incorrect answers. The author of the assessment/teacher will then explain what the pupil should have done with each question. It will then give the pupil at least one practice at each slight variation of sifted out questions. This is the formative learning stage. The next stage is to make a summative assessment by a new set of questions only covering the topics previously taught.

Learning design is the type of activity enabled by software that supports sequences of activities that can be both adaptive and collaborative. The IMS Learning Design specification is intended as a standard format for learning designs, and IMS LD Level A is supported in LAMS V2.elearning has been replacing the traditional settings due to its cost effectiveness.

Electronic Performance Support Systems (EPSS)

An Electronic Performance Support System is, according to Barry Raybould, "a computer-based system that improves worker productivity by providing on-the-job access to integrated information, advice, and learning experiences" (Raybould, 1991). Gloria Gery defines it as "an integrated electronic environment that is available to and easily accessible by each employee and is structured to provide immediate, individualized on-line access to the full range of information, software, guidance, advice and assistance, data, images, tools, and assessment and monitoring systems to permit job performance with minimal support and intervention by others." (Gery, 1989).

Electronic performance support systems are used for:

- task structuring support: help with how to do a task (procedures and processes),
- access to knowledge bases (help user find information needed)
- alternate forms of knowledge representation (multiple representations of knowledge, e.g., video, audio, text, image, data)

Content

Content is a core component of e-learning and includes issues such as pedagogy and learning object re-use. While there are a number of means of achieving a rich and interactive elearning platform, one option is using a design architecture composed of the "Five Types of Content in eLearning" (Clark, Mayer, 2007).

Content normally comes in one of five forms:

- Fact - unique data (e. g., symbols for Excel formula, or the parts that make up a learning objective)
- Concept - a category that includes multiple examples (e. g., Excel formulas, or the various types/theories of Instructional Design)
- Process - a flow of events or activities (e. g., how a spreadsheet works, or the five phases in ADDIE)
- Procedure - step-by-step task (e. g., entering a formula into a spreadsheet, or the steps that should be followed within a phase in ADDIE)
- Strategic Principle - task performed by adapting guidelines (e. g., doing a financial projection in a spreadsheet, or using a framework for designing learning environments)

Pedagogical Elements

Pedagogical elements are defined as structures or units of educational material. They are the educational content that is to be delivered. These units are independent of format, meaning that although the unit may delivered in various ways, the pedagogical structures themselves are not the textbook, web page, video conference, Podcast, lesson, assignment, multiple choice question, quiz, discussion group or a case study, all of which are possible methods of delivery.

Pedagogical approaches

Various pedagogical perspectives or learning theories may be considered in designing and interacting with e-learning programs. E-learning theory examines these approaches, including social-constructivist, one application of which was One Laptop Per Child, Laurillard's conversational model including Gilly Salmon's five-stage model, and cognitive, emotional, behavioural, and contextual perspectives. In 'mode neutral' learning online and classroom learners can coexist within one learning environment, encouraging interconnectivity. Self-regulated learning refers to several concepts that play major roles in e-learning. Learning courses should provide opportunities to practice these strategies and skills. Self-regulation and structured supervision both enhance e-learning.

Learning Object Standards

Much effort has been put into the technical reuse of electronically based teaching materials and in particular creating or re-using learning objects. These are self-contained units that are properly tagged with keywords, or other metadata, and often stored in an XML file format. Creating a course requires putting together a sequence of learning objects. There are both proprietary and open, non-commercial and commercial, peer-reviewed repositories of learning objects such as the Merlot repository.

Sharable Content Object Reference Model (SCORM) is a collection of standards and specifications that applies to certain web-based e-learning. Other specifications such as Schools Framework allow for the transporting of learning objects, or for categorizing metadata (LOM). These standards themselves are early in the maturity process with the oldest being 8 years old. They are also relatively vertical specific: SIF is primarily pK-12, LOM is primarily Corp, Military and Higher Ed, and SCORM is primarily Military and Corp with some Higher Ed. PESC- the Post-Secondary Education Standards Council- is also making headway in developing standards and learning objects for the Higher Ed space, while SIF is beginning to seriously turn towards Instructional and Curriculum learning objects.

In the US pK12 space there are a host of content standards that are critical as well- the NCES data standards are a prime example. Each state government's content standards and achievement benchmarks are critical metadata for linking e-learning objects in that space.

An excellent example of e-learning that relates to knowledge management and reusability is Navy E-Learning, which is available to Active Duty, Retired, or Disable Military members. This on-line tool provides certificate courses to enrich the user in various subjects related to military training and civilian skill sets. The e-learning system not only provides learning objectives, but also evaluates the progress of the student and credit can be earned toward higher learning institutions. The Internet allows for learning to be directed at one's current objectives. This reuse is an excellent example of knowledge retention and the cyclical process of knowledge transfer and use of data and records.

Applications

Preschool: Various forms of electronic media are a feature of preschool life. Although parents report a positive experience, the impact of such use has not been systematically assessed.

The age when a given child might start using a particular technology such as a cellphone or computer might depend on matching a technological resource to the recipient's developmental capabilities, such as the age-anticipated stages labeled by Swiss psychologist, Jean Piaget. Parameters, such as age-appropriateness, coherence with sought-after values, and concurrent entertainment and educational aspects, have been suggested for choosing media.

K–12

E-learning is utilized by public K–12 schools in the United States as well as private schools. Some e-learning environments take place in a traditional classroom, others allow students to attend classes from home or other locations. There are several states that are utilizing virtual school platforms for e-learning across the country that continue to increase. Virtual school enables students to log into synchronous learning or asynchronous learning courses anywhere there is an internet connection.

Technology kits are usually provided that include computers, printers, and reimbursement for home internet use. Students are to use technology for school use only and must meet weekly work submission requirements. Teachers employed by K–12 online public schools must be certified teachers in the state they are teaching in. Online schools allow for students to maintain their own pacing and progress, course selection, and provide the flexibility for students to create their own schedule.

E-learning is increasingly being utilized by students who may not want to go to traditional brick and mortar schools due to severe allergies or other medical issues, fear of school violence and school bullying and students whose parents would like to homeschool but do not feel qualified. Online schools create a safe haven for students to receive a quality education while almost completely avoiding these common problems. Online charter schools also often are not limited by location, income level or class size in the way brick and mortar charter schools are.

National private schools are also available online. These provide the benefits of e-learning to students in states where charter online schools are not available. They also may allow students greater flexibility and exemption from state testing.

Virtual education in K-12 schooling often refers to virtual schools, and in higher education to virtual universities. Virtual schools are "cybercharter schools" with innovative administrative models and course delivery technology.

Higher Education

In the United States, e-learning has become a predominant form of post-secondary education. Enrollments for fully online learning increased by an average of 12–14 percent annually between 2004–2009, compared with an average of approximately 2 per cent increase per year in enrollments overall. In 2006, 3.5 million students participated in on-line learning at higher education institutions in the United States. Almost a quarter of all students in post-secondary education were taking fully online courses in 2008. In 2009, 44 percent of post-secondary students in the USA were taking some or all of their courses online, this figure is projected to rise to 81 percent by 2014. During the fall 2011 term, 6.7 million students enrolled in at least one online course. Over two-thirds of chief academic officers believe that online learning is critical for their institution. The Sloan report, based on a poll of academic leaders, indicated that students are as satisfied with on-line classes as with traditional ones.

Although a large proportion of for-profit higher education institutions now offer online classes, only about half of private, non-profit schools do so. Private institutions may become more involved with on-line presentations as the costs decrease. Properly trained staff must also be hired to work with students online. These staff members need to understand the content area, and also be highly trained in the use of the computer and Internet. Online education is rapidly increasing, and online doctoral programs have even developed at leading research universities.

Although massively-open online courses (MOOCs) may have limitations that preclude them from fully replacing college education, such programs have significantly expanded. MIT, Stanford and Princeton University offer classes to a global audience, but not for college credit. University-level programs, like edX founded by Massachusetts Institute of Technology and Harvard University, offer wide range of disciplines at no charge.

Private organizations also offer classes, such as Udacity, with free computer science classes, and Khan Academy, with over 3,900 free micro-lectures available via YouTube. There already is at least one counterstream to MOOC; Distributed open collaborative course or DOCC challenges the role of the Instructor, the hierarchy, the role of money and role of massiveness. DOCC recognizes that the pursuit of knowledge may be achieved better by not using a centralized singular syllabus, that expertise is distributed throughout all the participants in a learning activity, and does not just reside with one or two individuals.

Coursera, an online-enrollment platform, is now offering education for millions of people around the world. A certification is consigned by Coursera for students who are able to complete an adequate performance in the course. Free online courses are administered by the website- fields like computer science, medicine, networks and social sciences are accessibly offered to pursuing students. The lectures are recorded into series of short videos discussing different topics and assignments in a weekly basis.

This virtual curriculum complement the curriculum taught in the traditional education setting by providing equality for all students, despite disability, and geographical location and socioeconomic status.

According to *Fortune* magazine, over a million people worldwide have enrolled in free online courses.

Corporate and Professional

E-learning has now been adopted and used by various companies to inform and educate both their employees and customers. Companies with large and spread out distribution chains use it to educate their sales staff about the latest product developments without the need of organizing physical onsite courses. Compliance has also been a big field of growth with banks using it to keep their staff's CPD levels up. Other areas of growth include staff development, where employees can learn valuable workplace skills.

Advantages and Disadvantages

Motivation: There are several advantages and disadvantages with regards to motivation in e-learning.

For many students, e-learning is the most convenient way to pursue a degree in higher education. A lot of these students are attracted to a flexible, self-paced method of education to attain their degree. It is important to note that many of these students could be working their way through college, supporting themselves or battling with serious illness. To these students, it would be extremely difficult to find time to fit college in their schedule. Thus, these students are more likely and more motivated to enroll in an e-learning class. Moreover, in asynchronous e-learning classes, students are free to log on and complete work any time they wish. They can work on and complete their assignments at the times when they think most cogently, whether it be early in the morning or late at night.

However, many teachers have a harder time keeping their students engaged in an e-learning class. A disengaged student is usually an unmotivated student, and an engaged student is a motivated student. One reason why students are more likely to be disengaged is that the lack of face-to-face contact makes it difficult for teachers to read their students' nonverbal cues, including confusion, boredom or frustration. These cues are helpful to a teacher in deciding whether to speed up, introduce new material, slow down or explain a concept in a different way. If a student is confused, bored or frustrated, he or she is unlikely to be motivated to succeed in that class.

Other Advantages and Disadvantages

Key advantages of e-learning include:

- Improved open access to education, including access to full degree programs
- Better integration for non-full-time students, particularly in continuing education,
- Improved interactions between students and instructors,
- Provision of tools to enable students to independently solve problems,
- Acquisition of technological skills through practice with tools and computers.

Key disadvantages of e-learning, that have been found to make learning less effective than traditional class room settings, include:

- Potential distractions that hinder true learning,
- Ease of cheating,
- Bias towards tech-savvy students over non-technical students,
- Teachers' lack of knowledge and experience to manage virtual teacher-student interaction,
- Lack of social interaction between teacher and students,
- Lack of direct and immediate feedback from teachers,
- Asynchronic communication hinders fast exchange of question,
- Danger of procrastination.

Distance Education

This article is about education over a distance. For learning that is spaced over time, see Distributed learning. Distance education, distance learning, dlearning, or D-Learning is a mode of delivering education and instruction, often on an individual basis, to students who are not physically present in a traditional setting such as a classroom. Distance learning provides "access to learning when the source of information and the learners are separated by time and distance, or both." Distance education courses that require a physical on-site presence for any reason (including taking examinations) have been referred to as hybrid or blended courses of study. Massive open online courses (MOOCs), aimed at large-scale interactive participation and open access via the web or other network technologies, are a recent development in distance education.

History and Development: Distance education dates back to at least as early as 1728 when an advertisement in the Boston Gazette promoted "Caleb Phillips, Teacher of the new method of Short Hand," who sought students who wanted to learn through weekly mailed lessons. Similarly, Isaac Pitman taught shorthand in Great Britain via correspondence in the 1840s. Distance education has a long history, but its popularity and use has grown exponentially as more advanced technology has become available. By 2008, online learning programs were available in the United States in 44 states at the K-12 level.

Correspondence Courses: The University of London was the first university to offer distance learning degrees, establishing its External Programme in 1858. This program is now known as the University of London International Programmes and includes Postgraduate, Undergraduate and Diploma degrees created by colleges such as the London School of Economics, Royal Holloway and Goldsmiths.

In the United States William Rainey Harper, first president of the University of Chicago, developed the concept of extended education, whereby the research university had satellite colleges of education in the wider community. In 1892 he also encouraged the concept of correspondence school courses to further promote education, an idea that was put into practice by Columbia University.

Enrollment in the largest private for-profit school based in Scranton, Pennsylvania, the International Correspondence Schools grew explosively in the 1890s. Originally founded in 1888 to provide training for immigrant coal miners aiming to become state mine inspectors or foremen, it enrolled 2500 new students in 1894 and matriculated 72,000 new students in 1895. By 1906 total enrollments reached 900,000. The growth was due to sending out complete textbooks instead of single lessons, and the use of 1200 aggressive in-person salesmen. By 1916 it was spending $2 million a year on magazine advertising. The dropout rates were high; only one in six made it past the first third of the material in a course. Only 2.6% of students who began a course finished it. The students dropped out because they underestimated the difficulty, had little encouragement, and had poor study habits. There was a stark contrast in pedagogy:

"The regular technical school or college aims to educate a man broadly; our aim, on the contrary, is to educate him only along some particular line. The college demands that a student shall have certain educational qualifications to enter it, and that all students study for approximately the same length of time, and when they have finished their courses they are supposed to be qualified to enter any one of a number of branches in some particular profession. We, on the contrary, are aiming to make our courses fit the particular needs of the student who takes them."

Education was a high priority in the Progressive Era, as American high schools and colleges expanded greatly. For men who were older or were too busy with family responsibilities, night schools were opened, such as the YMCA school in Boston that became Northeastern University. Outside the big cities, private correspondence schools offered a flexible, narrowly focused solution. In 1916 efficiency was enhanced by the formation of the National Association of Corporation Schools.

Universities around the world used correspondence courses in the first half of the 20th century, especially to reach rural students. Australia with its vast distances was especially active; the University of Queensland established its Department of Correspondence Studies in 1911. The International Conference for Correspondence Education held its first meeting in 1938. The goal was to provide individualized education for students, at low cost, by using a pedagogy of testing, recording, classification, and differentiation.

Radio and Television: The very rapid spread of radio in the United States in the 1930s led to proposals to use it for distance education. By 1938, at least 200 city school systems, 25 state boards of education, and many colleges and universities broadcast educational programs for the public schools. One line of thought was to use radio as a master teacher.

> *" Experts in given fields broadcast lessons for pupils within the many schoolrooms of the public school system, asking questions, suggesting readings, making assignments, and conducting tests. This mechanizes education and leaves the local teacher only the tasks of preparing for the broadcast and keeping order in the classroom."*

A typical setup came in Kentucky in 1948 when John Wilkinson Taylor, president of the University of Louisville, teamed up with the National Broadcasting Corporation to use radio as a medium for distance education, The chairman of the Federal Communications Commission endorsed the project and predicted that the "college-by-radio" would put "American education 25 years ahead." The University was owned by the city, and local residents would pay the low tuition rates, receive their study materials in the mail, and listen by radio to live classroom discussions that were held on campus.

Charles Wedemeyer of the University of Wisconsin–Madison also promoted new methods. From 1964 to 1968, the Carnegie Foundation funded Wedemeyer's *Articulated Instructional Media Project* (AIM) which brought in a variety of communications technologies aimed at providing learning to an off-campus population. According to Moore's recounting, AIM impressed the UK which imported these ideas when establishing in 1969 The Open University, which initially relied on radio and television broadcasts for much of its delivery. Athabasca University, Canada's Open University, was created in 1970 and followed a similar, though independently developed, pattern. The Open University inspired the creation of Spain's National University of Distance Education (1972) and Germany's FernUniversität in Hagen (1974). There are now many similar institutions around the world, often with the name "Open University" (in English or in the local language). All "open universities" use distance education technologies as delivery methodologies and some have grown to become 'mega-universities', a term coined to denote institutions with more than 100,000 students. In 1976, Bernard Luskin launched Coastline Community College as a college beyond walls, combining computer assisted instruction with telecourses proceed by KOCE TV, the Coast Community College District public television station. Coastline has been a landmark strategic success in helping to establish online distance learning using modern technology for learning.

Internet: The widespread use of computers and the internet have made distance learning easier and faster, and today virtual schools and virtual universities deliver full curricula online. In 1996 Jones International University was launched by Glenn Jones, CEO and Bernard Luskin, Chancellor and was the first accredited fully online university accredited by a regional accrediting association in the US. Jones had also developed Mind Extension University that offered courses and degree programs in partnership with colleges and universities and distributed them over the many Jones cable companies.

Dr. Bernard Luskin developed the education services support system for MEU and examples of partnership programs were a distance learning AA degree program with Seattle Community Colleges, a nursing program with California State University at Dominguez Hills, and a BA program in Restaurant management with The University of Delaware and an MA degree program in instructional technology with George Washington University. These distance learning courses, called telecourses at the time, were the precursors of the online degree programs of today.

Between 2000 and 2008, undergraduate enrollment in at least some distance programs became more and more common. The share of students "in at least one distance education class expanded from 8 percent to 20 percent, and the percentage enrolled in a distance education degree program increased from 2 percent to 4 percent."

Many private, public, non-profit, and for-profit institutions worldwide now offer distance education courses from the most basic instruction through the highest levels of degree and doctoral programs. Levels of accreditation vary: Widely respected universities such as Stanford University and Harvard now deliver online courses—but other online schools receive little outside oversight, and some are actually fraudulent, i.e., diploma mills. In the US, the Distance Education and Training Council (DETC) specializes in the accreditation of distance education institutions.

In the United States in 2011, it was found that a third of all the students enrolled in postsecondary education had taken an accredited online course in a postsecondary institution. Even though growth rates are slow, enrollment for online courses has been seen to increase with the advance in technology. The majority of public and private colleges now offer full academic programs online. These include, but are not limited to, training programs in the mental health, occupational therapy, family therapy, art therapy, physical therapy, and rehabilitation counseling fields.

Technologies: Although the expansion of the Internet blurs the boundaries, distance education technologies are divided into two modes of delivery: synchronous learning and asynchronous learning.

In synchronous learning, all participants are "present" at the same time. In this regard, it resembles traditional classroom teaching methods despite the participants being located remotely. It requires a timetable to be organized. Web conferencing, videoconferencing, educational television, instructional television are examples of synchronous technology, as are direct-broadcast satellite (DBS), internet radio, live streaming, telephone, and web-based VoIP. Online meeting software such as Adobe Connect has helped to facilitate meetings in distance learning courses.

In asynchronous learning, participants access course materials flexibly on their own schedules. Students are not required to be together at the same time. Mail correspondence, which is the oldest form of distance education, is an asynchronous delivery technology, as are message board forums, e-mail, video and audio recordings, print materials, voicemail, and fax.

The two methods can be combined. Many courses offered by The Open University use periodic sessions of residential or day teaching to supplement the remote teaching. The Open University uses a blend of technologies and a blend of learning modalities (face-to-face, distance, and hybrid) all under the rubric of "distance learning." Distance learning can also use interactive radio instruction (IRI), interactive audio instruction (IAI), online virtual worlds, digital games, webinars, and webcasts, all of which are referred to as eLearning.

Benefits: Distance learning can expand access to education and training for both general populace and businesses since its flexible scheduling structure lessens the effects of the many time-constraints imposed by personal responsibilities and commitments. Devolving some activities off-site alleviates institutional capacity constraints arising from the traditional demand on institutional buildings and infrastructure.

Furthermore, there is the potential for increased access to more experts in the field and to other students from diverse geographical, social, cultural, economic, and experiential backgrounds. As the population at large becomes more involved in lifelong learning beyond the normal schooling age, institutions can benefit financially, and adult learning business courses may be particularly lucrative. Distance education programs can act as a catalyst for institutional innovation and are at least as effective as face-to-face learning programs, especially if the instructor is knowledgeable and skilled.

Distance education can also provide a broader method of communication within the realm of education. With the many tools and programs that technological advancements have to offer, communication appears to increase in distance education amongst students and their professors, as well as students and their classmates.

The distance educational increase in communication, particularly communication amongst students and their classmates, is an improvement that has been made to provide distance education students with as many of the opportunities as possible as they would receive in in-person education. The improvement being made in distance education is growing in tandem with the constant technological advancements. Present-day online communication allows students to associate with accredited schools and programs throughout the world that are out of reach for in-person learning.

By having the opportunity to be involved in global institutions via distance education, a diverse array of thought is presented to students through communication with their classmates. This is beneficial because students have the opportunity to "combine new opinions with their own, and develop a solid foundation for learning.". It has been shown through research that "as learners become aware of the variations in interpretation and construction of meaning among a range of people [they] construct an individual meaning," which can help students become knowledable of a wide array of viewpoints in education. To increase the likelihood that students will build effective ties with one another during the course, instructors should use similar assignments for students across different locations to overcome the influence of co-location on relationship building.

The high cost of education effects students in higher education, to which distance education may be an alternative in order to provide some relief. Distance education has been a more cost-effective form of learning, and can sometimes save students a significant amount of money as opposed to traditional education. Distance education may be able to help to save students a considerable amount financially by removing the cost of transportation. In addition, distance education may be able to save students from the economic burden of high-priced course textbooks. Many textbooks are now available as electronic textbooks, known as e-textbooks, which can offer digital textbooks for a reduced price in comparison to traditional textbooks. Also, the increasing improvements in technology have resulted in many school libraries having a partnership with digital publishers that offer course materials for free, which can help students significantly with educational costs.

Within the class, students are able to learn in ways that traditional classrooms would not be able to provide. It is able to promote good learning experiences and therefore, allow students to obtain higher satisfaction with their online learning. For example, students can review their lessons more than once according to their need. Students can then manipulate the coursework to fit their learning by focusing more on their weaker topics while breezing through concepts that they already have or can easily grasp.

When course design and the learning environment are at their optimal conditions, distance education can lead students to higher satisfaction with their learning experiences. Studies have shown that high satisfaction correlates to increased learning. Students who are enrolled in distance education with high satisfaction in their online coursework are then motivated intrinsically to learn, which often means that their performance in class will improve.

For those in a healthcare or mental health distance learning program, online-based interactions have the potential to foster deeper reflections and discussions of client issues as well as a quicker response to client issues, since supervision happens on a regular basis and is not limited to a weekly supervision meeting. This also may contribute to the students feeling a greater sense of support, since they have ongoing and regular access to their instructors and other students.

Distance learning may enable students who are unable to attend a traditional school setting, due to disability or illness such as decreased mobility and immune system suppression, to get a good education. Distance education may provide equal access regardless of socioeconomic status or income, area of residence, gender, race, age, or cost per student.

Applying universal design strategies to distance learning courses as they are being developed (rather than instituting accommodations for specific students on an as-needed basis) can increase the accessibility of such courses to students with a range of abilities, disabilities, learning styles, and native languages.

Distance education graduates, who would have never have been associated with the school under a traditional system, may donate money to the school. Distance Learning may also offer a final opportunity for adolescences that are no longer permitted in the General Education population due to behaviour disorders. Instead of these students having no other academic opportunities, they may continue their education from their homes and earn their diplomas, offering them another chance to be an integral part of society.

Criticism

Barriers to effective distance education include obstacles such as domestic distractions and unreliable technology, as well as students' program costs, adequate contact with teachers and support services, and a need for more experience. Some students attempt to participate in distance education without proper training of the tools needed to be successful in the program. Students must be provided with training on each tool that is used throughout the program. The lack of advanced technology skills can lead to an unsuccessful experience. Schools have a responsibility to adopt a proactive policy for managing technology barriers.

The results of a study of Washington state community college students showed that distance learning students tended to drop out more often than their traditional counterparts due to difficulties in language, time management, and study skills.

Distance Learning benefits may outweight the disadvantages for students in such a technology driven society however before indulging into e-learning a few more disadvantages should be considered. Some may a negatice to distance education is the lack of social interaction. If the classroom environment is what you love most about learning you may want to take a step back and reconsider distance learning. Another downfall to distance learning or -learning is that format isn't ideal for all learners. Not everyone is an ideal candidate for online learning.

If you know you have problems with motivation, procrastination and needs lots of individual attention from an instructor you may want to think long and hard before enrolling in an online learning program. Not all courses required to complete a degree may be offered online. Health care profession programs in particular, require some sort of patient interaction through field work before a student may graduate. Studies have also shown that students pursuing a medical professional graduate degree who are participating in distance education courses, favor face to face communication over professor-mediated chat rooms and/or independent studies. However, this is little to correlation between student performance when comparing the previous different distance learning strategies.

There is a theoretical problem about the application of traditional teaching methods to online courses because online courses may have no upper size limit. Daniel Barwick noted that there is no evidence that large class size is always worse or that small class size is always better, although a negative link has been established between certain types of instruction in large classes and learning outcomes; he argued that higher education has not made a sufficient effort to experiment with a variety of instructional methods to determine whether large class size is always negatively correlated with a reduction in learning outcomes. Early proponents of Massive Open Online Courses (MOOC)s saw them as just the type of experiment that Barwick had pointed out was lacking in higher education, although Barwick himself has never advocated for MOOCs.

Finally, there may also be institutional challenges. Distance learning is new enough that it may be a challenge to gain support for these programs in a traditional brick-and-mortar academic learning environment. Furthermore, it may be more difficult for the instructor to organize and plan a distance learning program, especially since many are new programs and their organizational needs are different from a traditional learning program.

Bibliography

Ambrose, Susan A., Bridges, Michael, DiPietro, Michele, Lovett, Marsha C., and Norman, Marie, K.: *How Learning Works: Seven Research-Based Principles for Smart Teaching*, Jossey-Bass, San Francisco, 2010.

Arends, Richard: *Learning to Teach*, McGraw-Hill, Boston, 1998.

Barkley, Elizabeth F.: *Student Engagement Techniques: A Handbook for College Faculty*, Jossey-Bass, San Francisco, 2009.

Blackmore, C., van Deurzen, E., & Tantam, D.: *Teaching Mental Health*, John Wiley & Sons, Ltd., Hoboken, NJ, 2007.

Byrne, T. C.: *Athabasca University The Evolution of Distance Education*, University of Calgary Press, Calgary, Alberta, 1989.

Chute, Alan G., and Melody Thompson, Burton Hancock: *The McGraw-Hill Handbook of Distance Learning: A "How to Get Started Guide" for Trainers and Human Resources Professionals,* McGraw-Hill, NY, 1998.

Cole, Robert A.: *Issues in Web-based Pedagogy: A Critical Primer*, Greenwood Press, Westport, Conn., 2000.

Daniel, Sir John S. *Mega-Universities and Knowledge Media: Technology Strategies for Higher Education*, Routledge, 1998.

Delanty G.: *Challenging Knowledge*, Open University Press, London, 2001.

Dillon, Connie L., Rosa Cintrón: *Building a Working Policy for Distance Education*, Jossey-Bass, San Francisco, 1997.

Eisenstadt, Marc: *The Knowledge Web: Learning and Collaborating on the Net*, Stylus Pub., London, 2000.

Ferguson, Vernice: *Educating the 21st Century Nurse: Challenges and Opportunities,* National League for Nursing Press, New York, 1997.

Garrison, D.R.: *E-Learning in the 21st Century: A Framework for Research and Practice*, Taylor & Francis, New York, 2011.

Harry, Keith: *Higher Education through Open and Distance Learning* , Routledge, New York, 1999.

Iverson, K. M.: *E-Learning Games,* Pearson Prentice Hall, Upper Saddle River, NJ, 2005.

Johnson, W. B. & Ridley, C. R.: *The Elements of Mentoring,* Palgrave Macmillan, NY, 2004.

Katz, Richard N.: *Dancing With the Devil : Information Technology and the New Competition in Higher Education,* Jossey-Bass Publishers, San Francisco, 1999.

King R.: *The University in the Global Age,* Palgrave Macmillan, London, 2004.

Landow, George P.: *Hypertext: The Convergence of Contemporary Critical Theory and Technology,* Johns Hopkins UP, Baltimore, 1992.

McVay, Marguerita: *How to be a Successful Distance Learning Student: Learning on the Internet,* Pearson Custom Pub., Needham heights, Mass, 2000.

Moore, Michael Grahame and William Anderson: *Handbook of Distance Education,* Psychology Press, 2012.

Picciano, Anthony G.: *Distance Learning: Making Connections Across Virtual Space and Time,* Merrill Prentice Hall, Upper Saddle River, N.J., 2001.

Richardson, W.: *Blogs, Wikis, Podcasts, and other Powerful Web Tools for the Classroom,* Corwin Press, Thousand Oaks, CA, 2006.

Schank, R.: *Designing World-Class E-Learning : How IBM, GE, Harvard Business School, And Columbia University Are Succeeding At E-Learning,* McGraw-Hill, NY, 2001.

Shea, G. F.: *Making the Most of being Mentored: How to Grow from a Mentoring Partnership,* Crisp Publications, Menlo Park, CA, 1999.

Shea-Schultz, H. & Fogarty, J.: *Online Learning Today,* Berrett-Koehler Publishers, San Francisco, 2002.

Salmon, Gilly: *E-moderating: the Key to Teaching and Learning Online,* Kogan Page, London ; Sterling, VA, 2000.

Weiss, R., Knowlton, D. & Speck, B.: *Principles of Effective Teaching in the Online Classroom,* Jossey-Bass, San Francisco, 2000.

Wilson, Arthur L. and Elisabeth R. Hayes: *Handbook of Adult and Continuing Education,* Jossey-Bass, San Francisco, 2000.

Wolfe, C., & Wolfe, C. R.: *Learning and teaching on the World Wide Web,* Academic, San Diego, Calif. ; London, 2001.

Index

K

L

M

N

O

P

Q

R

S

T

V

W

❑❑❑